21世纪英语专业系列教材
外交实务系列丛书

国际公关

(英汉双语版)

肖 肃 总主编
周思邑 主编

图书在版编目(CIP)数据

国际公关:汉英对照/周思邑主编. —北京：北京大学出版社，2016.8
(21世纪英语专业系列教材)
ISBN 978-7-301-27441-5

Ⅰ.①国… Ⅱ.①周… Ⅲ.①国际关系—公共关系学—教材—汉、英 Ⅳ.①D802.2

中国版本图书馆CIP数据核字(2016)第199151号

书　　　名	国际公关（英汉双语版） GUOJI GONGGUAN（YING HAN SHUANGYU BAN）
著作责任者	周思邑　主编
责 任 编 辑	刘文静
标 准 书 号	ISBN 978-7-301-27441-5
出 版 发 行	北京大学出版社
地　　　址	北京市海淀区成府路205号　100871
网　　　址	http://www.pup.cn　新浪微博:@北京大学出版社
电 子 信 箱	liuwenjing008@163.com
电　　　话	邮购部 62752015　发行部 62750672　编辑部 62759634
印 刷 者	三河市博文印刷有限公司
经 销 者	新华书店
	787毫米×1092毫米　16开本　18.75印张　300千字 2016年8月第1版　2016年8月第1次印刷
定　　　价	48.00元

未经许可，不得以任何方式复制或抄袭本书之部分或全部内容。
版权所有，侵权必究
举报电话: 010-62752024　电子信箱: fd@pup.pku.edu.cn
图书如有印装质量问题，请与出版部联系，电话:010-62756370

序 1

  四川外国语大学秉承"外语内核,多元发展"的办学特色定位,一直在积极探索建设适应国家和地方发展需求、服务国家对外开放事业的特色学科专业。我校国际关系学院以提高质量为根本、内涵发展为核心、凝练特色为抓手、适应需求为导向,积极探索融合外交学、国际关系和英语及部分非通用语种等外语专业为一体,培养"国际事务导向,外语与专业能力并重"的复合型人才,实现人才培养"打通学科、按需发展、追求卓越"的目标。

  当今世界,中国正在作为一个世界大国和强国崛起,国家的发展对高校人才培养提出了更高、更全面、更多元的要求。对于外语院校而言,过去那种单一专业、单一方向、单一目标、封闭式的人才培养模式已明显不能适应时代的需求。有鉴于此,近年来,我校国际关系学院把培养"厚基础、宽口径、强能力、高素养、复合型"的"大外语"类国际交流型人才作为自己的奋斗目标,大力建设和发展跨外语及其他专业的融合性课程体系和相应师资团队,大力开展国际合作办学,积极推动素质和能力导向的教育教学改革,长期坚持适需对路的教材体系建设,以学生为中心、以学习为重心,为学生倾力打造各种课内、课外学习平台,如外交外事实验教学平台、模拟联合国大会活动、外交风采大赛活动、模拟APEC活动、中外合作办学项目、国际组织人才实验班等等,形成能有力保障教学和学习,富有特色的人才培养平台体系。

  "外交实务系列丛书"正是在这样的背景下应运而生,是国际关系学院教育教学改革和特色教材建设的重要成果之一。

  国际关系学院教师们编写的"外交实务系列丛书"是根据这些年教师们课程改革和教学实践的经验,结合国家发展战略和外交外事实践,采用英汉双语模式编写而成的。目前完成编写的有《国际礼仪》《国际会议》《国际公关》《外交谈判》和《外交文书》等五本教材。这套丛书旨在通过对外交实务的学习和体验,逐步实现业务技能的提升。同时对发展学生的英语能力,特别是专门用途英语能力也十分有帮助。

由于国际关系学院的人才培养模式还在不断探索和改革中,作为改革的成果,"外交实务系列丛书"难免存在一些不足,还需要在改革中不断地完善。但瑕不掩瑜,探索精神难能可贵。

作为同行和同事,与丛书编写团队共勉——路漫漫其修远兮,吾将上下而求索!

四川外国语大学副校长
王鲁男

序 2

新中国成立初期,周总理对中国外交人员的基本素质提出了"站稳立场、掌握政策、熟悉业务、严守纪律"的十六字方针,成为新中国培养外交外事人才的目标要求。

由四川外国语大学国际关系学院年轻教师所编写的"外交实务系列丛书"无疑践行了十六字方针的内容。丛书所体现出来的国际规范、中国特色是站稳立场的表现,形态多样的正反案例是对掌握政策的具体阐释,双语特色是业务能力的一种体现,为此而展开的讨论则体现了学术无禁区、讨论有底线,诠释了外交外事工作的纪律。

《中华人民共和国国民经济和社会发展第十三个五年规划纲要》指出,"如期实现全面建成小康社会奋斗目标,推动经济社会持续健康发展,必须遵循坚持统筹国内国际两个大局。全方位对外开放是发展的必然要求。必须坚持打开国门搞建设,既立足国内,充分运用我国资源、市场、制度等优势,又重视国内国际经济联动效应,积极应对外部环境变化,更好利用两个市场、两种资源,推动互利共赢、共同发展。"当下,举国上下正掀起学习和讨论十三五纲要精神的热潮。

笔者曾经先后在外向型企业和高等学校教学一线工作多年,随后转战向外交第一线,担任驻外大使、总领事,如今重回高校工作,深感国际事务导向、语言能力并重的国际化人才对于当下中国的意义。国际化人才是事关中华民族伟大复兴,实现两个一百年目标的智力资源。"外交实务系列丛书"则是中国国际化人才培养上的一次积极尝试,它将为中国的国际化人才培养提供一种新视角。该套丛书着眼于外交事务中的重大事项,通过形态多样的案例来展现外交、外事工作,既有明显的学术性,也有较强的可操作性,不仅易于在校学员学习,也是在职外交、外事人员的有益读物。

欣闻该丛书付梓,是为序。

外交学院党委书记

袁南生

Preface
前　言

　　现代公共关系学科和职业起源于美国。20世纪80年代,现代公共关系理论和实务伴随改革开放进入中国,虽然起步较晚,但发展迅速,目前,国际公关公司、专业课、培训班、网站、杂志、书籍等大量涌现,可谓掀起了一股"公关热"。

　　国际公共关系是全球化时代的公共关系,是国际行为体与他国公众的交往中,通过国际间各种信息传播活动,增进该主体与他国公众之间的了解和信任,维护和发展该主体的良好国际形象的一种公共关系。作为"外交实务系列丛书"中的一册,《国际公关》聚焦国际舞台上各类行为体,研究政府、国际组织、企业、个人行为体的公关活动,通过案例结合理论、模拟呼应案例的路径总结各类国际政治行为体公关的技巧和方法,探索公关规律,服务公关实践。

　　《国际公关》一书,内容丰富,资料翔实,有很多创新之处。其特点可总结为"新、美、专、用"。"新"体现为体系新,案例新,编排新。以国际公关行为体作为本书的结构体系,不仅内容全面,而且层次鲜明;双语的公关书籍编排新颖,更好地回应了新时期兼具语言技能和专业素质的新型复合公关类人才的需求。塑造和维护形象就是一项"美"的工程,也是国际公关的核心。"专",本书不仅对公关理论进行了梳理,而且在研究视角方面实现了政治学、新闻学、传播学等多学科融合,超越了现有公关教材的单一视角。多学科的融合不仅丰富了公关教材的理论基础,而且使读者接触到不同学科的基本知识,为其深入研究公关或从事公关工作打下坚实的理论基础。"用",通过练习题,尤其是情景模拟提供了理论结合实践的机会,使跃跃欲试的读者感受全真的公关模拟。

　　值得一提的是,《国际公关》书中有很多可圈可点的公关理论和案例,基础理论和双语案例相结合,双语案例和情景模拟相呼应,实践性强又引人深思。例如在"公众人物国际公关"章节,编者在基础知识部分引入了公关演讲,双语案例中选取了刘翔退役演讲和克林顿演讲。"国家公关"中的国家形象宣传片,"外国企业国际公关"中的企业社会责任,"普通人物国际公关"中的提高人际交往能力等等,很值得思考。

《国际公关》是编者在借鉴国内外学者有益成果的基础上,形成了自己的理论体系和内容,颇有独特的见解和新意。书中的公关理论、技巧以及原则可作为初学者的入门基础教材,又可将每部分视为独立的章节,为国家和社会层面的不同群体提供些许参考,以解决他们所面临的公关问题,因其富有趣味的案例亦可作为公关爱好者的读物。

在本书付梓之际,我们要衷心地感谢各方的支持和帮助。

首先,感谢给予本书编写工作指导和建议的各位领导、专家和朋友,你们在本书的构思、写作和修改过程中提出了大量宝贵的建议,使得本书能够不断地完善并得以出版。其次,感谢在资料收集、校正方面做出重要贡献的四川外国语大学国际关系学院师生,特别是外籍教师Daniel、马军兰、严和、汤雪霏、阳天天和张玲同学。再次,感谢北京大学出版社的编辑们,你们认真负责的态度和辛勤的工作保障了本书的顺利出版。最后,还要感谢我的家人,你们的爱给了我不断前进的动力。

在本书的编写过程中,我们参考借鉴了国内外有关教材和研究成果、网络资料等,引用了很多优秀的案例和理论,在此不一一列举,谨向有关作者表示最深切的谢意。尽管付出了极大的努力,但由于编纂人员能力有限,在相关问题上难免有疏漏和理解偏颇之处。在此,我们希望广大读者和学界同行提出批评和指正,一同把本书编得更好。

周思邑

2016年8月

Contents
目　录

Chapter 1　Introduction and Framework of the Book
　　国际公关绪论 ·· 1
　　1.1 Basic Knowledge 基础知识 ··· 2
　　　　1.1.1 Definition 定义 ·· 2
　　　　1.1.2 Features 属性 ·· 3
　　　　1.1.3 Elements 要素 ··· 4
　　　　1.1.4 Development 发展 ·· 5
　　　　1.1.5 Practice 实施 ·· 6
　　　　1.1.6 Theme Activities 专题活动 ··· 8
　　1.2 Bilingual Case Studies 双语案例 ··· 11
　　　　1.2.1 Chilean Mining Accident PR ·· 11
　　　　1.2.2 杭州城市品牌国际公关 ·· 15
　　1.3 Further Reading 拓展阅读 ··· 17
　　　　1.3.1 Disneyland Resort IPR Campaign ····································· 17
　　　　1.3.2 麦当劳"3·15"事件公关 ··· 20
　　1.4 Simulation 情景模拟 ··· 22
　　　　1.4.1 "International IT Hub" PR ··· 22
　　　　1.4.2 含氯可乐事件公关 ·· 23
　　Exercises 本章练习题 ·· 24

Chapter 2　International Public Relations of Nation
　　国家公关 ·· 30
　　2.1 Basic Knowledge 基础知识 ·· 31
　　　　2.1.1 Definition 定义 ·· 31

2.1.2 Features 属性 ·· 31
2.1.3 Classification 分类 ······································· 33
2.1.4 Evolution 演变 ·· 35
2.1.5 Practice 实施 ··· 37
2.1.6 Public Relations Planning 公关策划 ·················· 40
2.2 Bilingual Case Studies 双语案例 ··························· 42
2.2.1 "9.11" Incident PR ······································ 42
2.2.2 创意英国公关 ·· 46
2.3 Further Reading 拓展阅读 ···································· 48
2.3.1 Maldives' Underwater Cabinet Meeting ············ 48
2.3.2 MH370 事件公关 ·· 52
2.4 Simulation 情景模拟 ·· 55
2.4.1 Chernobyl Disaster PR ································· 55
2.4.2 墨西哥形象公关 ··· 56
Exercises 本章练习题 ·· 57

Chapter 3　International Public Relations of Local Government 地方政府国际公关 ·············· 64

3.1 Basic Knowledge 基础知识 ··································· 65
　3.1.1 Definition 定义 ·· 65
　3.1.2 Features 属性 ·· 66
　3.1.3 Classification 分类 ······································· 67
　3.1.4 Evolution 演变 ·· 68
　3.1.5 Practice 实施 ··· 69
　3.1.6 Games and Competitions 赛事申办 ·················· 70
3.2 Bilingual Case Studies 双语案例 ··························· 73
　3.2.1 Brazil World Cup PR ···································· 73
　3.2.2 汶川地震公关 ·· 76
3.3 Further Reading 拓展阅读 ···································· 78
　3.3.1 Hurricane Katrina PR ···································· 78
　3.3.2 2011 年西安世界园艺博览会 ·························· 81
3.4 Simulation 情景模拟 ·· 83
　3.4.1 Paris Hijacking ·· 83

3.4.2 第x届潍坊国际风筝节 ··· 85
　Exercises 本章练习题 ··· 86

Chapter 4　International Public Relations of Intergovernmental Organization 政府间国际组织国际公关 ············ **91**

- 4.1 Basic Knowledge 基础知识 ··· 92
  - 4.1.1 Definition 定义 ··· 92
  - 4.1.2 Features 属性 ··· 92
  - 4.1.3 Classification 分类 ·· 94
  - 4.1.4 Practice 实施 ··· 97
  - 4.1.5 International Meeting 国际会议 ······························· 98
- 4.2 Bilingual Case Stuides 双语案例 ···································· 100
  - 4.2.1 World Health Day Campaign ································· 100
  - 4.2.2 马德里"3·11"事件公关 ·· 104
- 4.3 Further Reading 拓展阅读 ·· 107
  - 4.3.1 UN Oil-for-Food Scandal PR ································· 107
  - 4.3.2 2014 APEC 峰会公关 ·· 111
- 4.4 Simulation 情景模拟 ·· 113
  - 4.4.1 IMF Scandal PR ··· 113
  - 4.4.2 第X届东盟首脑会议公关 ··· 114
- Exercises 本章练习题 ·· 116

Chapter 5　International Public Relations of Non-Governmental Organizations 非政府间国际组织国际公关 ··········· **120**

- 5.1 Basic Knowledge 基础知识 ·· 121
  - 5.1.1 Definition 定义 ··· 121
  - 5.1.2 Characteristics 特征 ·· 124
  - 5.1.3 Objective 目标 ··· 125
  - 5.1.4 Principles 原则 ·· 126
  - 5.1.5 Practice 实施 ··· 127
  - 5.1.6 Fund Raising 募集资金 ·· 129

5.2 Bilingual Case Studies 双语案例 ………………………………… 132
　5.2.1 WWF Giant Panda Conservation PR ……………………… 132
　5.2.2 国际奥委会盐湖城丑闻公关 ……………………………… 135
5.3　Further Reading 拓展阅读 …………………………………… 137
　5.3.1 Sanishop PR ………………………………………………… 137
　5.3.2 绿色和平组织"我是一棵树"公关 ……………………… 139
5.4 Simulation 情景模拟 …………………………………………… 141
　5.4.1 FIFA Corruption Crisis PR ………………………………… 141
　5.4.2 "地球一小时"公关 ……………………………………… 143
Exercises 本章练习题 ……………………………………………… 144

Chapter 6　Public Relations of Foreign Transnational Corporations
　　　　　　外国跨国企业国际公关 …………………………… **148**

6.1 Basic Knowledge 基础知识 …………………………………… 149
　6.1.1 Definition 定义 …………………………………………… 151
　6.1.2 Types of Company 分类 ………………………………… 151
　6.1.3 Objectives 目标 …………………………………………… 152
　6.1.4 Evolution of PR for Foreign TNCs 演变 ………………… 155
　6.1.5 Methods 方法 ……………………………………………… 156
　6.1.6 Corporate Social Responsibility 企业社会责任 ………… 157
6.2 Bilingual Case Studies 双语案例 ……………………………… 160
　6.2.1 Nestle : The Baby Killer? ………………………………… 160
　6.2.2 联邦快递公关 ……………………………………………… 164
6.3 Further Reading 拓展阅读 …………………………………… 168
　6.3.1 Shell and Its Environmental Issues ……………………… 168
　6.3.2 "速成鸡"事件公关 ……………………………………… 171
6.4 Simulation 情景模拟 …………………………………………… 174
　6.4.1 "BP Oil Spill" Issue ……………………………………… 174
　6.4.2 宜家：为大众创造美好的生活 …………………………… 176
Exercises 本章练习题 ……………………………………………… 177

Chapter 7 International Public Relations of China Transnational Corporation
中国跨国企业国际公关 ························· **181**

7.1 Basic Knowledge 基础知识 ························· 182
- 7.1.1 Definition 定义 ························· 182
- 7.1.2 Features 属性 ························· 183
- 7.1.3 Classification 分类 ························· 184
- 7.1.4 Evolution 演变 ························· 186
- 7.1.5 Practice 实施 ························· 187
- 7.1.6 PR Advertising 公关广告 ························· 189

7.2 Bilingual Case Studies 双语案例 ························· 190
- 7.2.1 Haier Branding Strategy ························· 190
- 7.2.2 "大白兔"甲醛危机公关 ························· 194

7.3 Further Reading 拓展阅读 ························· 197
- 7.3.1 Sany Group Sued Barak Obama ························· 197
- 7.3.2 阿里巴巴美国IPO上市公关 ························· 200

7.4 Simulation 情景模拟 ························· 203
- 7.4.1 WeChat PR ························· 203
- 7.4.2 华为芭蕾舞鞋广告 ························· 204

Exercises 本章练习题 ························· 206

Chapter 8 International Public Relations of Public Figures
公众人物国际公关 ························· **209**

8.1 Basic Knowledge 基础知识 ························· 210
- 8.1.1 Definition 定义 ························· 210
- 8.1.2 Features 属性 ························· 211
- 8.1.3 Classification 分类 ························· 212
- 8.1.4 Evolution 演变 ························· 213
- 8.1.5 Practice 实施 ························· 215
- 8.1.6 Public Speech 公关演讲 ························· 216

8.2 Bilingual Case Studies 双语案例 ························· 217
- 8.2.1 Putin's Hard-Man Image ························· 217
- 8.2.2 刘翔退赛危机公关 ························· 221

8.3 Further Reading 拓展阅读 ··· 224
  8.3.1 Lewinsky Scandal PR ··· 224
  8.3.2 陈光标慈善公关 ··· 228
8.4 Simulation 情景模拟 ··· 230
  8.4.1 Jolie's Breast Surgery PR ··· 230
  8.4.2 名人吸毒危机公关 ··· 232
Exercises 本章练习题 ··· 234

Chapter 9 International Public Relations of Ordinary Figure
普通人物国际公关 ··· 238

9.1 Basic Knowledge 基础知识 ··· 239
  9.1.1 Definition 定义 ··· 239
  9.1.2 Nature 属性 ··· 241
  9.1.3 Classification 分类 ··· 243
  9.1.4 Evolution 演变 ··· 243
  9.1.5 Process of Practice 实施过程 ··· 246
  9.1.6 Interpersonal Relationship 人际交往能力 ··· 248
9.2 Bilingual Case Studies 双语案例 ··· 250
  9.2.1 David Chang: The Road to Fame ··· 250
  9.2.2 "布鞋院士"李小文 ··· 253
9.3 Further Reading 拓展阅读 ··· 256
  9.3.1 Luxor Temple Carving Issue PR ··· 256
  9.3.2 斯诺登:"棱镜门"前后的系列公关 ··· 259
9.4 Simulation 情景模拟 ··· 261
  9.4.1 Jiang's Kiss in the Airport ··· 261
  9.4.2 请吃切糕:大学生最可爱的危机公关 ··· 263
Exercises 本章练习题 ··· 264

参考答案 ··· 268
英文参考文献 ··· 276
中文参考文献 ··· 280

Introduction and Framework of the Book
国际公关绪论

Gist
内容概览

As globalization strengthens transnational interdependence and international exchanges, many types of actors spring up and play important roles in global affairs. They frequently interact and communicate with the public at home and abroad to build dynamic relationships. However, due to natural and man-made disasters, cultural differences, conflicts of interests and so on, crises of international public relations often happen. Therefore, how to prevent crises, shape actors' image and cultivate a favorable environment for development is the hottest issue faced by all types of international actors at present.

This chapter introduces general knowledge and academic research on international public relations, encapsulates essential findings on a theoretical and practical level from various perspectives, such as contextualized studies in bilingual cases of governments, multinational corporations, organizations, and public figures. This chapter aims to build an overall framework for international public relations, and lay a cognitive foundation for subsequent chapters.

全球化的深入发展促进了国与国之间的互相依存,加强了跨国联系与交往。各类国际行为体也随之不断涌现,在全球事务中扮演着重要角色。然而由于自然或人为灾害、文化差异、利益分歧等原因,在国际交往和合作中,公关危机难以避免。因此,各个国际行为体如何应对危机,维护自身的形象,营造有利的发展环境,是目前亟需探讨的热点话题。

本章内容以国际公关为主题,通过理论与案例结合的方式,概括国际公关的基础理论,介绍不同国际行为体开展国际公关的实践策略,意在构建国际公关的总体框架,为后面章节奠定认知基础。

1.1 Basic Knowledge
基础知识

1.1.1 Definition 定义

In the relatively brief period leading up to today, international public relations (IPR) has been defined in many different ways, and the definition often evolves alongside international public relations' changing roles and technological advances. The earliest definition emphasized press agentry and publicity, while more modern definitions incorporate the concepts of "engagement" and "relationship building."

According to International Public Relations Association (IPRA), international public relations is a strategic communication process that builds mutually beneficial relationships between public relations actors and their publics. Simple and straightforward, this definition focuses on the basic concept of international public relations—as a communication process, one that is strategic in nature and emphasizing "mutually beneficial relationships." Specifically speaking, "process" is preferable to "management function," which can evoke ideas of control and top-down, one-way communications. "Relationships" relates to public relations' role in helping to bring together actors and individuals with their key stakeholders. "Publics" is preferable to "stakeholders."

But in the 21st Century international public relations, with the advent of new media, is embedded in everything from politics and business to celebrity. Gone are the days when IPR was an afterthought, it is now firmly at the heart of strategic planning.

国际公共关系是指各种国际行为体在与目标国际公众的交往中,通过各种国际信息传播活动,增进公关主体与公关公众之间的沟通和信任,维护和发展公关主体的良好国际形象,建立对主体和公众双方有益的公共关系。

国际公共关系与国内公共关系不同,它是跨国界的公共关系活动。在全球化时代,随着新媒体的发展,国家、国际组织、企业和个人都积极参与国际

国际公关绪论 | Introduction and Framework of the Book

公共关系活动。国际公共关系活动的地域大致可分为三种情况：一是主体母国境内与境内国际公众开展公共关系活动，二是在主体母国国境外的一国与该国公众开展公共关系活动，三是在多个国家同时开展的针对所有国际公众的公共关系活动。随着公共关系的日趋国际化，如何有效地开展国际公共关系工作，实现主体公关目的，是所有国际行为体所面临的一个新课题。

1.1.2 Features 属性

IPR actors are no longer limited to interact and communicate with home publics (where their main offices are located), but additionally with host (where they operate internationally) and transnational publics (simultaneously acting in several locations and communication dimensions or media platforms). Therefore, Institute for Public Relations defines international public relations as strategic communications and actions carried out by private, government, nonprofit organizations and celebrities to build and maintain relationships with publics in socioeconomic and political environments outside their home location. The feature goes hand-in-hand with Wakefield's conceptualization of international public relations: The important elements in an international program, therefore, boil down to where the entity is located and to which publics it must build relationships. If the public are located down the street or only within the same nation as the actors' home base, interacting with them does not constitute international public relations. Additionally, some scholars illustrate that global public relations is also simultaneous strategic communications and actions with home, host and transnational publics. That is, actors must take pre-emptive steps to ensure their voices are heard in cross-national conflicts, particularly through the cultivation of relevant media representatives, both at home and in host countries.

国际公共关系具有以下五个属性：

（1）Not Domestic 非本土性

国际公共关系活动不是仅仅在本国开展，还需在所在国以外的国家和地区开展。国际公共关系有可能在几个本土以外的地区同时开展，公关主体面临的公众包括外国人或侨民。

（2）Cross Cultural 跨文化性

各国、各地区由于地理位置、交通条件、地形、气候等的差异,加之长期的历史沉淀,形成了丰富多彩的民族文化或区域文化。跨国家、跨地区进行的国际公共关系活动,必然具有跨文化的特征。国际公共关系的成功,既有赖于对目标国公众文化的了解,又有赖于对目标国公众文化的主动适应或必要的诱导。

(3) Targeted 针对性

为了达到国际公关的目的,在国际公众中树立良好形象,任何国际公关活动必须有的放矢,如沟通方式和内容应视公众的文化背景不同而不同,公关主题应针对不同目标公众而调整等等。

(4) Diversified Actors 主体多样性

在全球化时代,各种社会组织或团体参与到国际交往中,天然地产生了对组织形象的维护和塑造活动,这些国际公关主体既包括传统的主权国家、跨国企业,也包括国际组织、地方政府或城市,甚至在一些特殊的情况下,参与国际交往的个人也成为国际公关的主体。

(5) Metabolic Time and Place 时空性

由于"国际政治国内化"和"国内政治国际化"的趋势日益明显,很多公关事件的发生发展都在变化中。在全球化的时代,很多国际公关的区域可能从一个区域变化到另一个区域,危机事态的发展可能挣脱边界的限制,时间的变化也可能不可控,这些都对公关主体提出了更高的要求。

1.1.3 Elements 要素[①]

(1) Actors 国际主体:国际公共关系活动的发动者、组织者、控制者、实施者和利益者,在国际公关行为过程中处于主动和主导地位。主要包含主权国家、国际组织、地方政府、企业和个人等,这些主体中有营利性的,也有非营利性的,有集体的,也有个人的。

(2) International Public 国际公众:国际公共关系活动的对象,与公关主体发生直接或间接联系,对该主体的生存和发展具有现实的或潜在影响力的个人、群体或社会团体,主要是外国的公司企业、顾客用户、技术合作者、金融信贷机构、政府部门、民间团体、各界知名人士等,而这些组织或公众处在不同的国家和地区,各有不同的语言、风俗和生活方式。

(3) Communication 传播:个人间、群体间或群体和个人之间交换和传递

[①] 周安华、苗晋平,《公共关系:理论、实务与技巧(第4版)》。北京:中国人民大学出版社,2013年。

国际公关绪论 | Introduction and Framework of the Book

新闻、事实、意见、感情的信息过程,双向性的信息交流与分享。由于公众的国际性,因地制宜地选择合适的信息传播渠道和方式至关重要。

1.1.4 Development 发展

Numerous examples of public relations-like activities were identifiable in the early days of American settlement as each of the colonies used publicity techniques to attract settlers. In 1641, Harvard College initiated the first systematic U.S. fund-raising campaign, which was supported by the first fund-raising brochure, New England' First Fruits. In 1758, King's College (now Columbia University) issued the first press release—to announce graduation exercises.

Not-for-profit organizations, including colleges, churches, charitable causes, and health and welfare agencies, began to use publicity extensively in the early 20th century. In 1899, Anson Phelps Stokes converted Yale University's Office of the Secretary into an effective alumni and public relations office. Harvard president Charles W. Eliot, who spoke as early as 1869 on the need to influence public opinion toward advancement of learning, was among the Publicity Bureau's first clients in 1900. By 1908, the Red Cross and the National Tuberculosis Association were making extensive use of publicity agents. The New York Orphan Asylum was paying a publicity man $75 per month.

As early as 1883, AT&T leader Theodore Vail expressed concern about the company's relationship with the public and the public's conflicts with the company. He built support from the middle class for AT&T programs by implementing cut-rate phone bills, friendly greetings from the telephone operator, employee morale programs and paid advertising. In 1907, he hired James Drummond Ellsworth for AT&T's public relations. Ellsworth promoted efficient operation and consideration of customers' needs, a systematic method for answering complaints and acceptance of governmental regulation as the price for operating a privately owned natural monopoly.

The greatest early governmental public relations effort in history, up to its time, was the one mounted in support of the U.S. effort in World War I. The military had utilized publicity for several years; the Marine Corps established a publicity bureau in Chicago in 1907. Never before had such a massive, multifaceted, coordinated program been mounted. Moreover, though often used by big business in a defensive fashion, public relations took the offensive when it came to war.①

1.1.5 Practice 实施

It is important for the international public relations actors to use strategic planning to guide this practice. Planning provides more exciting and interesting strategies because no situation and no brief are taken at just face value—they are examined from all angles, they are investigated, and they are thought about. Planning also encourages people to view IPR as a more cerebral discipline, more than just sending out a press release, more than just fluff' or spin. This, in turn, can create opportunities for IPR to take a more fundamental role in the decision making and running of organizations.②

Stage 1 Subject	Understanding the subject (eg company, product, service)	Position in marketplace Planned developments Competitor activity Issues (eg environmental, community, political etc)	Set overall quantified objective Identity key PR issues
Stage 2 Audiences	Get to grips with the target audiences	Who are they and how many of them are there? Their lifestyle, attitudes etc Their views on the subject	How do we reach them? Media and other means Identify key insights
Stage 3 Responses	The responses we want to generate in the audiences	What we want them to know, think, feel and do	
Stage 4 Objectives	Define the PR objectives	Must contribute to overall objective (as defined in stage 1)	Must be measurable and realistic
Stage 5 Strategy	The plan of how to achieve the PR objectives	Take account of everything learned	Add creativity and imagination

表1.1　战略规划过程中的5个步骤(source: *Strategic Planning in Public Relations*)

---

① Juan-Carlos Molleda. "Global Public Relations". Institute for Public Relations.(web) March 19, 2009
② Kieran Knights. *Strategic Planning of International Public Relations*. London: Thorogood, 2001.

国际公关绪论 | Introduction and Framework of the Book

Following a step-by-step process means that IPR actors have a series of manageable tasks rather than something to boggle the mind, and by strictly sticking to each stage of the process there it is less likelihood that they will miss something essential. On occasion actors will inevitably give in to the temptation to rush off in pursuit of some vague hunch, but if they have to return to the process there is less of a danger of getting stuck in a blind alley.

Besides, as a management function, IPR campaign also encompasses the following:

(1) Anticipating, analyzing and interpreting public opinion, attitudes and issues that might impact, for good or bad, the operations and plans of the organization.

(2) Counseling management at all levels in the organization with regard to policy decisions, courses of action and communication, taking into account their public ramifications and the organization's social or citizenship responsibilities.

(3) Researching, conducting and evaluating, on a continuing basis, programs of action and communication to achieve the informed public understanding necessary to the success of an organization's aims. These may include marketing, financial, fund raising, employee, community or government relations, and other programs.

(4) Planning and implementing the organization's efforts to influence or change public policies. Setting objectives, planning, budgeting, recruiting and training staff, developing facilities—in short, managing the resources needed to perform all of the above.

国际公关的实施应遵照"ROPE原则",即Research——调查、Objective——目标、Practice——实施以及Evaluation——评估。社会组织针对某一事件开展公关活动时,需要先查清该事件的具体情况,制定出科学可行的公关目标,之后朝着这个目标多角度、多层次、全方面地采取公关措施,并且要在活动末期对此次公关活动的效果进行合理化评估。

(1) IPR Research 国际公关调查

国际公关调查是国际公关全过程的首要步骤,是国际公关工作的基础,也是国际公关活动的重要方式。国际公关调查涉及组织所处内外环境、组织内部基本情况、组织外部公众及传播媒介的调查。国际公关的调查过程遵循科学性和逻辑性相统一的原则,可以采用访问调查、问卷调查、抽样调查、网络调查、观察调查以及文献调查等多种调查方式。

（2）IPR Objective 国际公关目标

国际公关目标是指组织通过策划和实施公关传播活动所追求和渴望达到的一种状态或目的，是国际公关全部活动的核心和公关工作努力的方向。整个公关实务工作的过程就可以理解为制定公关目标和实现目标的过程。根据国际公关的主要工作内容，派生出国际公关的三大基本目标，即形象设计与塑造、关系协调、传播与沟通，其中形象设计与塑造是整个公关工作的核心目标。具体国际公关的目标，则因不同的任务和要求而有所不同。

通常而言，知名度和美誉度是评价国际公关的两个最基本的标准。国际公关的知名度，就是国际公关发起者及其政策或措施被国际社会和国际公众所了解、知晓的程度，被了解广泛就是知名度高，反之则是知名度低；而所谓国际公关美誉度，就是指国际社会或国际公众对某个跨国组织及其政策或措施做出高度肯定的评价的程度。

（3）IPR Practice 国际公关实施

国际公关实施是指国际公关主体为了实现既定的目标，充分依据和利用实施条件，对国际公关的创意策划进行实施策略、手段、方法设计并实际操作与管理的过程。国际公关实施的关键在于，建立指挥系统，选取恰当的管理方法，实施的领导与控制。有效的公关实施，不仅能执行创意策划，还能创造性地修改和弥补策划的不足。

（4）IPR Evaluation 国际公关评估

国际公关评估，就其科学性而言，指的是有关专家或机构依据某种科学的标准和方法，对国际公关的整体策划、准备过程、实施过程以及实施效果进行测量、检查、评估和判断的一种活动。其目的是取得国际公关工作进程、工作效益和工作效率的信息，作为改进公关工作的重要依据。

1.1.6 Theme Activities 专题活动

Public relations specialists establish and maintain relationships with target audience, the media and other opinion leaders. Common responsibilities include designing communications campaigns, writing news releases and other content for news, working with the press, arranging interviews for company spokespeople, writing speeches for company leaders, acting as spokesperson, preparing clients for press conferences, media interviews and speeches, writing website and social media content, managing company reputation (crisis management), managing internal communications and marketing activities like brand awareness and

国际公关绪论 | Introduction and Framework of the Book

event management. Success of public relations requires a deep understanding of the interests and concerns of each of the IPR actors' many publics. The public relations actors must know how to effectively address those concerns using the most powerful tool of the public relations trade, which is publicity.

Building and managing relationships with those who influence international actors' audiences has a central role in doing IPR. After the actor has been working in the field, they accumulate a list of relationships that become an asset, especially for those in media relations. Within IPR campaign, typical activities include publicity events, speaking opportunities, press releases, newsletters, blogs, social media, press kits and outbound communication to members of the press. Video and audio news releases are often produced and distributed to TV outlets in hopes they will be used as regular program content.

国际公关的专题活动是公关行为体与广大公众之间进行沟通,塑造组织自身形象,扩大影响,提高声誉的有效途径。国际公关专题活动施加影响的对象并非所有公众,而是以其中某一部分公众为重点。在这种情况下,尤其是当公关发起者与公众的关系出现或可能出现不协调时,公关专题活动将会起到很好的协调和沟通作用,以便与这部分急亟协调的公众保持良好的关系。[1]

(1) Press Conference 召开新闻发布会

新闻发布会,是社会组织和某一个人向新闻记者发表某种新闻信息,并就此展开问答的一种特殊会议。新闻发布会是社会组织与新闻界保持联系的一种重要活动方式,也是国际公关人员广泛传播各类新闻信息的最好工具之一。

目前,发达国家的许多新闻媒介都已成为跨国性的大企业,在世界各地采访报道新闻、发行报刊、播放广播电视节目等。其中有美国的美联社、合众国际社、《纽约时报》《华尔街日报》《时代周刊》《新闻周刊》及三大广播电视公司;英国有路透社、《泰晤士报》《经济学家》杂志、《远东经济评论》杂志;法国有法新社、《世界报》等。在开展国际公共关系时,公关人员要充分运用这些新闻媒介,传播有利于我们的信息。当前需要全面了解这些新闻机构,有条件时要与之建立联系,并邀请他们的记者前来采访。

---

[1] 周安华、苗晋平,《公共关系:理论、实务与技巧(第4版)》。北京:中国人民大学出版社,2013年。

（2）Publicity Film 放映宣传片

宣传片是一种很好的公共关系传播工具,其目的就是介绍组织或企业。宣传片可以在下列情况下使用:组织或企业负责人到国外访问时放映;借给当地的分公司或代理人向有关方面放映;在国外举办展览会、博览会时放映;提供给国外电视台放映等。

（3）Exhibition 举办展览会

展览会是一种综合运用各种媒介推广产品、宣传组织形象和建立良好公共关系的大型公共关系专题活动。展览会的突出特点是:生动直观,能给公众留下深刻印象;具有一定的趣味性和知识性,能广泛吸引公众参加;便于新闻媒介采访报道;在展览会能充分与公众进行双向交流。

（4）Visiting 开放参观活动

开放参观活动,指的是社会组织邀请外部公众参观本组织的工作条件、环境设施、成就展览等,是国际公关实务中经常使用的一种团体性专项公关活动。其目的是增进组织与某类重要公众之间的双向了解;消除某些公众对组织的一些偏见和误解;亲善社区或邻里关系,增强组织与公众的联系。

（5）Celebration 组织庆典活动

庆典活动是指公关行为体在其内部发生值得庆祝的重要事件或围绕重要节日而举行的庆祝活动。它可以是一种专题活动,也可以是大型公共关系活动的一项程序。庆典活动往往给公众留下"第一印象",如一家跨国企业举行一个气氛热烈、庄重大方的开业典礼,这是在国际公众面前的第一次亮相,这个"相"亮得好,可以为该企业创造良好的形象。随着社会的发展,能够举办庆典的节日也越来越多。

（6）Meeting 举行会议

会议是指有组织、有目的的言语沟通活动方式,是围绕一定目的进行的、有控制的集会,有关人士聚集在一起,围绕一个主题发言、插话、提问、答疑、讨论,通过语言相互交流信息,表达意见,讨论问题,解决问题。筹划和召开国际会议,利用会议形式来传递信息,沟通意见,协调关系,也是国际公关常用的一种传播方式。会议的形式有例行工作会议、专题性会议、布置工作和总结性会议等。

国际公关绪论 | Introduction and Framework of the Book

1.2 Bilingual Case Studies
双语案例

1.2.1 Chilean Mining Accident PR①

The 2010 Copiapó mining accident, also known then as the "Chilean mining accident," began in the afternoon of Thursday, 5 August, 2010, as a significant cave-in at the troubled 121-year-old San José copper-gold mine. Thirty-three miners were trapped inside the San José copper-gold mine for 69 days at 2300 feet deep, about 5 kilometers away from the mine entrance. Initially, however, no one knew exactly where the miners were located. The mining company was slow to acknowledge the problem, and had a history of safety problems. And family members of the miners told stories about their loved ones. All the factors seemed for a human tragedy and a public relations disaster. So how did Chilean government turned this unexpected national image crisis into a fame-building triumph?

Chilean government first adopted regular rescue measures, but they failed. Later Chilean government began again to research their current conditions.

First, this mining disaster had aroused the complaints of public, especially the family members of the trapped miners. It was necessary to console them in case of erupting conflicts later. Second, rescuing the trapped miners was so challenging that it was even impossible for Chile alone to complete this rescue. Therefore, relying on other rescue forces is imminent and urgent. Third, as international community, especially media had cast much attention on this mining disaster, practicing proper and efficient media communications is of significance for the sake of shaping good national image.

Having figured out a general outline for this emergent and tough rescue, the Chilean government devoted to practical rescue.

Chilean government took two steps to achieve the successful rescue. In general, President Pinera personally directed the communications aspect of the rescue operations to give his mining minister a more focused mindset in

---

① Heather Yaxley. "An international view of crisis management of the Chile mine disaster".PR Conversations, http://www.prconversations.com/author/heather-yaxley/December 16, 2015.

carrying out the rescue mission. The Chilean president took charge of communication responses, such as handling the press interviews and in getting hold of the professionals and technological experts that the international community could provide. The mining minister, on the other hand, was at the helm of the actual rescue operation responses.

Initial Tactics

The Chilean president was on top of the disaster situation by being available at moment's notice to approve all proposals. His initial step was to make a public commitment that they would see the operation through, at all costs, without let-up and with the best professional and technological help available.

On the other hand, the mining minister arrived at the disaster site within 24 hours and stayed there to organize what turned out to be a chaotic conglomeration of miners' families, reporters, volunteers and an assortment of organizations that wanted to offer their expertise and know-how.

The Chilean government also regarded the US National Aeronautics and Space Administration (NASA) as the best resource. NASA sent its deputy chief medical Michael Duncan to bring his expertise regarding long-duration and enclosed-space flights. The conditions that were being experienced by the miners were considered similar to those experienced by astronauts during space flights.

The government had 33 modular units brought to the site, which served as temporary homes for each of the families of the thirty-three miners. In Chile, a family means more than just the spouses and their children but likewise includes an entire clan. Other family members were asked to go home, to give more room for the rescue operations that were about to take place.

Calling on assistance from experts from many countries extended support for the rescue effort and engaged media from Canada to Australia, where local angles enhanced the coverage.

Continuing Tactics

Precision Company, an oil-drilling service provider who had the technology to perform the hole-drilling operations via computer-aided equipment, was tasked to drill holes. The company initially used poke drills to allow the emanation of any foul smell that would indicate signs of decaying bodies. On

国际公关绪论 | Introduction and Framework of the Book

the 17th day of the rescue operations, one of the poke drills came up with a note coming from the miners that stated all 33 workers were alive, safe and sound.

NASA Chief Duncan and his team of expert engineers designed and developed an escape capsule that was fully equipped with oxygen masks and monitoring equipment complete with audio and visual appendages.

The Chilean government also had organized the following measures.

Each of the trapped miners was made to take-in a high-calorie drink that would allow the miners to stand the spinning motion of the capsule as it ascended.

The closest family of the ascending miners was brought nearer to the hole's surface area as part of the welcoming party.

Traffic going to the site was closed to allow the rescue helicopter pilots enough night vision and landing areas. Their task was to transport each worker to the nearest hospital for proper medical examination after each haul.

Paramedics of the Navy Special Forces were at hand in case of emergencies.

The miners were brought up divided into three groups: The first was composed of the most skilled and expert in the group. This group was tasked to provide any information that would warn the NASA team of possible technical troubles that might crop-up. The second team comprised those who were considered the weakest in the group, while the third were those considered the strongest.

The whole world watched and applauded as each miner, looking happy and in the best disposition, appeared. This successful mission was a great triumph not only for the rescue of mining disaster, but also for the public relations of Chile.

The French credit rating agency Coface declared that the dramatic mining rescue will have a positive impact on Chile's economic reputation. "It provides with international investors an image of a country where you can do safe business," Coface's UK managing director, Xavier Denecker said, "It gives a good impression in terms of technology, solidarity and efficiency." On March 2011, the first of the expected books on the rescue, *Under the Earth: The 33 Miners that Moved the World*, is nearing completion. Another book called *33 Men, Buried Alive: The Inside Story of the Trapped Chilean Miners*, by Jonathan

Franklin, a writer for UK-based *The Guardian*, is due for release in early 2011. In a word, Chile received a lot of praises and applauses from the international community, which facilitated the improvement of its national image and the spreading of international fame.

> **Case Study 案例分析**
>
> It is a typical case of national crisis management. The IPR actor is the Chilean government, and the target public are trapped miners, their families, as well as the media. Finally, the Chilean government transferred a mining disaster into a successful promotion.
>
> Here are several points we can learn from this case. First, speed and attitude. After the disaster, the central government reacted immediately and took emergency measures to rescue the trapped miners. The Chilean president was on top of the rescue operation by being available at moment's notice to approve all proposals. Second, information disclosure. Facing doubts from the domestic public and the international community, the Chilean government didn't hide the facts or attempt to cover up this tense situation. Instead, the government actively issued a press conference and allocated those relatives of the victims to the accident spot. Third, cooperation. When the rescue was stuck into deadlock due to the technology problems, the Chilean government appealed to international community and received professional assistance from the U.S.A, which managed rescue efforts and at the same time, attained sympathy and support from outside the country. Finally, the media. When the miners were rescued from the mining well, the Chilean government took full advantage of the domestic and international media to present the rescue achievement to the world. Therefore, it is undoubted that Chilean government gained global approval.

国际公关绪论 | Introduction and Framework of the Book

1.2.2 杭州城市品牌国际公关[①]

杭州,是浙江省政治、经济、文化中心,中国东南重要交通枢纽。杭州经济发达,2014年GDP为9201.16亿元,经济综合实力跻身全国大中城市前十位。

2004年,杭州开始实施"旅游国际化"战略,2008年,杭州提出"城市国际化"战略,目标瞄准世界一流城市,用世界眼光谋划未来的发展,用国际化的理念贯穿城市发展的各个方面。随着杭州战略定位的调整,杭州树立了自己的城市品牌——"生活品质之城"。但是,确定城市品牌仅仅是做好城市形象的开头。如何丰富城市品牌的内涵,有效传播城市品牌,让城市品牌在全球化的浪潮中进行国际化的传播并创造价值仍是杭州开展国际公关的重要议题。为此,杭州基于城市形象的国际定位,结合国际一流城市的形象塑造经验,制定并实施了城市品牌国际公共关系策略。

杭州借助各种契机和要素,运用多种手法对城市形象进行整体传播,不仅仅单单发挥政府部门的作用,还广泛利用城市各种资源,将城市形象传播推进到了整合营销传播(IMC)的层次。

（1）建立城市形象识别系统

历史上对杭州有很多美誉,比如"人间天堂""丝绸之都"等等。在杭州确定城市品牌的过程中,充分考虑了全球化因素。比如,"人间天堂"这一品牌在翻译上可能出现问题。因为西方国家对"天堂"的翻译和我们理解不同,如果"人间天堂"翻译成英文,就容易引起国外人士的歧义。在广泛征集意见和专家论证的基础上,经过多次筛选、比较,最后确定了"生活品质之城"的城市品牌。

在实际中,杭州还将"生活品质"这个城市品牌广泛地与各种大型活动、行业相结合,成倍放大了城市品牌的效应。例如应用于旅游业为"东方休闲之都,品质生活之城",应用于高新行业为"天堂硅谷、品质生活",西博会的口号为"西湖博览会,品质生活城"。

（2）媒介宣传型公关

新闻报道：组织新加坡亚洲新闻台、凤凰卫视、中国台湾《联合早报》、中国香港新闻中心、英国TBP杂志等记者到杭采访,在相关报纸、杂志、电台上免费刊播杭州旅游宣传内容。

专题栏目：与中央人民广播电台合作开设《东方休闲之都——杭州》专栏；与新华网合作建设杭州旅游品牌形象推广网站——新华网杭州旅游

[①] 谢婧,《杭州城市品牌国际公关策略》,《公关世界》,2014年第7期,第22-25页。

频道。

形象广告：在中央电视台中文国际频道和英文国际频道投放 15 秒杭州形象广告。

宣传画册：旅游部门制作发放了《杭州旅游指南》《杭州休闲导图》等九种各针对不同受众的多语言旅游宣传手册，共计 185 万余册。

（3）交际型公关

2006 年，杭州以举办世界休闲博览会为契机，组织促销团或派员参加国家旅游局或浙江省旅游局组织的国外促销团 8 次，接待国外交流团体 60 余批。2008 年 7 月，杭州以招商之旅推进城市国际化，市长率团出访美国、加拿大，借鉴国际经验，加快推进杭州的城市国际化进程，吸引更多的国际知名企业和海外留学人才来杭投资创业，进一步扩大对外交流和合作。2008 年，杭州还举办了"国际友好城市市长峰会"论坛，国际友城 19 个代表团和国内友城 12 个代表团共商"城市与旅游"，推进国际友好城市合作。

（4）活动体验型公关

连续多年，杭州每年都举办"生活品质国际交流日"的活动，并将把这个活动打造为杭州城市形象国际化公关的精品节目。该活动的特色是，第一，邀请的都是外籍人士，目的不仅是让这些国际友人体验杭州的生活品质，更重要的是这些人可以承担杭州形象"二级传播"的舆论领袖，其影响力可以为杭州传播城市形象助一臂之力。其次，这种体验式的传播活动不仅能够展示杭州外在的美好形象，更能让这些国际友人深入了解杭州的文化内涵。

（5）会展营销型公关

西湖博览会从恢复之日开始，就承载了杭州城市营销的责任。西湖博览会在 2008 年正式更名为"西湖国际博览会"（简称"西博会"），增加了很多国际性的活动，例如"西湖国际音乐节""西湖国际睡眠论坛""西博会国际旅游节""杭州国际友城'城市与旅游'市长峰会"等等。除了西博会，杭州还举办了"中国国际动漫节""国际休闲博览会""国际丝绸博览会"等等各种类型的博览会，充分借助行业的展会推动城市形象的国际化传播。

（6）体育赛事型公关

大型体育赛事如奥运会等，对于城市形象的传播能够起到巨大的推动作用。杭州今年也开始借用国际体育赛事传播城市形象，如杭州国际马拉松赛，来自中国、韩国、日本等国家和地区的 50 多支代表队，环绕西湖，途径柳浪闻莺、南屏晚钟等著名景点进行比赛，赛事路线被誉为"世界上最美丽的马拉松线路"之一。

国际公关绪论 | Introduction and Framework of the Book

在杭州多管齐下的国际城市形象塑造活动中,杭州愈加显现出充满魅力的"国际范"。杭州每周有超过400架次的国际航班在空中起飞、穿梭、降落;每年数以百亿的资本和财富以进出口贸易的形式在杭州与世界之间流动;每年11000多个国际、国内会议在这里上演"头脑风暴";每年320万人次的"洋面孔"带着好奇和憧憬走进这座城市,其中不少人选择留下来,在这里学习、生活、创业,成为了"新杭州人"。

> **Case Study 案例分析**
>
> 杭州城市品牌国际公关属于地方政府国际公关,目的是在全球化环境下,更好地传播城市形象,提高城市的国际知名度和美誉度。
>
> 杭州城市品牌国际公关成功之处主要有两点。第一,精准定位品牌形象。杭州的城市特征,从单方面讲,山水可能不及桂林、黄山;经济可能不如上海、深圳;文化遗产不如北京、西安,但杭州的优势是自然环境、经济、文化互为渗透融合,经过多方面的考虑,杭州最终选用"生活品质之城"这一城市品牌作为杭州的国际定位。第二,整合公关手段,实施多重公关。经过调研城市现状与可用资源后,杭州巧妙地利用媒介宣传型公关、交际型公关、活动体验型公关、会展营销型公关以及体育赛事型公关等公关方式,全方位、多层次地向国际社会积极展现"品质生活城市"的方方面面,促进了杭州国际形象的推广以及国际化的深入发展。

1.3 Further Reading 拓展阅读

1.3.1 Disneyland Resort IPR Campaign[①]

Background

As the Disneyland Resort's Hispanic agency of record, VPE, a public relations company, was tasked with generating media interest that strengthens the park's standing as a prime destination for Hispanic families. In 2011, the park established a Three Kings Day (Día de los Reyes Magos) weekend long

---

① Danny Moss & Barbaba Desanto, (ed.). *Public Relations Cases*. London: Routledge, 2002

event, a highly popular Hispanic holiday held annually in early January. Disneyland is one of the most popular destinations for Hispanic families in Southern California, and adding this celebration was designed as a way of strengthening ties with Latino guests and extending the park's highly-popular holiday period an additional week.

Strategy

The Disneyland Resort Holiday Season was extended through January 6, 2013, which made Three Kings Day Celebration (Jan 6) a perfect and natural fit. The Three Kings Day Celebration would continue to set Disneyland Resort apart from the competition by providing a unique offering for the Hispanic segment. This presented the opportunity to create a "Disney-only" event that appealed directly to Hispanic guests and generated widespread Hispanic media interest that would increase visitors during the popular holiday season.

Practice

Following the success of first Three Kings Day Celebration in Disneyland in 2012, the event moved to the larger Big Thunder Ranch Jamboree in Frontierland 2013. Big Thunder Ranch Jamboree was transformed into an authentic Three Kings Day-themed area, adorned with statues of the Three Kings in an altar with bright jewel-toned décor including Paper Mache flowers, Papel Picado, florals and garlands. The area also included appearances by Mickey Mouse and Minnie Mouse and other Disney characters in fiesta costumes. Entertainment highlights included a variety of local folklorico ballet troupes and musical performers including the Grammy-winning Mariachi Divas. Children's activities included face-painting, coloring, crown decorating and other activities. Special food carts served traditional Three Kings Day treats. The seasonal menu at Rancho del Zocalo restaurant included tamales, Mexican hot chocolate and rosca de reyes, the special cake associated with the holiday. Three Kings Day entrance was free with Disneyland park admission.

Disneyland Resort and VPE implemented a two-week media relations campaign to secure media attendance for live remotes prior to the event in order to maximize the event's exposure, built around the following angles: Due to a successful premiere of the first Three Kings Day at Disneyland Resort, the park is celebrating a second year with a special celebration with themed décor and entertainment showcasing Mexican heritage, with food and children's activities themed to the holiday.

Disneyland provided various satellite paths from 4 a.m. to 1 p.m. in the Big Thunder Ranch Jamboree area to conduct live interviews on local morning shows. The Mariachi Divas and Disney characters were also available to add color to the segments. A Disneyland Resort chef was also on hand to give an interactive demonstration of Latin American Foods and Three Kings Day desserts to the media.

Through January 6, Dia de Reyes will be celebrated at Disneyland Park in a themed area at Big Thunder Ranch Jamboree with themed decorations, special food and treats, cultural entertainment and children's activities that celebrate this important Hispanic holiday.

Three Kings Day was the kick-off featured event to initiate the 2013 park campaign, Limited Time Magic. Limited Time Magic will surprise and delight guests in fanciful and unexpected ways at Disney Parks throughout 2013 with new entertainment and imaginative events for a span of a few days.

Evaluation

The 2013 Three Kings Day Media Event exceeded expectations for a second year in a row, generating a total of 1264196510 impressions and coverage from 46 Hispanic Media Outlets including the following.

Univision's national morning show Despierta America, Hispanic America's morning show for almost 15 years, aired a six-minute segment LIVE from Disneyland Park for the Three Kings media event with an exclusive food demo with Chef Jorge Sotelo. The segment positioned Disneyland as one of the top venues celebrating this important holiday in the country.

Agency EFE News Wire Service covered the event for the second year in a row, distributing the stories and photos to hundreds of outlets across the country.

16 Hispanic TV Stations covered the event reaching 13358696 Million viewers.

4 Hispanic Print outlets generated 632034 Impressions.

15 Online/Wire unique outlets generated 1249843260 Impressions.

11 Blogs generated 362520 Impressions.

Thinking:

1. What was VPE's primary goal to achieve for the Disneyland Resort? And in order to accomplish this goal, how did Disneyland Resort do with the guidance of VPE?
2. Holiday marketing is frequently utilized by companies to promote their products. According to this case, please list its features and common measures.
3. Write a case study on Disneyland Resort IPR Campaign.

1.3.2 麦当劳"3·15"事件公关

3月15日是国际消费者权益日。1991年3月15日,中央电视台(简称"央视")经济部首次推出现场直播"3·15"国际消费者权益日消费者之友专题晚会。作为中央电视台的品牌节目,它唤醒了消费者的权益意识,成为规范市场秩序、传播国家法规政策的强大平台。专题调查、权威发布等,都成为广大观众最期待的节目亮点。上央视"3·15"晚会,对于品牌来说,是一个致命的打击。

2012年"3·15"晚会,麦当劳被曝将超过保质期限的食品再利用,甚至更改生产时间。据央视"3·15"晚会报道,麦当劳对每种食材都有在保温箱内存放时间的限制,并且规定在保温箱中的食材如果存放超过规定时间就要扔掉。但央视记者暗访的结果却是,在北京三里屯麦当劳店内,食材在保温箱中存放超过规定时间,但并没有被扔掉,而是被重新放回了保温箱,再次加工销售。麦当劳各类甜品派是颇受消费者喜欢的,麦当劳的派在包装上都有一个数字,它是这个派的过期时间。央视记者发现,这些数字可以被员工随意更改,原本只有90分钟保质期的派,可能三四个小时之后仍在待售。此外,记者在暗访中还发现,有些麦当劳员工会把掉在地上的牛肉饼、过期变硬的吉士片、已经过期的鸡翅当做正常的原料使用。

在社会化媒体时代,危机蔓延的范围无边界,其传播速度也更加快速;但同时也给了品牌快速回应,在最短时间内回应和弱化危机影响的机会,这就考验企业的公关能力。

从央视"3·15"晚会开播到三个小时,被曝光的品牌中,麦当劳第一个站出来回应。麦当劳在问题被曝光后,一个小时候后迅速在新浪微博的官方微博上做出了第一个回应:

国际公关绪论 | Introduction and Framework of the Book

> @麦当劳：央视"3·15"晚会所报道的北京三里屯餐厅违规操作的情况，麦当劳中国对此非常重视。我们将就这一个别事件立即进行调查，坚决严肃处理，以实际行动向消费者表示歉意。我们将由此事深化管理，确保营运标准切实执行，为消费者提供安全、卫生的美食。欢迎和感谢政府相关部门、媒体及消费者对我们的监督。

截至写这篇文章的2012年3月15日23点20分，在@新浪财经等众多媒体的带动下，@麦当劳官方微博这条信息获得了8400多次的转发量，直接一次转发覆盖的人数超过1000万。获得了在社交媒体时代的最大程度的信息传递速度和效率。

（图片来自市场部①）

麦当劳的品牌官方微博声明被微博和互联网媒体广泛转发，从回应速度和态度上，已经获得媒体的响应。这也给麦当劳最大范围免费扩散反映和弱化负面影响的机会。在"3·15"晚会的第二天，各大传统媒体不会是一边倒的负面曝光声音，麦当劳在中国的粉丝群也稳定了下来。

麦当劳的微博公关取得了很好的效果。据媒体报道，"3·15"晚会之后，各地记者走访麦当劳，发现生意依旧火爆。在被曝光的麦当劳三里屯店，一边有记者和工商局的人员在质询，一边消费者还在排队购买。有顾客表示：被曝光出来的问题并不严重，不妨碍自己继续在麦当劳消费。而在美股上市的麦当劳股价，也仿佛穿上了防弹衣，当天甚至每股上涨0.75美元。

思考题：

1. 阅读麦当劳"3·15"事件公关案例后，再结合你的社交经验，总结出社交媒体对企业危机的利与弊。
2. 假设某地方本土品牌快乐基被媒体曝光存在食品变质问题，请模仿麦当劳回应被央视曝光的问题的140字微博，为快乐基公关团队撰写一条申明

---

① http://www.shichangbu.com/article-3784-1.html 2015年10月15日。

微博。

3. 试从公关主体类型、公关技巧等方面写麦当劳"3·15"事件公关案例分析。

1.4 Simulation 情景模拟

1.4.1 "International IT Hub" PR

In the early 2000s, the Singapore government launched a major policy initiative to promote the island state as the primary location for leading international IT and telecommunications companies wishing to establish head offices, joint ventures and manufacturing facilities in the Asian market. Success in this potentially means billions of dollars to the Singapore economy.

With China widely predicted to become the world's largest market, much attention has turned to Beijing and Shanghai, while Hong Kong continues to vie for international investment, and new emerging economies such as Malaysia and India are also competing for international investment dollars.

Through the InfoComm Development Authority of Singapore (IDA), working in conjunction with the Economic Development Board of Singapore and other government agencies, Singapore launched an international public relations campaign to promote key messages that position Singapore positively as an "IT investment hub" in Asia, including: government support and incentives for international investment; the wide availability of technology infrastructure, including broadband, in Singapore; a skilled workforce; geographic centrality to the emerging economies of China and India; multicultural and multilingual capabilities with Singapore having large Indian and Chinese speaking populations as well as English; a safe, secure environment to invest and establish facilities.

Simulation:

1. According to the classification of International Public Relations actors, what actor does this case involve?

2. Singapore government finds media are influential within its targeted audiences in this public campaign. If you are in charge of this campaign, which media will you choose to convey Singapore's PR idea?
3. Divide the whole class into two groups, of which one team were the Singapore government, and the other team were the honored guest include famous media and IT giant, the government team simulate a press conference to show how fit Singapore is for IT investment.

1.4.2 含氯可乐事件公关

2012年4月17日,可口可乐(山西)饮料有限公司的员工对媒体的爆料引发热议。该员工称公司在管道改造中,将消毒用的含氯处理水误混入饮料中,涉及9个批次、12万余箱可口可乐,价值可能高达500万元,目前这部分被疑含氯饮料可能已经流入市场。

新华网报道称,记者就此事向可口可乐(山西)饮料有限公司核实时,该公司给记者提供了一则声明,称所谓"公司内部信息"经查并不符合事实,并保留依法追究的权利。该公司声明称,鼓励员工通过合适的渠道向公司反映其关心的问题,并确保该渠道畅通。该公司公共事务及传讯部经理高旭峰表示,公司不接受当面采访,对于记者提出的任何疑问,可以通过电子邮件提问并予以答复。从16点40分通过电子邮件提出采访问题,新华网记者等待近两个小时,该公司未给出任何答复。

山西省质监局网站4月28日通告称,针对媒体披露的"可口可乐(山西)饮料有限公司含氯软化水混入部分批次饮料产品"中的问题,山西省质监局于4月19日组成调查组,通过现场检查、抽检样品、查阅记录、询问员工等方式,认定媒体报道情况属实。同时在调查中,还发现该公司存在个别生产条件不符合相关规定的问题。根据相关法律法规规定,4月28日,山西省质监局对可口可乐(山西)饮料有限公司做出了停产整改的行政处罚。

模拟:

1. 按国际公关主体划分,"含氯可乐"公关属于哪一种公关?
2. 若你担任可口可乐大中华区的总裁,下车后遇到等待近两个小时的新华网记者,你将如何回答记者的质疑?如何应对日益升级的"含氯可乐"事件?

3. 此次"含氯可乐"事件影响了可口可乐在中国的形象,请一组同学模拟可口可乐公关团队,应采取哪些专题活动修复该组织在中国的形象?

Exercises
本章练习题

Gap Filling 填空题

Directions: Fill in the blanks with the correct form of the words and expressions provided.

| practice | public | press release |
| strategic communication process | press agent | settle |

1. Numerous examples of public relations—like activities were identifiable in the early days of American settlement as each of the colonies used publicity techniques to attract (   ).
2. The earliest definition emphasized (   ) and (   ), while more modern definitions incorporate the concepts of "engagement" and "relationship building."
3. According to International Public Relations Association (IPRA), International public relations is a (   ) that builds mutually beneficial relationships between organizations and their public.
4. (   ) must take pre-emptive steps to ensure their voices are heard in cross-national conflicts, particularly through the cultivation of relevant media representatives, both at home and in host countries
5. In 1758, King's College (now Columbia University) issued the first (   )—to announce graduation exercises.

True or False 判断题

Directions: In the answer sheet, write T or F to indicate whether the statement is true or false.

1. 各国、各地区由于地理位置、交通条件、地形、气候等的差异,加之长期的历史沉淀,形成了丰富多彩的民族文化或区域文化。跨国家、跨地区进行

国际公关绪论 | Introduction and Framework of the Book

的国际公共关系活动,必然具有跨文化的特征。( )
2. 国际公关三要素由国际行为体(国际主体)、国际社会环境以及传达的信息组成。( )
3. 目前,发达国家的许多新闻媒介都已成为跨国性的大企业,在世界各地采访报道新闻、发行报刊、播放广播电视节目等。其中有美国的美联社、合众国际社、英国的路透社、法国的法新社、俄罗斯的卡塔尔等媒体。( )
4. 国际公关调查是国际公关全过程的首要步骤,是国际公关工作的基础,也是国际公关活动的重要方式。( )
5. 国际公关评估是指国际公关主体为了实现既定的目标,充分依据和利用实施条件,对国际公关的创意策划进行实施策略、手段、方法设计并进行实际操作与管理的过程。( )

Table Completion 表格题
请按照国家公关的实施程序填充下列表格。

阶段	实施内容
	了解该国在国际公众心目中的形象地位,对开展公关活动的条件、困难、实现目标的可能性等情况进行了解,可以为决策提供科学依据。
目标——Objective	
操作——Practice	
	主要是在活动末期从准备过程、实施过程、活动影响等方面开展工作。准备过程中,要考虑到背景资料、调查形式等因素;实施过程要考虑媒体参与数量、信息发送数量、影响公众数量,活动影响则要将最终结果纳入考虑范围内。

Reading Comprehension 阅读理解

Directions: Read the following passage and choose the best answer from A,B,C and D.

A Case Study Analysis of the Tiger Woods Scandal[①]

In 2009, Tiger Woods, an American professional golfer, was caught amidst one of the most high-profile sex scandals of all time. Since the beginning of his

---

① Blair Bernstein, "Crisis Management and Sports in the Age of Social Media: A Case Study Analysis of the Tiger Woods". *Elon Journal of Undergraduate Research in Communication* 2012(3):2.

professional career in 1996, Woods was regarded as one of the best—if not the best—golfer in history.

His fame and popularity made his fall from grace in 2009 that much harder. Reports of infidelity with a woman named Rachel Uchitel surfaced on Thanksgiving Day of that year from a tabloid magazine. It was immediately met with disbelief, but the situation became increasingly suspicious following a 2:30 a.m. car accident two days later. It was reported his wife, Elin Nordegren, was chasing his Cadillac Escalade with a golf club. Over the next several weeks, 10 other women came forward admitting to having had affairs with the married-Woods. *The New York Daily News* reported there were 120 allegations of adultery. The mistresses ranged from prostitutes to porn stars to waitresses. Woods saw several big-name sponsors like Accenture, Gillette and Gatorade drop him as a spokesperson, stating that he no longer represented the values of their organizations.

Social Media's Reaction to the Woods Scandal

In the days immediately following the accident, traditional media outlets allotted 2% to 7% of its coverage to the Woods scandal, good for the second leading story between November 30 and December 6. Since the details of Woods' infidelity took the back seat to President Obama's speech on the War in Afghanistan, the level of traditional media coverage did not accurately reflect the fervor the Woods' scandal created among social media users. Online communications saw dramatic spikes in how often Woods' name was mentioned and how often it was mentioned on issues unrelated to golf performance. According to a Nielsen Wire report (2010), Woods' name was almost always associated with words like "cheater" "infidelity" and "crash" on social media sites.

Crisis Management Strategies by Statement

Statement 1, November 29, 2009: On November 29, 2009, two days after the initial crash and four days after the report of infidelity, Woods' PR staff issued their first public statement on the rumors circulating in the media. The statement was written as a direct letter from Woods. By explaining the accident and the injuries he sustained from it, he took sole responsibility for its occurrence. Woods used mortification strategies, like accepting blame for the

国际公关绪论 | Introduction and Framework of the Book

incident and apologizing, but did so referring exclusively to the car accident. He avoided any mention of infidelity and went so far as to use non-existent strategies like denial and attacking the accuser when addressing those allegations.

Statement 2, December 2, 2009: The statement issued by Tiger Woods on December 2, 2009, marked the first apology for his implied extramarital affairs. Though he never specifically mentioned infidelity or cheating, he alluded to his "transgressions." He used mortification strategies at great length in the second statement. Not only did he apologize to his family and fans but made a promise to do better by both parties in the future.

Statement 3, December 11, 2009: Woods announced on December 11, 2009, that he would be taking a hiatus from professional golf. He stated that it was a decision he came to after much thought and that he needed to focus his attention on becoming a better husband, father and person. It was also the first time Woods directly took responsibility for cheating, rather than just implying it. It took a total of 15 days from the time of the accident until Tiger would specify he had betrayed his wife, a period of silence that would earn him heavy public criticism. He used mortification strategies exclusively throughout the remainder of the statement.

Statement 4, February 17, 2010: The fourth statement from Woods' staff announced that Tiger would address the media publicly for the first time since the scandal on February 19 in Ponte Vedra Beach, Fla. It was not a news conference, therefore, eliminating the opportunity for a question and answer period. This was the first report from Woods in more than two months, which allowed for long periods of speculation and criticism. Though it was a brief statement, his staff utilized the opportunity to employ mortification strategies like atonement and remediation once again.

Statement 5, February 19, 2010: The speech given by Tiger Woods on February 19, 2010, was the most extensive made during the scandal. It was written and designed to signal the end of the acute crisis stage and transition into a period of recovery and regrouping. He began with more mortification strategies, primarily atoning for his sins wherever possible. Woods made an effort to not only acknowledge the hurt he caused family and fans, but his business partners as well. It is then that he included a reference to his foundation and the good work it had done in the past, an ingratiating strategy known as bolstering. Many media members criticized him for his attempt to pitch his foundation during a speech that was meant to center around his apology.

Statement 6, March 16, 2010: On March 16, 2010, Woods announced that he would return to professional golf at the Masters. He reminded readers of the therapy he had undergone and the efforts he made to restore his family life. Woods also offered an apology for the tournaments he had to miss as a result of his rehabilitation, the use of yet another mortification strategy.

Statement 7, April 8, 2010: After completing day one at the Masters, Woods held a press conference open to all reporters. It was the first time he took questions from the media since the scandal. During the duration of the interview, Tiger was able to deflect all questions that related back to the scandal and spoke specifically on his golf game. He mentioned the warm reception he received from the fans out on the course. There were no identifiable crisis management strategies used throughout the duration of the interview.

Statement 8, August 23, 2010: The final statement in the 2010 Tiger Woods scandal was a joint statement by both him and his wife. It announced that they were divorced and that though they were no longer married, they would remain wonderful parents to their two children. The statement called for sympathy from the public, a suffering strategy, as a way to encourage others to respect their privacy and move on from the scandal.

Summary

Woods relied predominately on mortification strategies to manage the crisis and restore public perception. Of the eight statements made, six included mortification strategies and often more than one instance of them. Four of the five types of crisis management strategies were incorporated into his statements throughout the lifespan of the crisis, all with the exception of distance strategies. The media drew attention to his attempt at "bolstering" with the mention of his foundation and his repeated use of suffering tactics. Traditional media coverage was common, but not as potent as the discussion of the scandal on social media. Woods' name was mentioned frequently in association with his wrongdoings up until his first press conference. Though it may have been a prolonged process,

国际公关绪论 | Introduction and Framework of the Book

research indicates that discussion of Woods and the scandal has died down on social media sites. Woods' slightly restored image has landed him two new sponsorships with Rolex and Fuse Science Inc. since the scandal.

1. According to a Nielsen Wire report (2010), Woods' name was almost always associated with words like ( ) on social media sites.
   A. "cheater" "fidelity" and "incrash"
   B. "cheater" "fidelity" and "crash"
   C. "cheat" "infidelity" and "crash"
   D. "cheater" "infidelity" and "crash"
2. By explaining the accident and the injuries he sustained from it, he took ( ) responsibility for its occurrence.
   A. sole   B. no
   C. part   D. none
3. The statement issued by Tiger Woods on December 2, 2009, marked the ( ) apology for his implied extramarital affairs.
   A. third   B. second
   C. first   D. fourth
4. After completing day one at the Masters, Woods held a ( ) open to all reporters.
   A. press conference B. meeting
   C. forum   D. discussion
5. Woods relied predominately on ( ) strategies to manage the crisis and restore public perception.
   A. mortification   B. ingratiating
   C. non-existent   D. suffering

Thinking 思考题
1. 国家、地方政府、企业、个人在实施国际公关时有哪些技巧？
2. 各类国际公关主体在实施公关时有哪些不同？
3. 搜索一个你喜欢的国际公关案例，按照ROPE的步骤编辑并分享。

International Public Relations of Nation
国家公关

Gist
内容概览

As the most important actors in international community, nations change the international community from day to day by their diversified activities. In the era of globalization, all nations need to cope with endless natural and man-made disasters and the task of image-building. The colorful public relations activities of nations highlight the international public relations stage.

This chapter discusses public relations activities of nations. Students can learn the purposes, methods and techniques of national public relations from many up-to-date bilingual cases, including "9.11" Incident, Think UK, Maldives' underwater cabinet and so on. Students are required to discuss and analyze the successful experiences and failed lessons, and then apply what they have learned in simulated activities, which cultivates students' practical public relations skills.

国家是国际社会中最重要的国际行为主体,它的活动推动着国际社会日新月异的变化。在全球化浪潮日益加深的当今世界,所有国家都面临着天灾人害等公关危机和塑造国家形象的任务,形式多样的国家公关活动是国际公共关系舞台上浓墨重彩的部分。

本章以国家为公共关系行为主体,介绍了不同国家公共关系的目的、方法和技巧,选取了有代表性的国家公关双语案例,如"9·11"事件公关、创意英国和马尔代夫水下内阁公关等。学生在学习完本章内容后,应熟知和学会运用国家公关的方法和技巧,尝试解决情景模拟的问题。

国家公关 | International Public Relations of Nation

2.1 Basic Knowledge 基础知识

2.1.1 Definition 定义

A nation is a union composed of people, territory, sovereignty and government. National Public Relations (NPR) is a method of intercultural communication management between extensive international public and the sovereign country. From a dynamic point of view, National PR is two-way communication activity spreading between government agencies and the international public community; from a static point of view, National PR is both a behavior or state of information exchange, and a communication and dissemination between the government and the international public. Traditionally, the public relations activities supported by governments have been interest-oriented.

现代英语中对国家的表述有三个词汇：领土意义上的国家为country，民族意义上的国家为nation，政治（主权政府）意义上的国家为state。一般用nation表述国际法中的民族国家。国家是由人口、领土、主权和政府组成的统一体。

国家公关是主权国家与广泛的国际公众之间的跨文化传播管理。从动态上看，国家公关即政府机构与国际社会公众之间的双向传播沟通活动；从静态上看，国家公关是发生在政府与国际公众之间的一种信息交流、沟通与传播的行为和状态。

2.1.2 Features 属性

National public relations have the following features.

(1) NPR as an Extension of Diplomacy

The first of the feature of NPR is the one that is least frequently stated explicitly. That is the view that foreign external communication activity is an extension of diplomacy.

(2) NPR as a Matter of National Projection

External communications exists to create an image of the nation in the minds of foreign nationals, which will make them to support the nation's policies, visit (or emigrate) to that country, and invest in that country's industries or buy that country's goods and services.

(3) External Communication for Cultural Relations

The central proposition of the cultural relations paradigm is that cultural connections can have political or economic effects.

(4) External Communication as Political Warfare

The fourth type is a conflict in which communication becomes the tool of military or ideological struggle. In this mode of action, the overall objective is the defeat of the opponent.

根据国家公关的定义,可以总结出的国家公关的属性主要有七点:主体的排他性、客体的复杂性、方式的差异性、领域的广泛性、目标的公益性、环境的全球性、资源的整合性。

(1) The Exclusiveness of the Subject 主体的排他性

一方面,国家对国内政治、经济、军队和暴力机关的垄断,为国家的统治能力提供了坚实的基础。另一方面,国家作为国际社会的个体,国家对他国和国际体系也有自身的利益诉求。所以,国家对内的垄断性和对外的利益表达,决定国家在公关中,只能由代表国家的相关政府机构进行策划和决策。

(2) The Complexity of the Object 客体的复杂性

国家公关的客体,既包括社会公众,又包括国际公众。不同群体中公众的文化素质、生活方式、价值观念有极大差异性,这种差异性直接导致不同公众对同一事件的不同态度。因此,国家在公关中应该注意宣传形式和媒体选择。

(3) The Difference of the Manner 方式的差异性

国家实力与国家性质影响国家公关的风格。一方面,国家软实力与硬实力的强弱直接影响国家公关方式、态度的强硬与妥协。另一方面,国家是极权主义、权威主义还是民主主义,同样在潜意识里决定国家公关的风格。

(4) The Universality of the Domain 领域的广泛性

国家的主权特性,决定国家有义务处理国内和涉外的政治、经济、文化和公共服务等领域的危机。所以国家公关就是如何高效地处理本国与他国发生的利益纠葛。在这一方面,它属于国家公共外交和国内公共管理的交集。因此它的范围既有涉外交往也有国内管理,例如"9·11事件"、白宫关门事件、跨国界的水污染事件。

(5) The Commonweal of the Objective 目标的公益性

国家政府作为公关部门,在实现本国利益诉求的过程中。其本质是在维护和实现国家内部的公共利益与社会利益。一方面,公共利益是公民利益的直接反映,包括安全、医疗、教育等。另一方面,国际国内环境的稳定,为本国社会利益的实现提供和谐稳定的环境。

(6) The Globalization of the Circumstance 环境的全球性

这里的环境包括两个方面,一是国际舆论;二是国家环境。国家公关策略的制定,既要考虑各个主权国的国家利益,又要考虑国际组织的宗旨与原则。同时国家的性质、稳定和繁荣程度会间接地影响公关效果。因此,国家公关,既要考虑到本国的利益与形象,又要考虑不同层次的环境。

(7) The Integration of the Resource 资源的整合性

国家的主权性和权威性,决定国家对国内资源的垄断。一方面,政府公关的实施既包括公共资源也包括公共资源以外的资源,比如,专业性强的公关顾问或公司。另一方面,国家掌握着大量传播工具,各类媒体由国家管理,政府可以有效地整合不同媒体的优势,从而有效的传播国家信息,起到引导公众舆论的作用。

2.1.3 Classification 分类

The categories of NPR are extensive and various. Here are several kinds of classifications listed below.

According to the classification and international status of different nations, the NPR can be classified as: Superpower PR, Great Power PR, Middle Power PR and Small Power PR.

According to the forms of NPR, it can be divided into two perspectives. From a narrow perspective, NPR activities can be divided into two aspects: one is information activities, which is using all kinds of media to expand the influence of the state. The other is education and cultural exchange. The exchange of students, teachers and scholars will promote the transfer of information. Both sides can gain a mutual benefit, and promote a good national image. In a broad sense, the content of NPR activities is very extensive. The government, economy, sports and even an individual can play a significant role in NPR activities.

According to the purpose of NPR, there are two types: One is the proactive type, which means a nation-sate takes PR activities initiatively to maintain its positive image. And the other is the reactive type, which refers to a nation which takes PR activities in the face of a crisis in order to extricate them from a passive situation.

According to the content of NPR, it can be classified as: Government PR, Media PR, Culture PR, Economy and Trade PR, Public PR and so on.

按照不同的标准,国家公关可以分为不同的类别。以下列举了几种不同分类。

根据国家分类的不同,以一国的国际地位和全球影响力为尺度,国家公关可分为:超级大国(Superpower)公关、大国(Great Power)公关、中等国家(Middle Power)公关和弱小国家(Small Nations)公关。按国家的不同意识形态,可分为:资本主义国家公关和社会主义国家公关。按国家所属不同文明和地域的差别,又可分为:西方文明(Western Civilization)国家公关、伊斯兰文明(Islamic Civilization)国家公关、儒家文明(Confucian Civilization)国家公关、印度教文明(Hindu Civilization)国家公关、日本文明(Japanese Civilization)国家公关、非洲(African Civilization)文明国家公关和拉美文明(Latin America Civilization)国家公关。

根据国家公关活动的不同形式,可分两个层面上的国家公关。从狭义上讲基本上包括两个方面,一是信息活动(Information Activities),也就是利用各类媒体和传媒手段来扩大国家的影响。主要是通过无线电、出版物、电台、电视台、各种新闻记者招待会或其他舆论渠道介绍国家的基本信息和情况,加强与外国公众的交流,达到传播本国的价值观的目的,起到一个导向作用。二是教育文化交流活动(Educational and Cultural Exchange),利用学生、教师和学者的学术教育交流来增进国家间的信息传递,推广了国家间的思想交流,相互之间扩大影响,促进国家形象的塑造。从广义上讲,国家公关的内容十分广泛,除去信息活动和文化教育交流之外还有政府公关、经贸公关、体育公关,甚至个人行为也能在国家公关中起到重要的作用。

按国家公关的目的,可以分为:主动性公关(Proactive Type),指国家为维护国家形象采取的以攻为守的策略;被动性公关(Reactive Type)指国家在危机面前,为了摆脱被动局面,防止自身的公共关系失调而采取的一种公共关系活动方式。

按国家公关的内容不同,可以分为政府公关、媒体公关、文化公关、经贸公关、公众公关。

(1) Government Public Relations 政府公关

国家公关 | International Public Relations of Nation

政府公关是由政府为主体,用比较正式的公关形式开展国家公关,如国家间的领导人互访、国家媒体的对外宣传等,来塑造良好的国家形象。

(2) Media Public Relations 媒体公关

运用大众传播媒介和内部沟通方法,开展宣传工作,使更多的外国公众能够了解公关国家的信息,进而直接开展与外国民众的交流活动。

(3) Culture Public Relations 文化公关

文化是影响一国民众思想意识的重要因素之一。文化交流可以使其他国家的民众增进对本国的了解,长期的接触和交流有利于传播本国的价值观和意识形态。文化公关已成为国家公关的重要内容。

(4) Economics and Business Public Relations 经贸公关

在全球化日益加深的世界,经济的重要作用不言而喻。用经济贸易手段,增进与其他国家的联系,通过市场的运作机制和规则,以官方或非官方的方式加大与外国各界的交流,从而可以塑造良好的国家形象,消除外国民众的无知或误解。

(5) The Public PR 公众公关

主要发生在一些西方国家,利用游说的方式开展演讲和宣传,增加信息的交流,消除外国公众的偏见和误解,获得多数人的支持,从而成功开展公关活动。

2.1.4 Evolution 演变

在古代中国的类国家公关思想中,商王盘庚迁都时进行了宣传与动员活动;西周末年针对周厉王的暴政,《国语·周语上》中的《召公谏厉王弭谤》左丘明记载道:"防民之口,甚于防川",社会舆论的好坏直接关系到政权的稳定;春秋战国,则有百家争鸣,各派皆有国家施政之策。中国古代国家公关主体的内在修为很重要,如孔孟之道,偏重政治、军事和道德;但古代中国的类公关思想中缺乏具体操作规范和方法。

而在古代西方的类国家公关思想中以古希腊和古罗马为代表。古希腊的贝壳放逐法①体现对民众意见的重视,其注重具体方法技术研究,如演讲、修辞、逻辑,旨在说服他人,如亚里士多德的修辞学强调怎么用语言影响听众的技术。由此看来西方古代公关注重效益和实用性,传播手段多样。正

---

① 又称陶片放逐法,陶片放逐法是古希腊雅典等城邦实施的一项政治制度,由雅典政治家克里斯提尼于公元前510年左右创立,约公元前487年左右陶片放逐法才首次付诸实施。雅典公民可以在陶片上写上那些不受欢迎人的名字,并通过投票表决将企图威胁雅典民主制度的政治人物予以政治放逐。

因如此,国家公关可以说是起源于西方并且最初发展于西方。

公共关系最早可以追溯到古罗马先哲们"权力在民"的政治思想,但真正成为一种工具和职业,还是应该回到19世纪末的美国。美国独立战争期间的政治游说、宣传鼓动、资金募集等活动为公共关系这一工具的推广使用起了很好的示范效果,20世纪初美国媒体针对资本家、企业主的大规模"揭丑"运动则直接导致了公共关系职业的诞生。19世纪以马戏团老板巴纳姆为代表,信奉"公众要被愚弄"的主张,激起了新闻界的"扒粪运动",由此成为现代公共关系的导火索。

20世纪初,在此期间诞生了艾维·李和爱德华·伯奈斯这两个公关先驱。1903年,艾维·李成立"宣传顾问事务所",以收费的方式为客户提供有效的传播沟通服务,标志着公共关系职业在美国的诞生,也是在世界范围内的诞生。他主张"说真话",奠定了诚信传播的职业道德基础,第一次把公众放在平等的位置上。伯奈斯主张"投公众所好",根据公众的特点要求确定传播政策和计划,著有《公众舆论的形成》,使公共关系理论化、系统化、完整化。

A significant contribution to the development of public relations came from Edward Bernays in the 1920s. He promoted a more sophisticated one-way approach to communications by contending that public relations attempts to engineer public support through the use of information, persuasion and adjustment. For many public relations practitioners, persuasion is the desired outcome of their activities, whether it is to change the attitude of government towards a client, promote an employers' point of view or create awareness of a product or service and thus support sales. It is also the judgment applied by clients who ask whether the PR effort made changes that were both beneficial and made an impact on profits. Yet Bernays did not simplistically advocate crude, one-way communications. His aim was to apply social science methods first to research the situation and then to create the most effective methods of communication. Absent from these early approaches was an application of a developed concept of two-way communication, of strategy and of feedback applied to the program of activity. From 1950s onwards, notions such as "mutual benefit" and "goodwill" became more widespread and public relations began to move away from its roots in publicity towards a more planned approach.

20世纪50年代后,卡特利普和森特著有《有效的公共关系》,正式提出双向对称式传播模式,标志公共关系走向成熟。

一些国家的国家公关活动走在了世界前列,例如:美国早在1945年,就全面启动了国家公关战略,至今已经建构了两个主要的公关等式,即"自由=美国精神""美国精神=普世价值"。韩国政府为了塑造国家形象,不仅聘请了国际公关公司游说世界,而且成立了由总理直接负责的专门的国家形象委员会。日本为了挽回第二次世界大战后形象的损失,利用奥林匹克运动会(简称"奥运会")、世界博览会(简称"世博会")、国际足联世界杯(简称"世界杯")等国际性活动,向世界全方位地展现日本战后的新形象,同时,风靡全球的动漫也是日本开展国家公关的重要方式。为了在世界传播法兰西的文化价值观,法国大力开展文化公关,目前已在近百个国家建立了一百五十多个的文化中心来推行法语和法国文化。而俄罗斯近年来也大力支持俄语推广和俄罗斯文化研究,将语言当做增强国家公关的重要工具。

2.1.5 Practice 实施

(1) The Basis of Practice 实施的基础

国家公关是以国家综合实力为基础进行的跨文化传播管理,国家硬实力和国家软实力在国家公关的开展过程中扮演着至关重要的角色。硬实力是一国利用其军事力量和经济实力强迫或收买其他国家的能力,软实力则是由文化、价值观、意识形态和民意等构成的影响力。

(2) The Purpose of Practice 实施的目的

展示国家真实形象

国家形象是国家的内部要素与外显形态的总和,反映了社会公众对一个国家的认同、喜好和支持的程度。国家形象作为一种软实力,通过政治制度、文化价值观、国民素质和外交关系体现出来,已成为国家利益的重要力量。

促进文化传播

国家公关利于展示一国的文化底蕴。有利于该国文化的对外传播和争取国际公众对其文化的理解,促进文化软实力的提升。一国政府通过一系列公关活动,能够增强中外文化与意识形态领域的交流,促进不同文化之间的相互融合。

提升国际地位

国家公关不仅有助于实现特定时限的目标,并且有助于解决现阶段的国际事务,实现一国长期战略所必不可少的组成部分,它通过公关信息项目和其他软实力资源的比较优势,使得其对外政策目标得以实现与巩固。

引导国际舆论,实现国家利益

国际舆论日益成为一种无形资源被世界各国所重视,其对于某个国家而言,既可能成为富有积极意义的推动力量,也可能成为带来消极后果的反对力量。国家公关的最终目的和最高境界,是公关实施国在有利的国际舆论环境下实现国家利益。

(3) The Procedure of Practice 实施的步骤

一国针对外国公众开展公关活动时,需要先查清该事件的具体情况,制定出科学可行的公关目标,之后朝着这个目标多角度、多层次、全方面地采取公关措施,并且要在活动末期对此次公关活动的效果进行合理化评估。

Research of NPR

Research reveals the perceptions, interests and opinions of targeted audiences; produces evidence used to select from among competing solutions; and provides a benchmark from which to evaluate campaign success. Research also allows campaign planning and evaluation based on facts rather than on intuition, rule of thumb, or past practices. NPR Practitioners find research particularly useful as the costs and importance of a campaign increase or as the certainty concerning an issue or public decreases.

Objective of NPR

What does the nation want to say?

The message is crucial. Before promoting the objectives of the NPR, establish what message, what angle the nation wants to try to put across. Bear in mind that it should be "newsy" or controversial to stand a reasonable chance of making any impression or being taken up by the media.

Who is the nation trying to reach?

Clearly this must depend on the message the nation is trying to put across. Don't forget that there are many distinct and separate target groups that the message should seek to influence, but even this target group needs to be broken down into smaller targets.

How can the nation get your message across?

This is where NPR comes into its own. Professionals who are professional know which medium to aim for: trade or national press, or radio and television.

They can also suggest when it will be more effective to use sponsorship, exhibitions, direct mail, or a combination of several, to do the job.

Practice of NPR

Informal methods often provide nations with inexpensive ways to listen to the critical public. Despite these potential benefits, practitioners take a sizable risk when they use informal research methods as the sole basis for communication campaign planning and problem solving. Because these methods lack the rigors of scientific research, they have a much greater likelihood of producing inaccurate results. The most obvious and common form of informal research involves talking to people. Practitioners can learn a surprising amount simply by asking people— ideally surveying those who are members of a target audience or other relevant group—for their opinions and ideas.

Broadly all NPR tactics can be categorized into five different types or methods to carry a government's chosen messages. These are hard news, soft news, news events, promotional content and direct news.

Each of these methods is in essence a form of media content. The choice of method or methods will depend on a government's already established message and media selection. Before looking at each of these methods it is worth recalling what the media is looking for.

In some nations, the use of the media as a primary communication tool has encountered several obstacles. Thus, it seems important to study: Media outreach in a nation; Media control by government or business; Media access.

Evaluation of NPR

There are many possible tools and techniques that NPR practitioners can utilize to begin to measure NPR outputs, but there are the four that are most frequently relied on to measure NPR impact at the output level:

Media Content Analysis

This is the process of studying and tracking what has been written and broadcast, translating this qualitative material into a quantitative form through some type of counting approach that involves the coding and classifying of specific messages.

Cyberspace Analysis

What appears in print is frequently commented about and editorialized about on the Web. Therefore, one component of PR output measurement ought to be a review and analysis of Web postings.

Trade Shows and Event Measurement

For shows and events, obviously one possible output measure is an assessment of total attendance, not just an actual count of those who showed up, but also an assessment of the types of individuals present, the number of interviews that were generated and conducted in connection with the event, and the number of promotional materials that were distributed.

Public Opinion Polls

Although most surveys that are designed and carried out are commissioned to measure NPR outcomes rather than NPR outputs, public opinion polls are often carried out in an effort to determine whether or not to target a specific audience.[①]

（4）The Technique of Practice 实施的技巧

国家公关技巧包含了传播公众选择适当、传播议程设置合理、传播方式本土化、传播媒介多样化。而大国和小国的公关技巧侧重点不同：大国借助自身强大的经济实力和政治影响力，通过多样化的媒介渠道和活动方式，希望在国际社会的大范围内产生实质性影响。而小国由于自身实力限制与目的相对单一集中，通常会利用国际多边话语平台，选择性地影响公众，从而达到公关目标。

2.1.6 Public Relations Planning 公关策划

公共关系策划是公共关系战略的核心。国家公关策划是对国家公共关系活动项目的形式和内容出谋划策与设计行动方案的泛指，是国家公关实施者根据国家形象的现状和目的要求，分析现有条件，谋划、设计公关战略、专题活动和具体公共关系活动最佳行动方案的过程。

国家公共关系策划无论是创意或制订方案，还是实施活动的全过程，都是一个运用科学思维，特别是创造性思维的过程。国家公共关系策划者应该灵活运用科学思维的技巧和方法。

（1）直接效仿法

直接效仿法就是借别人成功的招法为我所用，是一种模仿或借鉴之法。

---

① Jim Dunn, *Public Relations Techniques that Work*. London: Hawksmere, 1999.

对于国家公关策划的新手来讲,模仿他人的策划手段和方法,不能不说是一种比较实际的方法;对于国家公关策划的专家来讲,适时应用他人成功的策划招数,往往也能产生很好的效果。

遵循这种思路进行活动的策划应注意以下两点:第一,要进行仿效,原则上应有相似条件;第二,仿效不等于照搬,应该是在借鉴的基础上进行创造性的发挥。

(2)目标延伸法

目标延伸法是根据国家的具体公共关系目标来延伸推导,寻求实现目标的最佳途径的公共关系策划方法。这是一种顺向的发散性思维过程,思维顺序是:国家目标——影响实现目标的主要因素或条件——创意。

运用目标延伸法的关键是使目标和手段相适应,手段要确实能够推进目标的实现,也需注意公共关系活动的目标和实现目标的手段都具有可操作性。

(3)借名播誉法

借名播誉法是借助国际名流的知名度和美誉度来提高国家知名度和美誉度的方法,是一种借势法。国际名流往往是新闻界追踪的对象,社会公众关注的焦点,通常会产生所谓的名人效应。

利用借名播誉法进行国家公关活动策划不乏经典之作,但是要注意两点,第一,要创造性地发挥。如利用歌星、影星和体育明星等做当前策划热点时,要巧妙地应用其他领域的知名人士进行公关宣传,反而会产生新意。第二,一般要名誉相符。选择名人参与公关活动时,要注重其正面形象,要结合其自身特性及魅力,注重发挥名人的积极影响力。

(4)借题发挥法

借题发挥法是利用某种时机、某种态势,因势利导地进行国家公关策划的方法,也是一种借势法。"借题发挥"法中的"题"是指特定的时机、场合和事件。

借题发挥在应用时,要注意以下几点:第一,要善于识别机会、把握机会、利用机会;第二,一般来讲,所发挥的内容应同题相符;第三,要有独创性。

(5)制造新闻法

制造新闻法是通过国家公关实施者精心策划出具有轰动效应的事件来吸引国际媒体及国际公众注意的方法,是一种求同存异的思路,是一种造势之法。此种思路在应用过程中的关键是具有轰动效应的事件制造,这也是此法的根本价值所在。制造轰动效应就是要利用创造性思维,借机造势,或者借势造势,就是要标新立异、出奇制胜,但切忌无中生有和过度离奇。[①]

2.2 Bilingual Case Studies
双语案例

2.2.1 "9.11" Incident PR

Background

The grave unfolding of the events of September 11, 2001 began in the early hours of the morning. The first high-jacked passenger jet, American Airlines Flight 11 out of Boston, Massachusetts, crashed into the north tower of the World Trade Center at 8:45 a.m. Eastern Standard Time. A second plane, American Airlines Flight 175 also from Boston, followed shortly after and hit the south tower of the World Trade Center at 9:03 a.m. Both impacts tore gaping holes in the building, setting them on fire. At 9:43 a.m., American Airlines Flight 77 struck the Pentagon, lighting it on fire and causing significant damage. Immediately following the collision, the Pentagon and the White House were evacuated. The final blow came when United Airlines Flight 93 crashed in Somerset County, Pennsylvania.

Research

A sense of shock, fear and confusion swept the nation. Speculation about who was responsible for the devastation grew. The "9.11" terrorist attacks at its essence was successful in destroying a clear symbol of American prosperity and military might, calling into question the security and peace enjoyed by the greatest superpowers of world. This inevitably created the situation in which a response from the American government was not only required, but also extraordinarily significant.

Objective

It was vital for the American government to take emergency measures in order to, on the one hand, console the American people and deal with the chaotic scenes after the attack, and on the other hand, to reassure the foreign countries and reshape America's image on the international stage.

---

① 周安华、苗晋平,《公共关系:理论、实务与技巧(第4版)》。北京:中国人民大学出版社,2013年。

国家公关 | International Public Relations of Nation

Practice

At the time of attack, President George W. Bush was speaking at an elementary school in Sarasota, Florida. When informed of the attack, the president made a statement to the public declaring that the country had suffered an apparent terrorist attack before leaving the elementary school.

As the morning ended and the chaos continued, President Bush made a public statement from Barksdale Air Force Base in Louisiana at 1:04 p.m. He assured the American people that the government was taking all of the appropriate security, safety and rescue measures. This included placing the U.S. Military on high alert status worldwide, and he also asked for prayers for the victims of this horrific event.

Coverage of the September 11 attacks began almost instantaneously, with news stations and bystanders capturing video footage of the second plane crashing into Twin Tower II, victims leaping out of windows to their deaths, the collapse of the towers, and fire fighters, police officers, rescue workers, and volunteers pulling victims out of the rubble and helping them to safety. Throughout the coverage, however, the media also focused on the president, reporting on his utterances, actions and intentions, thus illustrating the importance of the president's role in this drama for the American public.

New York Governor George Pataki closed all government offices. Mayor Rudolph Giuliani urged New Yorkers to stay at home the day following the attacks. The American Stock Exchange, the NASDAQ, and the New York Stock Exchange were all closed and announced that they would remain closed the following day.

Once President Bush arrived back at the White House, he scheduled an address to the nation at 8:30 p.m. This address, coming directly from the Oval Office in the White House, was very short—only lasting five minutes—and to the point. In this speech, the president made the bold statement that the U.S. government would not make any distinction between the terrorists who committed the acts and the countries and leaders who harbor them. Finally, he assured the nation that administration and government bodies would continue to function, announcing that government offices in Washington were reopening for essential personnel Tuesday night and for all workers Wednesday.

In the days following the attack, the president promptly declared a national emergency the day of the attacks, and a national day of remembrance in response to the event. He also activated 50000 National Guard and reserve members to help with recovery and security. The president even traveled to the Pentagon that day to visit the victims and the relief workers, despite the security risks to his life.

A memorable rhetorical event for the president came three days following the attacks in what would become known as his bullhorn moment. Visiting the World Trade Center and standing on the rubble where the towers once stood, the president visited with the volunteers and people of New York. Holding up a bullhorn, and making a few general conversational comments with the people working there, there was a mustering of "We can't hear you" arising from the crowd. President Bush promptly said, "Well, I can hear you. All of America can hear you. And soon, the people who did this will hear us all."

As normal life began to resume in New York and Washington D.C., the president was very involved with ceremonial events. On the Friday after the attacks, President Bush led the nation in a national day of prayer and remembrance, giving a heartfelt meditation at a memorial service held in the National Cathedral. He even went as far as to stand in the middle of Yankee stadium, knowing the risks and dressed in full-body armor, to throw out the first pitch resuming the major league pennant race.

On September 20, nine days after the attacks, the president addressed a joint session of Congress broadcast live on primetime television to the American people. The president carefully described the situation surrounding the events and presented the next step for the United States, a nation that was just starting to come out of shock and comprehend the extent of the events of September 11.

Reports following President Bush's address to Congress were very clear and unified in focus and content. The news media continued to spotlight the president's efforts and actions in response to the terrorist attacks.

Evaluation

The pre-news coverage unveiled the reality described by network news. Coverage portrayed the dominant term of the drama, the scene, as a "warzone,"

国家公关 | International Public Relations of Nation

which became a popular term, comparing it to the likes of Pearl Harbor. The United States Congress, the American people, and even international community rallied around President Bush and the American government. The president played two roles in this scene: Commander-in-Chief and Consoler-in-Chief. According to the media, the president focused on preparing the nation for war and consoling a nation which was trying to make sense of the situation. Additional phrases highlighted by the news media and dictated by the scene were the president's vow to "defend freedom" and "bring the terrorists to justice" in this "war on terror."

The media relayed the administration's message in the pre-speech coverage, hence setting the president's public relations team's message up for success. President Bush continued with a consistent message, unifying the nation under the same purpose. Echoing President Bush, post-media coverage confirmed the government's depiction of the situation, reinforcing this narrative and the government's desire for unification. Based on the speculations of the new media, everyone expected Bush Administration to respond as he did, and he did it well.

The successful public relations campaign not only helped President Bush to succeed in the next presidential election, but also gained trust and good faith of the international community.

> **Case Study** 案例分析
>
> In a new century, a nation may face many natural and man-made crises, which test a nation's PR crisis management ability. The "9.11" incident is a PR crisis faced by American government.
>
> Immediately after the attacks, the Bush Administration set up a crisis center facilitating crisis warnings and strengthening national defense, and soothing the public's grief and anxiety. A leader is very important in the time of crisis. The president Bush played two roles in this scene: Commander-in-Chief and Consoler-in-Chief. Bush's address from the oval office, his bullhorn moment, and his primetime TV speech not only showed his resolution to respond actively to this crisis, but also

> strengthened unification. Throughout this crisis of public relations, media reported on the administration's actions, reinforcing national unity. The public in this case were the American people and the whole world, so successful public relations not only enabled President Bush to succeed in the next presidential election, but also earned him trust and good fame of the international community.

2.2.2 创意英国公关

案例调研

21世纪初,英国驻华使馆官员称,他们发现很多人对英国的印象还停留在"过去时"。英国驻华大使韩魁发爵士说:"当你们想到英国时,脑海中也许会出现在白金汉宫与女王陛下共进午茶,自以为是而又思想保守的英国绅士,笼罩伦敦的大雾,那些都已成为英国的过去。"除了英国在世人头脑中"老旧"的形象外,一位资深媒体人认为,英国在介入中国人生活方面已远远落后于其他国家,如果中国人对英国还有什么印象的话,那更多的是负面印象,尽管这种印象主要是政治层面上的。

公关目标

为了改变中国人对于英国的刻板印象,英国驻华使馆官员提出了"Think UK",即"创意英国"的方案。"创意英国"的创意思路在于:放弃传统,颠覆"负面印象",它的典型宣传目标定在中国16岁到35岁之间的、所谓的"接班人的一代,"进行"未来投资"。他们在不远的将来就会成为中国重要政策的决定者、执行者以及挑战者。同时,这类人群也对创意活动、新式展览有极大的兴趣,很容易参与其中并理解接受。英国政府相信,这些人就是他们需要讨好的对象,而这种做法的回报也将在未来体现。

"创意英国"项目策划者表示,选在这个时间段举办这样的活动是因为中国加入世界贸易组织(简称"世贸组织")、成功申办奥运会使得中国向国际化迈进了一大步,中国是英国非常重要的一个贸易伙伴,再加上2002年是中英建交30周年,又逢首相布莱尔访华,是对中英两国很有纪念意义的年份。

公关实施

2002年,在英国驻华大使韩魁发的帮助下,一个旨在为自己的英国老家争取更多拥趸的网站在中国建立,韩魁发把该网站誉为是"通往活力神州的

国家公关 | International Public Relations of Nation

信息大门"。英国最大的海外宣传推广活动——"Think UK"在2003年全面启动,该活动试图为英国塑造一个全新的形象:富于创新精神又站在科技的最前沿,并且乐意与世界上人口最多的国家发展贸易联系。托尼·布莱尔也在这场闪电般的宣传战中投入了100万英镑,其中的一半都由英国的几位极有分量的商业领袖买单。

"创意英国"以"中英共创未来"为口号,每一个核心项目都体现了"合作"的精神。这首先体现在本次活动标志的设计上。标志中的几个圆圈,有"思想泡沫"之意,也体现了一种新鲜的创意;左边的红色代表中国,右边的蓝色则代表英国,两者结合在一起便代表了两国间的合作;自下而上,圆圈逐渐变大,并最终融为一个圈,表示两国间的交流合作越来越扩大、越来越深入、越来越融洽。标志的寓意以及"中英共创未来"的标记,表明了该次活动无限美好的意图。

"'亚洲土地'雕塑巡回展",作品从中国的古老文明和农耕历史中汲取灵感,由20万个手掌大小的泥人组成,这些小泥人在英国艺术家安东尼·葛姆雷的指导下,由来自广州东北部地区的300位不同年龄的市民和来自英国的志愿者们亲手制作;"激情英伦时尚设计大赛",英方出创意,定主题,并实施奖励;中方出人才,并在获奖之后与英国人一道学习、工作。

自2003年4月份开始,在广州、北京、上海、重庆等地,英国驻华大使馆文化教育处及英国文化协会举办了英国"莫奇蓝乐队(Morcheeba)巡演""'亚洲土地'雕塑巡回展""激情英伦时尚设计大赛""纪念发现DNA结构50周年""中英太空天文系列活动"等二十多个涉及文化、教育、科技、商业的活动与展览,活动范围和领域十分广阔。

2003年9月24日,英国驻华大使馆及使馆文化教育处召开新闻发布会。即将在北京东方广场推出"设计盛宴",展出一百多个体现英国先锋技术和设计的产品,向中国观众展示英国最富创造力的技术和灵感背后的故事。"设计盛宴"是"创意英国"(Think UK)的又一项重要活动。

公关评估

"创意英国"活动取得了巨大的成功。大约4500000多名中国青年通过各种形式参与其中,无论是亲身体验活动,还是参观展览、参与竞赛或是其他由近100个中英合作伙伴共同组织的特别活动。现在"创意英国"活动已经结束了,但是英国仍然会保持一个与中国的长期合作的势头。

> **Case Study 案例分析**
>
> "创意英国"公关活动是英国实施的针对中国青年公众的主动性国家形象公关,公关目标是改变中国人对于英国的陈旧和负面印象,试图塑造一个全新的英国形象:富于创新精神又站在科技的最前沿,并且乐意与世界上人口最多的国家发展贸易联系。
>
> "创意英国"国家公关有几个亮点值得关注:目标公众明确,全程活动丰富多样,标志和口号新颖,选择良好时机,资金充足。"创意英国"公关活动的目标公众是中国16岁到35岁之间的"接班人的一代",他们年轻富有活力,乐于接受新鲜事物,同时影响中英关系未来。在活动设计方面,形式多样和参与性强的创意活动不仅展现了英国的魅力,也吸引了目标公众的兴趣,调动了广泛的参与。活动的口号和标志"中英共创未来"突出了合作精神,新颖且过目不忘。选择时机在公关设计中很关键,"创意英国"公关活动选择在中英建交30周年和布莱尔访华的重要年份。同时,公关实施中的充足资金保障了宣传和活动的顺利开展。

2.3 Further Reading 拓展阅读

2.3.1 Maldives' Underwater Cabinet Meeting

Research

The Maldives is an archipelago of almost 1200 coral islands south-southwest of India. Most of it lies just 4.9 feet (1.5 meters) above sea level. The United Nations' Intergovernmental Panel of Climate Change has forecast a rise in sea levels of at least 7.1 inches (18 cm) by the end of the century. The Maldives is grappling with the very likely possibility that it will go under water if the current pace of climate change causes the sea levels to continues to rise. The country's capital, Male, is protected by sea walls. But creating a similar barrier around the rest of the country will be cost-prohibitive.

The tourist nation, whose white sandy beaches lure well-heeled Westerners, wants to set aside part of its annual billion-dollar revenue towards buying a new homeland. "We will invest in land and we do not want to end up in refugee tents if the worst happens." The Maldivian President Mohamed Nasheed said at the time. "What do we hope to achieve? We hope not to die. I hope I can live in the Maldives and raise my grandchildren here," says Mr Nasheed.

Nasheed's government said it has broached the idea with several countries and found them to be "receptive." Lands owned by Sri Lanka and India were possibilities because the countries have similar cultures, cuisine and climate as the Maldives. Australia is also being considered because of the vast unoccupied land it owns. The president said repeatedly that the Maldives was a frontline state, and that this was not merely an issue for the Maldives but for the world. If we cannot save the Maldives today, we cannot save the rest of the world tomorrow.

The UN climate summit in Copenhagen, a meeting which sought solutions to handle the climate change, was held in December 2009. Maldivian President Mohamed Nasheed, Vice President Mohamed Waheed and 11 cabinet ministers donned scuba gear and submerged four meters below the surface of sea to hold the world's first underwater cabinet meeting on Oct. 17, 2009.

Objective

Why did the Nasheed's government hold the cabinet meeting underwater?

In a bid to push for a stronger climate change agreement in the upcoming U.N. climate summit in Copenhagen, "We are trying to send our message to let the world know what is happening and what will happen to the Maldives if climate change isn't checked," Nasheed said, according to his Website.

Practice

To prepare the world's first underwater cabinet meeting, the ministers learned the basics of scuba diving on the weekends. Nasheed is already a certified diver. The scuba lessons were going well; 12 of the 14 ministers had already been trained. "It has given them a whole different perspective to what climate change can do," Aminath Shauna, the deputy undersecretary in the president's office, said, "We are seeing quite drastic changes in coral (reef) bleaching—and having them see it in person is a completely different thing than seeing it on TV."

Before the dive, the president told the BBC that they had to get the message across through a course of action which resonated with ordinary people, and what they were trying to tell the people was that they hoped there would be a better deal in Copenhagen. Major Ahmed Ghiyaz, the coordinator from the Maldivian National Defence Force (MNDF), told to the BBC reporters that all measures had been taken to protect the president, which included checking the coral for dangerous creatures.

At the meeting, the president and his team took their seats at the bottom of the lagoon off Girifushi Island, about 35 km northeast of the capital Male, sitting at desks with name tags while colourful parrot fish and black and white damsel fish darted around them. During the 30-minute meeting held in the turquoise lagoon, Nasheed and his cabinet ministers signed a resolution calling for global cuts in carbon emissions, the President's Office of the Maldives said in a statement published on its official website. Nasheed and the ministers used a waterproof pencil to sign the declaration "SOS from the frontline" which was printed on a white plastic slate. The declaration will be presented before the UN climate summit in Copenhagen in December, calling for people to "unite in global effort to halt further temperature rises, by slashing carbon dioxide emissions to a safe level of 350 parts per million."

After the dive, a press conference was held, the president restated what was happening and what might and will happen to the Maldives if climate change is not checked. The president told the BBC he had seen a stingray swim nearby during the meeting, "I've never been worried about reef sharks and I've been diving for a long time," the 42-year-old added. Besides, the ministers signed their wet suits, which are being auctioned, to raise money for coral reef protection in the Maldives.

Evaluation

The underwater cabinet meeting was a hit in the media and effectively attracted the world's attention. After the meeting, media brought it up as a headline about 12 to 15 times per day for two or three weeks. The world has been talking about the environmental issue for long time.

Foreign Policy, one of the world's most prestigious magazines on global politics and economics, has selected President Mohamed Nasheed as one of its top 100 global thinkers of 2010. The magazine praises President Nasheed's

国家公关 | International Public Relations of Nation

efforts to bring the issue of climate change and cutting carbon emissions to the forefront of the global agenda, noting the success of the underwater cabinet meeting and the Maldives. "He has made his tiny country—a string of atolls in the Indian Ocean that sits an average of just 7 feet above sea level—a poster child for the need to stop global warming," FP said.

Thinking:

1. Complete the following table by ROPE.

	Maldives's Underwater Cabinet Meeting	Think UK
Research		
Objective		
Practice		
Evaluation		

2. In order to promote nation image, what PR activities did Maldives and UK take respectively? What are the differences between PR activities of big powers and PR activities of small powers?
3. As a small island country, Maldives held the world first underwater cabinet meeting, tried to push for a stronger climate change agreement in UN climate summit in Copenhagen and successfully attracted the world attention. What can other small powers learn from Maldives' PR activities?
4. UK has successfully transferred from a traditional country which was dependent on manufacturing industry to a creative country relied on cultural industry, and now China is also in the critical stage of transformation. What PR experiences can China learn from "Think UK" to promote Chinese image?

2.3.2 MH370事件公关

案例调研

北京时间2014年3月8日凌晨1时20分,由马来西亚飞往北京的马来西亚航空公司(简称"马航")MH370航班与地面失去联系,机上239人中包括153名中国大陆乘客。2时40分,马来西亚苏邦空中交通管制台证实航班失联。6时30分,失联航班没能按时抵达北京首都国际机场。8时左右,马航发布航班失联官方消息。

马航MH370失联后,事件不断发酵,各种真假消息漫天飞舞,国际公众对于马来西亚的措施失望至极,马来西亚政府的国际信度降至冰点,国际形象遭遇寒流。

公关目标

澄清国际上关于对马航MH370事件的假消息,减少国际公众对于马来西亚政府的指责,维护马来西亚政府的国际公信力,塑造马来西亚的国家形象,降低此事对于马来西亚旅游业发展,乃至整体经济发展的负面效应。

公关实施

飞机失事后

马航公司

3月8日凌晨2时40分,马来西亚苏邦空中交通管制台证实航班失联,而当天早上8时,马航才发布航班失联官方消息,直到上午11时马航公布乘客名单。而在此之前国际媒体已针对此事进行了广泛的报道。直到8日下午,马航召开首个新闻发布会,却比预定时间推迟两小时。发布会仅持续5分钟,发布的仍是"失去联系"的消息,也未给记者提问的机会。主持人离场时现场一片骚动,场外则一片混乱。

马来西亚政府官员

马来西亚交通部长8日否认了马航MH370航班已经坠毁的消息。在失联13个小时后,也就是8日16时,马来西亚总理纳吉布才就事故情况召开记者会。记者会又因故推迟数小时。

飞机搜索中

马航公司

马航公司第二次新闻发布会在8日23:30推迟2小时后举行,也并无任何实质内容。在记者的追问下,马航竟然用关闭现场灯光的方法,驱赶记者。而在3月10日的发布会上,马航的高管竟然一言不发。对于记者的关

国家公关 | International Public Relations of Nation

于各种最新传言的求证,马航均以"未得到当局的确切消息"来敷衍。这种做法不仅使乘客家属极其不满,也使马航丧失了整个事件中的舆论主导权。

马来西亚官员

在飞机失事搜索过程中,马方官员对于飞机失事原因和最终结果的回复,缺乏系统的危机应对策略,发布信息,否认,再发布,再否认,再承认,整个危机处理混乱不堪。

9日15时,马来西亚官方说吉隆坡国际机场现场监控已经锁定使用虚假护照信息登机的乘客画面。马方称用假护照登机的乘客为"亚洲面孔",晚些时候否认这一说法。11日,马来西亚警方公布监控视频截图。国际刑警组织证实,两人均为伊朗人,只是,他们的目的应该是偷渡欧洲,没有发现与恐怖组织关联。

3月15日,马来西亚总理纳吉布亲自出席发布会,并确认失联客机联络系统是被人为关闭的,而客机航线也是被蓄意改变的,卫星与飞机之间的最后一次通信为3月8日8时11分。针对客机的最后位置,纳吉布给出了两种可能,即南部走廊地带和北部走廊地带。而此前,美国媒体援引客机发动机制造商提供的数据报道,飞机失联后飞行了4个小时,遭马方否认。

3月23日,马来西亚政府称,法国当局当天提供的卫星图像显示,在印度洋南部海域发现可能与马航MH370航班有关的可疑漂浮物。

飞机终结后

3月24日晚10时,马来西亚总理纳吉布在吉隆坡就有关失联客机MH370的相关进展召开新闻发布会,根据最新的分析结果,MH370客机已坠落在南印度洋,机上无人生还。纳吉布表示,25日早上会开新闻发布会公布更多细节。马航已经向家属通报了相关进展,随后纳吉布的声明结束,未透露更多细节。

在北京丽都酒店守候了十余天的乘客家属在听到马来西亚官方宣布飞机失事的消息后悲痛欲绝,但鉴于以往马方在调查事件时的反复和滞后表现,一部分家属表示不信任这一说法,只有看到飞机残骸才能确信飞机失事。

25日上午,乘客家属举着自制标语步行前往马来西亚驻华大使馆进行抗议。下午3点半,马来西亚驻华大使在丽都饭店参加家属说明会,家属正对昨天马方宣布飞机坠海这一结果向马来西亚驻华大使提出质疑,马来西亚大使表示现在无法回答。家属要求大使现场给马来西亚总理打电话询问,马来西亚大使沉默,只称会转达问题。

公关评估

在整个事件过程中,马来西亚并未在第一时间发布权威官方信息,导致舆论真空期,谣言满天飞;同时,信息发布没有统一口径,信息来源多样,马方不断否认,给公众带来极大负面形象。而且,马方沟通态度缺乏诚意,几次发布会都是无故推迟,甚至单方面更改地点,草率应对,不给媒体提问机会,导致媒体形象极端负面。而且,自始至终,马方缺乏系统的危机应对策略,发布信息,否认,再发布,再否认,再承认,整个危机处理混乱不堪,将马来西亚航空以及马来西亚政府的形象跌入谷底。

马来西亚在马航MH370事件中的危机公关处理让国际社会失望至极,马航公司濒临破产,马来西亚政府形象一落千丈,马来西亚国家的国际声誉严重受挫。中国与马来西亚的双边关系也因马来西亚政府的办事不力而遭遇寒流。《华尔街日报》援引知名金融机构美林公司的研究报告称,今年赴马来西亚的中国旅客将减少40万至80万人次,马来西亚旅游业至少损失40亿至80亿人民币。

思考题:

1. 结合"9.11" incident PR 和MH370事件两个案例内容,总结两个案例的异同。

	"9.11" incident	MH370
Research		
Objective		
Practice		
Evaluation		

2. 如果你是马来西亚总理,你会如何利用新闻发布会等媒介方式传播有效信息,安抚国内外民众,维护国家形象?

3. 越来越多的自然和人为灾难事件考验着国家的危机处理能力,从"9·11事件"的应对措施中,你能够总结出哪些国家公关的危机处理经验?

国家公关 | International Public Relations of Nation

2.4 Simulation
情景模拟

2.4.1 Chernobyl Disaster PR

Background

The Chernobyl disaster was a catastrophic nuclear accident that occurred on 26 April, 1986 at the Chernobyl Nuclear Power Plant in Ukraine (then officially the Ukrainian SSR), which was under the direct jurisdiction of the central authorities of the Soviet Union. An explosion and fire released large quantities of radioactive particles into the atmosphere, which spread over much of the western USSR and Europe.

The Chernobyl disaster was the worst nuclear power plant accident in history in terms of cost and casualties, and is one of only two classified as a level 7 event (the maximum classification) on the International Nuclear Event Scale (the other being the Fukushima Daiichi nuclear disaster in 2011). The battle to contain the contamination and avert a greater catastrophe ultimately involved over 500000 workers and cost an estimated 18 billion rubles (18 billion $USD). During the accident itself, 31 people died, and long-term effects such as cancers and deformities are still being accounted for.

There're two views heavily lobbied by different groups, including the reactor's designers, power plant personnel, and the Soviet and Ukrainian governments. According to the IAEA's 1986 analysis, the main cause of the accident was the operators' actions. But according to the IAEA's 1993 revised analysis the main cause was the reactor's design. One reason there were such contradictory viewpoints and so much debate about the causes of the Chernobyl accident was that the primary data covering the disaster, as registered by the instruments and sensors, were not completely published in the official sources.

The Chernobyl accident attracted a great deal of interest. Because of the distrust that many people (both within and outside the USSR) had in the Soviet authorities, a great deal of debate about the situation at the site occurred in the first world during the early days of the event. Journalists mistrusted many professionals (such as the spokesman from the UK NRPB), and in turn encouraged the public to mistrust them.

After the incident, countries like Japan denounced the irresponsible action of the Soviet Union to let this thing happen, which seriously influenced the health of other countries. This denounces and concerns in a period were huge obstacles for countries to develop nuclear techniques.

Simulation

1. According to the classification of national PR, what type does this case involve?

2. Background: Divide the class into three groups: one group of students simulate journalists encouraging the public to mistrust professionals, the second group act the public, and the third are Soviet Union officials. What national public relations would the officials take to regain the public's trust, and relieve the nuclear panic of the international society?

Actors: journalists, the public, officials of Soviet Union, etc.

3. Background: The Calf family members are all victims of this disaster. Calf became a disabled person. Some students act the Calf family, and some students act the officials of the Soviet Union government. What measures the officials would take to make up for and settle the large number of refugees like Calf? And what kind of media the official would choose to report this case?

Actors: Calf, Calf's wife and children, officials of Soviet Union government, etc.

2.4.2 墨西哥形象公关

背景

随着墨西哥涉毒暴力愈演愈烈,凶杀等暴力事件几乎每天都在这个国家上演。德国海德堡大学国际冲突研究所最近已将墨西哥从"危机国家"提升至"战争国家"级别,列入全球六大暴力国家之一。墨西哥国家统计局的最新调查发现,2011年2月份公众对国家的不安全印象指数急剧攀升,57%的本国民众认为,社会治安比去年更加"糟糕"或"非常糟糕"。

墨西哥私企经济研究中心的数据显示,不安全因素已给墨西哥造成占国内生产总值(GDP)15%的经济损失,其中旅游业首当其冲。作为墨西哥第三大支柱产业,旅游业占其GDP总量的近10%,也是继石油出口和侨汇之后的

国家公关 | International Public Relations of Nation

第三大外汇来源,关乎全国750万个直接或间接工作岗位。

在墨西哥接待的外国游客中,有80%是美国人。每年3月,美国大学生一般会利用春假,成群结队赴墨旅行,形成墨西哥旅游的小旺季。但自2010年年底以来,美国当局频繁发布旅游警告,特别提醒美国公民谨慎前往阿卡普尔科,造成今年当地以接待美国学生团为主的酒店入住率只有10%。"根本就没人预订,父母出于安全考虑不允许孩子们到这里休假……"费德里科说。

接二连三的暴力事件令越来越多的游客对这个太平洋沿岸城市望而却步。在酒店区美丽的海滩上,记者零星看到一些外国游客正在享受日光浴。大街上的酒吧和餐厅也不似往日般热闹和喧哗,联邦警察和反毒军用车辆不时呼啸而过,缉毒军人的增多反倒成了街头一大"景观"。

因此在墨西哥反毒斗争开始不断深入的同时,墨西哥总统在全球发起公关活动,以期缓解涉毒暴力事件给本国形象带来的负面影响。

模拟:

1. 根据本章的理论,墨西哥的公关目标是什么?目标公众是谁?
2. 针对美国大学生,你们组会采取哪些媒体,拍摄什么内容的旅游宣传片?
3. 背景:将全班同学分为五组,四组同学分别代表不同的公关公司,分别演绎出你们公司策划的墨西哥旅游宣传方案,一组同学模拟墨西哥官员,选择最合适的国际公关公司全面综合开展公关合作,并说明选择原因。
   角色:墨西哥官员、四组不同公关公司代表等。

Exercises 本章练习题

Gap Filling 填空题

Directions: Fill in the blanks with the correct form of the words and expressions provided.

| forecast | broach | get...across | instantaneous | sweep |
| cost-prohibitive | drastic | evacuate | resume | tear |

1. The United Nations' Intergovernmental Panel of Climate Change has _____ a rise in sea levels of at least 7.1 inches by the end of the century.

2. Both impacts _____ gaping holes in the building, setting them on fire.
3. The Nasheed's government said it has _____ the idea with several countries and found them to be "receptive."
4. Immediately following the collision, the Pentagon and the White House were _____.
5. We are seeing quite _____ changes in coral bleaching—and having them see it in person is a completely different thing than seeing it on TV.
6. A sense of shock, fear and confusion _____ the government.
7. They had to _____ the message _____ through a course of action which resonated with ordinary people.
8. Coverage of the attack began almost _____, with news stations and bystanders capturing video footage.
9. Creating a similar barrier around the rest of the country will be _____.
10. As normal lifestyle routines began to _____ in New York and Washington D.C., the president was very involved with ceremonial events.

Multiple Choices 选择题

Directions: In this part there are 5 sentences. For each sentence there are four choices marked A, B, C and D. Choose the ONE answer that best completes the sentence.

1. These are the planes and their corresponding attacking consequences. Which one is correct?
   A. Flight 11: Hit the south tower of the World Trade Center.
   B. Flight 175: Hit the north tower of the World Trade Center.
   C. Flight 77: Light Pentagon on fire.
   D. Flight 93: Gap holes in the building in Somerset County, Pennsylvania.
2. Which word can describe the immediate reaction of the Malaysia Airlines.
   A. responsible   B. perfunctory   C. liable   D. initiative
3. _____ is confirmed by the Malaysian official.
   A. The boarding passenger with fake passport on MH370 has been locked in Kuala Lumpur International Airport through monitoring, and the passenger has "Asian face."
   B. American media reported that the plane had been flying for 4 hours after

国家公关 | International Public Relations of Nation

loosing contact.

C. The contact system of MH370 was closed by people, and the route was also deliberately altered.

D. The two Iranians were related to terrorism.

4. Which city or country below hasn't encountered the potential danger brought by rising sea level?

　A. Male　　　B. India　　　C. Sri Lanka　　　D. New Delhi

5. Reasons that Think UK was launched in 2002 do not include that_____.

A. China was one of Britain's most important trade partner.

B. 2002 marked the 30th anniversary of the establishment of bilateral diplomatic relations between Britain and China.

C. Chinese were badly fond of British culture.

D. China was stepping towards internationalization rapidly since it joined WTO and successful bade to host the Olympic Games.

Reading Comprehension 阅读理解

Directions: Read the following passage and choose the best answer from A,B,C and D.

China National Publicity Film

In October 2003, the first Chinese citizen saw his homeland from outer space and the mythology and dreams of thousands of years became a reality. Our songs of how the earth is our garden and our pride in surviving our long history suddenly became more vivid and clear. Who are the Chinese? What makes us who we are? But even before this momentous chapter in our history, Chinese people have always regarded themselves from multi-faceted angles. Is tradition a burden or kind of a driving force for development? Do we take our cultural heritage too seriously or not seriously enough? Do you see conflict or fusion, nostalgia or visions of the future?

Opening the door with confidence

In 1979, China opened the biggest window in the world to the outside and China suddenly dazzled people with the panorama of change. Some may argue under such huge material and mental stimulation, it would be hard to maintain equilibrium. In my mind, China is a country that has very strong inclusiveness.

59

She is a country with rich culture. She has a long history, but also changes everyday. But after 30 years, the world has seen how much China's profound history and cultural essence has given; lead us to flexibility and unity when facing fast transformation. After China's accession to the WTO, Chinese people are getting more and more confident because of the increasing national strength. Observers must admit in its meeting with the world, China has preserved its own special character. Thirty years of opening has been a time of bravely facing the new and stepping forward on a path of our own choosing. Several respective international polls rank us No.1 in terms of public confidence in the future. Is this confidence underpinned by GDP growth or thousands of years of culture or the efforts of many millions of people? We believe China will deliver an answer before too long

Growth with Sustainability

Over two thousando years ago, the great Chinese philosopher Mencius observed, "a refraining from over-fishing will ensure fishing last forever, and also cutting wood according to the season ensures healthier forest." Such century-resulted wisdom now goes by the name "sustainable development" In China today, you can see GDP increasing, personal income increasing, and with that the increase of people's dreams. You can also see people sharing the increase in educational opportunities. Recently, the development of Chinese education is amazing. The exam-oriented education is changing to quality-oriented education step by step. There will be more and more kinds of method for teaching and our children will get diversified education

Multiculturalism with Shared Prosperity

While living some 5000 km apart, the 55 ethnic minorities in the far North, South, East, West of China, over thousands of years, have mixed with Han culture and added to our cultural richness and diversity. Our new-found prosperity has given minorities more choices to enhance traditional lifestyles and increase mobility and communication. Minorities enjoy relative liberal regulations allowing them to pass their unique heritage on to their children. Such unique freedom further adds to our country's rich cultural diversity and blends the imaginations of east and west, ancient and modern. Painting, sculpture, music, architecture, movies, Chinese arts are unified by a clear national identity.

国家公关 | International Public Relations of Nation

China is more encouraging of unique individuals and styles. Such diversity is the corner stone of our brave and open-minded future.

Freedom with Responsibility

China today is home to 780000000 mobile phone users and 420000000 Internet users. And everyday many millions communicate and express themselves to a modern technology. Chinese netizens are becoming accustomed to influencing regional and global opinions.

From all over the globe, Chinese netizens are showing their instant compassion and eagerness to strengthen the society by helping those most in need. Our people's optimism and generosity is born of huge loyalty and love for their country.

Expanding Democracy with Stable Authority

Understanding a little of Chinese history shows that recent years have involved compression or even skipping over important stages of development. Heroes of China have always struggled during complex stages of development to build democracy. It's not hard to imagine how hard this has been. Today around 900000000 people in the Chinese countryside enjoy village voting rights. The world applauds such training for democracy. After all, before flourishing nationally, free elections must begin at the village level. The National People's Congress remains China's supreme legislate body. Since the late 1970s, far fair and more transparent margin elections have been used to elect NPC delegates. Here the most important decisions in the country are made.

This is China's period of greatest change. A proper legal framework is starting to replace the habit of personal relationships as the principle weapon and defense the people's interests.

Economic Differences with Mutual Respect

During an economic takeoff, difference between the rich and the poor can sometimes be seen. Is this something Chinese should worry about? Much Chinese new wealth calls a rags-to-riches story.

And people remember, not so long ago, they had only a dream in their pocket. People can transform from poverty to richness in a single day but it will never change the respect and love between people. And everyone who has a dream deserves respect. Improved living conditions ensure everyone can contribute to public service initiatives.

Prosperity with Prudence

Chinese people are shifting from being consumers of materials to non-material goods. Besides buying cars and houses, people are buying a modern life style.

As saving money has long been a national virtue, China can back its development with strong financial reserves. When celebrating China's 60th anniversary, the government also demonstrated the value of thrifty. The Shanghai Expo is similarly leading the way in recycling.

Chinese people understand future happiness must be built on the foundation of the past. Chinese people have never cherished their cultural heritage more than today, nor felt more its lingering charm which is why after so many generations we are still here. From tradition to revelation, inspired by the future, Chinese people are creating an even newer way of thinking: building this generation's new common spirit.

1. In which part mentioned above does China National Publicity Film introduce its admission to WTO?
   A. Prosperity with Prudence   B. Freedom with Responsibility
   C. Growth with Sustainability   D. Opening the Door with Confidence
2. According to section entitled "Expanding Democracy with Stable Authority," what is China's supreme legislative body?
   A. National People's Council
   B. The State Council
   C. National Politics Consultative Congress
   D. The Supreme Court of the People
3. Which facet does "Our new-found prosperity has given minorities more choices to enhance traditional lifestyles and increase mobility and communication" reflect?
   A. Multiculturalism with Shared Prosperity
   B. Freedom with Responsibility

国家公关 | International Public Relations of Nation

    C. Growth with Dustainability

    D. Opening the Door with Confidence

4. Which Chinese philosopher observed "A refraining from over-fishing will ensure fishing last forever, and also cutting wood according to the season ensures healthier forest."

    A. Confucius   B. Mencius

    C. Lao-tzu   D. Chuang-tzu

5. How many facets have been included in the fifteen-minute feature?

    A. 5   B. 6

    C. 7   D. 8

Thinking 思考题

1. 搜索不同国家的形象宣传片,分析它们的特点。
2. 如何利用国家形象宣传片进行国家公关?
3. 搜索一个国家公关案例,按ROPE编写并分享。

International Public Relations of Local Government
地方政府国际公关

Gist
内容概览

With the development of globalization, the local governments play a more and more important role in international public relations. The local governments attach importance to public relations, because these public relations will affect the opinion by investors and the public at home and abroad, as well as its own image and economy.

This chapter focuses on the international public relations of local governments. The basic knowledge outlines the definition, nature, classification, evolution and skills of local government's public relations. The bilingual cases and further reading highlight the strong points of successful campaigns and draw some lessons from failed cases. In addition, the exercises, especially the simulations, will help students better understand the theories and practical public relations knowledge of local governments.

随着全球化的发展,次国家行为体——地方政府在国家治理与对外事务关系中的地位日益显现,地方政府的公关能力将直接影响国内外投资者与公众对其整体形象的评价,从而间接地促进或阻碍地方的经济效益和城市美誉度。

本章以地方政府为行为主体,介绍地方政府公关的定义、属性、分类、演变与实施方法,突出地方政府公关活动的技巧和特点。选取公共危机治理公关、城市美誉度公关,主要涉及 Florida Hurricane、西安园艺博览会等典型案例,并结合 ROPE 原则、危机管理 4R、3T 原则等公关措施进行分析并做出

地方政府国际公关 | International Public Relations of Local Government

总结。情景模拟部分与双语案例相呼应,融合了理论与公关方式的精选案例,设置相关情景和问题,以考查学生对理论和实践的理解与操作能力。

3.1 Basic Knowledge
基础知识

3.1.1 Definition 定义

PR of local government is based on a specific social background, and it is for the purpose of maintaining and developing relations between the government and the public, creating a good self-image through its two-way information dissemination and ensuring the citizens a stable and lasting mutual understanding of the governmental work.

由于政府公关属于政府职能和公关外交的交叉领域,但是与其相关的理论并没有系统建立起来,所以对于政府公关的概念并没有完全统一,但是其共同点都是为树立和维护政府和国家的良好形象。如安世民给出的定义:"政府公共关系指国家行政机关及其公务员为树立良好形象和有效推行公务而与相关的社会公众进行的双向信息交流活动,是政府改善行政环境和政民关系的一项重要职能。"[①]美国的公共关系研究者雷克斯·哈罗认为:"公共关系是一种特殊的管理职能,它帮助一个组织建立并保持与公众之间的交流、理解、认可与合作;它参与各种问题与实践的处理、它帮助管理部门了解公众舆论,并对其做出反应。"[②]因此,"政府公关就是指在特定社会环境中,在维护社会利益前提下,政府为了维持和发展政府和公众之间关系的总体协调、塑造良好的自身形象,与它的公众进行双向信息传播沟通、建立稳定和持久的相互了解、相互信任的关系,争取公众对政府工作理解和支持的活动。"[③]由于地方政府缩小了政府行为体的范围,所以,地方政府公关主要是指省或州之下的行政单位或基层组织为维护、建设政府和城市形象,在公共危机管理和地区美誉度建设方面,积极与公众形成双向沟通,以达成共识做出决策。

---

① 安世民,《政府公关的特征和实施条件》,《甘肃理论月刊》,1999年第1期,第44页。
② 陈宪光编,《当代国际关系教程》。北京:知识产权出版社,2007。
③ 汤锋,《全球背景下的政府公关与国家形象塑造》,2008年,第7页。

3.1.2 Features 属性

The characteristics of Public relations of local government contain six aspects: Authority of Government Action、Accountability of Government Ability、Diversity of Objects、PR Transparency、Social Welfare、Universal Participation.

（1）政府行为权威性。政策导向型和传播垄断性,[①]确立了政府公关的权威性。政府作为国家统治管理地方的从属机构,在地方代表着国家的利益和尊严。同时,国家所具有的物力、财力和军事力量也为地方政府处理危机、塑造形象提供强大的后盾,这也是其他个人、企业和团体所无法比拟的。

（2）政府的责任性。一方面,政府作为公共服务的提供者,公共事务的管理者以及公共权力的行使者。有义务向本国公民提供稳定的社会秩序和维持国家运转的公共产品,从而保障他们的基本利益得到实现。另一方面,从民族国家层次来讲,政府所承担的责任又是其存在的合法性以及得到广泛认可、信任和支持的源泉。

（3）对象的多元性,地方政府国际公关的对象既包括地方本地区的公众也包括国家其他各行政区的公众;既包括本国的公众也包括国外的公众。由于政府公关涉及政府公共管理和社会治理问题,地方政府公关的对象既有广大市民也有企业和媒体。无论是危机处理还是形象塑造,个人、企业和媒体都起着举足轻重的作用。

（4）公关的透明性。在公共危机治理中公关的透明性尤其重要,英国危机公关专家杰斯特提出的危机处理的"3T"原则:"Tell your own tale"(以我为主提供情况);"Tell it fast"(尽快提供情况);"Tell all"(提供全部情况)[②]。正如杰里·A.亨德里克斯所说:"公共关系危机处理中心的任务就是为内部和外部公众提供信息,为媒体提供新闻信息,建立信息咨询部回答问讯和控制谣言的传播[③]。"

（5）社会公益性。政府的主要职能,一方面是管理社会,约束公众可能有害于国家稳定的行为,监督社会与市场的运行。另一方面是政府主动提供利民惠民的公共服务,例如各个城市缔结的友好城市,它在一定程度上既塑造了自身的良好形象,又加强了与友城的经济往来。从而提高市民的经济效益。这两方面都展现了政府为社会提供公共服务并保障公共利益。

[①] 周晓丽,《论政府公共关系与公共危机的治理》,《理论月刊》,2008年第5期,第97页。
[②] 同上书,第98页。
[③] 杰里·A.亨德里克斯编,《公共关系案例》。北京:机械工业出版社,2003.

（6）全民参与性。一方面。随着全球化和技术的不断革新,国际环境和国内环境已发生很大变化,政府在公共危机治理、形象塑造等方面的能力有所减弱。因此,必须依靠不同群体支持并参与到政府公关的方方面面,以提高政府的行政效率。例如,近年来的非传统安全——恐怖分子的袭击、环境污染问题。地方政府治理中的多中心治理就暗含着全民参与解决本社区的公共问题的方式。

3.1.3 Classification 分类

In this section, we classify the PR of local government according to the form of government, the contents of PR, and the ways taken by local government.

Firstly, in terms of regime, local governments can be divided into federal and unitary government, thus the PR of local government can be divided into PR of federal government and PR of unitary government. Secondly, from the content of the local government public relations, it can be divided into public crisis governance, namely the emergency crisis management, and city image shaping which aims at promoting local government image. Besides, according to Public Relations Strategy, there are also hard-power PR and soft-power PR. Technically speaking, there are traditional PR and new network PR of local government.

从不同政体划分地方政府,可分为联邦制的地方政府和单一制的地方政府。联邦制的地方政府有地方法律和法院,相对独立于联邦政府,有自我的决策权和更多的自治权。单一制的地方政府受中央政府的影响较大,更多是作为中央政策的执行者而非决策者,自主性比较小。因此,一般联邦制下的地方政府比单一制地方政府在公关过程中具有更多的权限。

从政府公关的内容划分,分为公共危机治理公关和城市美誉度公关,即突发事件的危机处理以及有意识地塑造和推广地方政府形象。如不可抗的自然灾害、城市的水污染、技术事故、权益纠纷等,都属于突发的公共危机事件。城市形象宣传片、重大活动的策划和举行、地方政府的对外合作和交流等,都属于有意识地塑造和推广城市美誉度公关,从而为地方的发展创造良好的外部环境。如奥运会、冬奥会、世界杯、上海世博会等活动的举行。

从形象塑造方面划分,分为强力政府公关和软力政府公关。(Power Public Relations)强力政府公关随着软实力应运而生。在20世纪90年代,Sandre Oliver提出战略公关理论(Public Relations Strategy)。强力政府公关

的"公共关系是社会组织为了塑造良好组织形象,全面构造软力量,通过对组织形象的策划、塑造、传播、维护和对组织机构凝聚力、文化力、传播力、协调力的整合,从而影响社会公众、调整社会关系的科学与艺术"。它注重在双向沟通平衡模式的基础上以凝聚力、文化力、协调力和参与力来整合沟通模式。软力政府公关指地方政府公关仍处于封闭状态,将其视为一种秘密活动,缺乏全面总体设计。仅仅从政治单方面制定公关策略。

从技术上可分为传统政府公关和网络政府公关。随着大数据时代的到来和网络的迅速传播,电脑通讯和数字交互式媒体技术在公关技术中逐渐突显出来,利用电子邮件、网上论坛、电子新闻、博客、微信等网络公关模式,能够更有效率的宣传政府政策,与公众进行有效沟通,从而获得公众的参与和支持。

3.1.4 Evolution 演变

Public relations of local government originate from the United States. And it went through three stages in total: infancy, development and maturation. With deepening globalization and the rapid development of information technology, the PR of local government pays more attention to the public and launch proactive PR campaigns with prepared content, it's more simple and efficient.

政府公关最早可追溯到美国,共经历三个阶段:萌芽时期、发展时期和成熟时期。

萌芽时期(19世纪30年代到20世纪初)

最早的政府公关产生于美国的政治活动中,这与美国的经济、政治和文化环境密不可分。美国经济在19世纪中后期已由自由竞争走向垄断。市场表现为更广泛的分工和协作,从而促使社会形成一个极具活力的开放式网络。政治方面,美国的民主制度使联邦政府和州政府必须获得广大公民的支持,政府的领导人方能当选,政府的政策才能顺利执行。文化方面,正如托克维尔在《论民主》中所描述的,美国公民参与政府管理的习俗普遍存在于镇里和社区中。这一时期政府公关集中于总统竞选采取的公关。"如以亚历山大、汉密尔顿为首的争取宪法获得批准的运动被称为"有史以来最杰出的的公共关系工作"。杰克逊总统任命新闻代理人肯德为宣传顾问,开创了总统新闻秘书的先河。

发展时期(20世纪初到第二次世界大战结束)

这一时期的政府公关的工具主要是广告和新闻发布。理论也逐渐系统化和科学化,主要著作有现代公共关系先驱爱德华·伯纳斯的《舆论的结晶》(*Crystallizing Public Opinion*)、李普曼的《舆论学》等。这些著作较为系统地介绍了政府公共关系的运作方法,为政府的有效治理提供了合理的思路和方法。

成熟时期(1945年到现在)

随着全球化和信息化突飞猛进的发展,这一阶段的政府公关在系统化的基础上,更加注重以公众为中心主动积极的策划公关内容,并且简洁高效,政府公关组织趋于扁平化。在此阶段,美国在1947年成立美国公共关系协会(*Public Relations Society of America*),由斯科特·卡特里普和艾伦·森特出版的《有效公共关系》(*Effective Public Relations*)系统阐述了公关管理操作的四阶段模式。

3.1.5 Practice 实施

The foundation of local government public relations has two aspects: one is authorized by the state, mainly embodied in the functions of government; the other is supported by the public, both sides are relevant to each other. Public relation aims to maintain a good image of the local government and the whole country. On the one hand, it will timely resolve external negative evaluation. On the other hand, it will help the government to regain the public's trust.

The PR of local government is conducted in line with ROPE, including research, objective, practice and evaluation. "4R" theory by Robert. Heath (reduction, readiness, response, recovery in crisis management) also provide some reference to the evaluation of crisis management PR.

Holding sports meeting, applying Expo, and establishment of sister cities are major activities of the proactive PR of local government.

(1) 实施的基础

地方政府公关的基础来源于两方面,一方面是国家的授权,主要体现在政府的职能上;另一方面来源于公众的支持。两者是息息相关的,只有地方政府履行好自身的职能,政府的公关策略才能获得公众的参与和支持,即政治学中的"合法性"和"认同性"以及公信力问题。

(2) 实施的目的

从地方政府的定义中,可得出公关的目的在于维护政府和国家的良好形象。在公关危机治理中,地方政府公关通过积极的挽救策略来化解危机,增强地方社会稳定性与安全度。一方面及时化解外部的消极评价,另一方面重新获得公众的信任。在形象塑造中,政府积极主动地承办策划相关活动,能够将政府的政策和绩效传播给公众和世界。从而吸引各个地区和国家的公众了解并参与本地区的创意公关,提高城市的知名度和美誉度。

(3)实施的方法

地方政府公关的实施也应遵照"ROPE原则",即Research——调查、Objective——目标、Practice——实施以及Evaluation——评估。但在具体事件的处理上还应结合罗伯特.希斯的危机管理理论,即危机管理由"4R"组成:缩减(Reduction)、预备(Readiness)、反应(Response)、恢复(Recovery)。

将两者融合来分析地方政府的公关策略和效果。

地方政府公关的不得力将导致政府公信力的下降。

(4)实施的技巧

主动塑造地方政府形象的公关活动很多,如城市形象宣传片、大型活动的策划和举行、地方政府的对外合作和交流等,简单列举三种:承办体育赛事、申请博览会、缔结友好城市。一、承办体育赛事,增强城市的软硬实力。硬实力主要表现在基础设施建设和经济增长方面,比如与赛事相匹配的交通运输系统建设、社会治安的整改、酒店的开发,同时,政府可以重点挖掘地方的文化特色、饮食特色,引导各国队员与观众深入体验所在城市的魅力。二、申请博览会,博览会既是展现地方经济实力与科技实力的平台,又是巩固和深化城市名片的重点公关措施,例如,上海世博会和西安园艺会,前者打造的是一座金融与科技的大都市,后者打造的是一座古色古香的历史文化名城。三、通过友好城市的交流活动进行形象塑造。

3.1.6 Games and Competitions 赛事申办

随着我国综合实力的增长,大型赛事在我国举办的项目逐年增加。它不仅促进了地方政府的经济和社会效益,而且能够提升城市的美誉度,打造城市的靓丽形象。大型赛事的申办既考察了城市的硬实力同时也考量软实力,既需要政府的官员的牵引力,也需要专业的公关人员的执行力。

地方政府大型赛事申办的影响因素如下:1、技术元素:拟申办赛事的地点、设施、预算、拟定日期、发起计划、重要途径;2、支持因素:人员服务、当地政府、城市或社区的作用、交通服务、食宿供应、媒体设施;3、文化因素:拟申办城市或地点、电视覆盖率、典礼、表演或展示、文化节目、规则或指导方针以及最终的报道等。

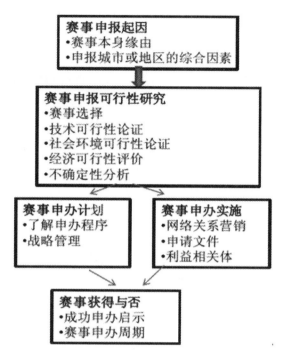

图3.1 地方政府大型赛事申办模式

图3.1为大型赛事申办的模式图,与地方政府公共关系密切相连的是赛事申办计划及实施[①]。

(1)赛事申办计划

了解申办程序

赛事申办程序是正确进行赛事申办计划的前提。以申办冬季奥运会(简称"冬奥会")为例。第一阶段为在国际奥林匹克委员会(以下简称奥委会)董事会授权下候选城市接受验收的程序,即申请城市通过各自国家奥委会向国际奥委会提交主办申请。每个国家奥委会的提名将会在国际奥委会董事会决定是否接受其为候选城市的前10个月,视为申请城市。申请城市必须通过问卷形式向国际奥委会提交信息。由专家和国际奥委会管理官员组成的评估工作小组将会对技术标准、政府组织、舆论、公共基础设施、安全、场地、住宿和交通等进行相关评估。通过申请验收程序,国际奥委会执委会将决定哪些城市可被接受为候选城市。在第二阶段,候选城市须向国际奥

---

① 殷细,《我国大型综合性体育赛事申办模式的研究》,2009年,第14-27页。

委会提交候选材料。该文件须经评估委员会检验和审查,评估委员会将会发布一份报告。

战略管理

战略管理主要包括:1、确定申办城市的目的、目标和战略,2、分析赛事申办的环境,包括赛事自身环境和赛事申办的外部环境,3、对申办赛事的正面的机会可能性和负面的威胁的识别,4、评估申办地区或城市的资源和赛事举办能力,5、识别可申办赛事的优势与劣势,6、根据上述内容,构造出赛事申办战略,7、实施赛事申办战略,8、评估申办战略的有效性,并适时做出调整。

(2) 赛事申办实施

网络关系营销

赛事的申办包括许多受益人的利益与冲突,联合广泛的合伙人是赛事申办成功的一个重要因素,两个主角之间赛事网络表现出一种重要的配对关系:第一位的关系包括与配对伙伴有直接关系的参与者,第二位的关系呈现为以配对伙伴影响彼此关系的组织,第三位的关系仅仅与一个配对成员相关。

初级关系包括赛事所有者和赛事申办者整合成为诸如国际体育组织、国家体育组织甚至赛事参与者等团组;次要关系包括重要配对合伙人之间的联系,如赞助人和大众媒体等。第三位关系反映拥有潜在支持者的亲密关系的形成。这些关系可能会发生在拥有重要政客、赞助人、城市官员和媒体的关系的形成中。

申请文件

成功的赛事需要明确注意赛事所有者阐明的要求,需要检查各个方面的要求并且用一种简洁明了的方式介绍重要信息。为了反映高质量的申办,国际奥委会建议基本信息应放在独特而又有魅力的重要人物之前。国际奥委会为候选城市申办奥运会举办权准备了手册。这份文件要求提交的信息通过一份"候选文件",描述组织奥运会的主要计划。每一个申办城市递交一份必须回答的含有18个主题,149个问题的调查问卷和一份显示城市作答的标准候选文件。

利益相关体

一项大型综合性体育赛事的申办及举行,必然会牵涉许多相关利益群体。从赛事主办国、赛事主办城市、赛事转播媒体、赞助商、参赛运动员、裁判员到观看比赛的观众,这些利益相关主体的协调与配合是获得赛事举办

地方政府国际公关 | International Public Relations of Local Government

权的关键。

3.2 Bilingual Case Studies
双语案例

3.2.1 Brazil World Cup PR[①]

Research

Football is the national sport in Brazil. There is a saying in Brazil that a person's character is defined by his loyalty to his football team. It is possible to change wives, political parties, religion and even sexual orientation but changing teams is unacceptable. Brazil is the country with the most world titles and has participated in all World Cups. But it has poor infrastructure to host major international sporting events such as the World Cup. And, Brazilian unemployment rate is 7.3%. Most of the people in the European countries can afford to buy a football team jersey paying more than € 80. But in Brazil and South Africa the majority of the people cannot afford this. So, they buy these jerseys from the informal market paying € 15 for them in Brazil. In accordance with FIFA rules this behavior is characterized as ambush marketing. But, those survival strategies developed by poor people, provide them with some income, although very low, which is critical to their survival.

One of Brazil's main problems is what has been called "Brazil Cost." Road transport is responsible for more than 60% of the inputs delivery to production and final products to consumer markets. The efficiency of the sector depends on stable investment flows for the construction, maintenance and operation of highways. This has not happened in the last thirty years. Only in the last three years has the investment in infrastructure increased due to the Growth Acceleration Program—PAC of the Brazilian Federal Government. But, its expenditures are still below what is needed. "Brazil Cost" includes actions such as regulations and rules edited by regulatory agencies that are very

---

① Luiz Martins de Melo, "Experiences from World Cup 2010 in South Africa—first thoughts about implication for Brazil 2014", Economics Institute, Federal University of Rio de Janeiro, http://www.ie.ufrj.br/datacenterie/pdfs/seminarios/pesquisa/texto1904.pdf 2015年10月30日

extensive and bureaucratic, making a hostile institutional environment for the investment in infrastructure.

Objective

The transportation costs in Brazil are very important for the World Cup logistic system because the distances between the host cities are extremely long. So, through hosting World Cup, not only the Infrastructure, but also Brazilian image can be improved.

Practice

The Brazilian federal, state and municipal governments have committed to invest a total of 5.0 billion USD for urban mobility in works aimed at the 2014 World Cup. Over two thirds (67.4%) come from the federal government via BNDES. According to the array of responsibilities, however, all these works will be performed by state and local governments. The Federal Government will be responsible solely for the supervision of the works of mobility, including airports. São Paulo will be the host city most benefited by federal funds. Caixa Econômica Federal—CEF, a federal government-owned financial institution, will provide US$ 0.6 billion for the construction of the monorail Gold Line, linking the Congon has airport to Morumbi stadium. The construction costs are US$1.5 billion, or 23% of the total invested in urban mobility, according to the document. Performing this work will be the responsibility of the state of São Paulo government.

The Getúlio Vargas Foundation—FGV and Ernst & Young Consulting have published an "ex-ante" multiplier effect study about the impact of the expenditures of The 2014 World Cup. They estimate that they will cause a chaining effect that can multiply the investments being made in the country for 5 times. An increase of U.S.$ 79 billion will be injected in the Brazilian economy over the next four years to meet the demands of hosting the World Cup. Out of this total, US$ 12.4 billion will be direct investments to ensure infrastructure and for the organization of the event.

The marketing of the 2014 FIFA World Cup included sale of tickets, support from sponsors and promotion through events that utilize the symbols and songs of the tournament. Popular merchandise included items featuring the official mascot as well as an official video game that has been developed by EA

地方政府国际公关 | International Public Relations of Local Government

Sports. The official song of the tournament was "We Are One (Ole Ola)" with vocals from Pitbull, Jennifer Lopez and Claudia Leitte. As a partner of the German Football Association, the German airline Lufthansa renamed itself "Fanhansa" on some of its planes that flew the German national team, media representatives and football fans to Brazil.

For fourth consecutive FIFA World Cup Finals, the coverage was provided by HBS (Host Broadcast Services), a subsidiary of Infront Sports & Media. Sony was selected as the official equipment provider and built 12 bespoke high definition production 40-foot-long containers, one for each tournament venue, to house the extensive amount of equipment required. Each match utilized 37 standard camera plans, including Aerial and Cablecam, two Ultramotion cameras and dedicated cameras for interviews. The official tournament film, as well as three matches, will be filmed with ultra high definition technology, following a successful trial at the 2013 FIFA Confederations Cup.

The broadcasting rights—covering television, radio, internet and mobile coverage—for the tournament were sold to media companies in each individual territory either directly by FIFA, or through licensed companies or organizations such as the European Broadcasting Union, Organización de Televisión Iberoamericana, International Media Content, Dentsu and RS International Broadcasting & Sports Management. The sale of these rights accounted for an estimated 60% of FIFA's income from staging a World Cup. The International Broadcast Centre was situated at the Riocentro in the Barra da Tijuca neighborhood of Rio de Janeiro.

Evaluation

Operational and tourists expenditures generate an additional US $ 3.9 billion. Another US$. 62.7 billion come out indirectly through various sectors of the economy. They examined 55 subsectors of industry, commerce, services and construction. What they called the "World Cup effect" is particularly strong in industry and in the labor market. A study foresees that the number of foreign tourists will reach 7.4 million people in 2014—an increase of 64.4% compared to the one recorded in 2009. The expectation is that industry revenue will jump from US$ 3.0 billion recorded in 2009 to US$ 5.0 billion in 2014. According to the study which evaluated the subsectors using the Gross Domestic Product (GDP) of each segment, manufacturers of appliances will have an increase in its

GDP by 10.2% between this year and 2014. This will also be high for strong traditional sectors of Brazilian industry like textiles, footwear, auto parts and furniture

> **Case Study 案例分析**
>
> This is an image-shaping case. Brazil's infrastructure construction in countryside and inland region lags behind that of the coastal cities, and it is wise for the local government to take advantage of the World Cup to improve its infrastructure and its reputation.
>
> Holding games and competitions is conducive to the enhancement of hard power and soft power of a city. Hard power is embodied in infrastructure and economic growth. Soft power is the charm and popularity of a city. In preparation of Brazil World Cup, federal and local government worked together for urban mobility, the host city benefited a lot from federal funds. And the "world cup effect" brought new vigor in Brazilian economy. The mascot, songs and singers, sports broadcast and media reports attracted public's attention, thus built the good reputation of host city.

3.2.2 汶川地震公关

案例调研

2008年5月12日14时28分,四川省阿坝藏族羌族自治州汶川县发生8.0级地震。震中位于汶川县映秀镇与漩口镇交界处,根据中国地震局的数据,此次地震的面波震级达8.0MS,矩震级达8.3MW,破坏地区超过10万平方千米,烈度达到11度。汶川大地震共造成69227人死亡,374643人受伤,17923人失踪。是继唐山大地震后最惨重的一次地震。

公关目标

及时进行抗震救灾,防止余震和地震引发的山体滑坡阻碍救灾进程。同时安抚受灾地区的民众,稳定民众的情绪,维护公共秩序,将地震损失降到最低。

公关实施

(1)通过媒体第一时间报道灾情,让民众及时了解危机状况安抚人心。

5月12日14时46分,新华网就发布消息:四川汶川发生7.8级强烈地震,

地方政府国际公关 | International Public Relations of Local Government

北京通州发生3.9级地震。十几分钟后,凤凰卫视就进入直播状态。中央电视台在32分钟后首发新闻,在52分钟后打开直播窗口。随后,国内各大电视台和主要门户网站都报道了这则消息,让全国人民对异常情况有了及时和全面的了解。第一时间满足了观众的信息需求,及时进行权威发布,对于地震的流言及时辟谣,稳定了人心。

（2）政府积极动员人力、物力和财力积极深入灾区展开危机救援。

5月12日深夜,政府就设立了由军地人员组成的救援组、预报监测组、医疗卫生组、生活安置组和生产恢复组等8个抗震救灾工作组。随后,各个负有法定职责的政府职能部门,也纷纷组织开展了积极、全面的救援行动。交通、铁路、民航等部门,迅速组织对被损毁道路、铁路、水港、空港和有关设施进行抢修；电力通讯部门,全力确保抗震救灾电力通信的畅通；医疗卫生部门,立即组织急救队伍,利用各种医疗设施全力抢救伤员,及时检查、监测灾区的饮用水源、食品；解放军、武警官兵、公安民警全力向一些交通已经瘫痪的灾区挺进,全面开展道路抢修与人员抢救工作。

（3）政府在重建过程中,发动社会资源,使广大民众加入灾后心理辅导工作。

灾后,地方政府制定了很多相关的制度。就经济体系来说,"有产权损失的补助制度、基础设施体系的重建制度、产业体系的重建制度；"①就行政体系来说,选派一些经验丰富的优秀干部和优秀的志愿毕业大学生到县、乡、村等行政组织中任职。就社会体系来说,首先是人的重建。如采取人口迁徙鼓励政策,对伤残者给予长期的生活救助和长期的精神救助。其次是家庭的重建。鼓励重建完整家庭,建立对孤儿、孤寡老人的认养、领养的奖励制度,实行特殊的计划生育政策。同时,采取了很多必要的措施,保证灾区人民吃、穿、住、行、教育、卫生等等,使灾区人民有勇气、有信心面对困难,重新生活。

公关评估

（1）媒体报道：随着国家配合地方政府迅速开展救灾活动,新华网、中央电视台、腾讯、凤凰卫视等各家媒体争相报道灾情的发展及地方政府的救灾活动,并呼吁社会积极参与救灾活动。政府在运用各种传播手段与社会公众进行信息沟通的过程中,政府与媒体间建立了积极的合作关系,满足了公众的知情权和话语权。政府、媒体、公众这三者之间形成的良性互动关系,

---

① http://www.xinhuanet.com/xhwenchuan/.2015年2月10日。

塑造了良好的政府形象,维护了最广大人民群众的利益。(2)公众反映:地震发生后,全国各地的志愿者和企业自发组织的救援小分队赶赴汶川为灾区捐赠所需的食物、水等生活必需品。同时全国的学校和社区也纷纷为灾区捐款。同时,社会公众给予汶川地方政府高度评价,一方面积极开展救灾活动,另一方面灾后运用专项资金为灾区人民修建房屋,保障了灾后重建工作。

> **Case Study 案例分析**
>
> 　　此案例属于地方政府公共危机治理公关,中央政府和汶川地方政府在此次公共危机公关中成功地塑造了政府形象,体现了地方政府公关的 4R 危机管理原则,即灾难缩减(Reduction)、灾难预备(Readiness)、灾难反应(Response)和灾后恢复(Recovery)。
>
> 　　地震发生后地方政府第一时间报告中央政府,并组织地方媒体进行实况报道,第一时间告诉民众。同时中央政府及时组织人力、物力、财力积极投入救灾过程中。得到社会各界的高度评价。地方政府在震后发挥重大作用,积极配合中央政府实施重建工作,并组织心理辅导医生为受害者诊疗。既注重重建外在的物质生活,又使受害者从心理上感受到生活的希望。

3.3 Further Reading 拓展阅读

3.3.1 Hurricane Katrina PR[①]

Background

Hurricane Katrina was the eleventh named storm and fifth hurricane of the 2005 Atlantic hurricane season. It was the costliest natural disaster, as well as one of the five deadliest hurricanes, in the history of the United States. Overall, at least 1245 people died in the hurricane and subsequent floods, making it the deadliest United States hurricane since the 1928 Okeechobee hurricane.

Katrina originated over the Bahamas on August 23, and headed generally westward toward Florida and strengthened into a hurricane only two hours

---

① Thomas J. Stipanowich, "Mediation Matters: Atates, Insurers Foucus on Adr for Katrina Relief", *Alternatives to the High Cost of Litigation* 2006(3): 59-64.

地方政府国际公关 | International Public Relations of Local Government

before making landfall Hallandale Beach and Aventura on August 25. After very briefly weakening to a tropical storm, Katrina emerged into the Gulf of Mexico on August 26 and began to rapidly deepen. The storm strengthened to a Category 5 hurricane over the warm waters of the Gulf of Mexico, but weakened before making its second landfall as a Category 3 hurricane on August 29 in southeast Louisiana. Katrina caused severe destruction along the Gulf coast from central Florida to Texas.

Practice

New Orleans is a city that lies below sea level; everyone knew it could flood anytime. But while the city had some plans for an impending disaster, its citizens were not really prepared for anything of such magnitude. The city had levees that were known to be vulnerable to torrential rains and flooding that would result from any category 5 storm. It was clear that none of the key players in the city, the surrounding states, or federal governments, were adequately prepared for the catastrophe.

Due to the slow response to the hurricane, New Orleans's top emergency management official called the effort a "national disgrace" and questioned when reinforcements would actually reach the increasingly desperate city. New Orleans's emergency operations chief Terry Ebbert blamed the inadequate response on the Federal Emergency Management Agency (FEMA). "This is not a FEMA operation. I haven't seen a single FEMA guy," he said. "FEMA has been here for three days, yet there is no command and control. We can send massive amounts of aid to tsunami victims, but we can't bail out the city of New Orleans." In the early morning of September 2 Mayor Ray Nagin expressed his frustration at what he claimed were insufficient reinforcements provided by the President and federal authorities.

Bush was criticized for not returning to Washington, D.C. from his vacation in Texas until after Wednesday afternoon, more than a day after the hurricane hit on Monday. On the morning of August 28, the president telephoned Mayor Nagin to "plead" for a mandatory evacuation of New Orleans, and Nagin and Gov. Blanco decided to evacuate the city in response to that request.

The evening of September 1, the Senate approved a 10.5 billion USD relief fund. The night of September 8, President Bush officially signed a total of 51.8 billion USD of the emergency relief appropriation bill. Bill Bush in September 23 signed an emergency for the amount of 6.1 billion USD in tax cuts after the disaster, to help the victims of Hurricane Katrina through.

President Bush also ordered 7200 active-duty troops to assist with relief efforts. However, some members of the United States Congress charged that the relief efforts were slow because most of the affected areas were poor. There was also concern that many National Guard units were short staffed in surrounding states because some units were deployed overseas and local recruiting efforts in schools and the community had been hampered making reserves less than ideal.

Local governments, who have primary responsibility for local disasters, including both Governor Blanco and Mayor Nagin were criticized for allegedly failing to execute the New Orleans disaster plan, which called for the use of the city's school buses in evacuating residents unable to leave on their own. The city never deployed the buses, which were subsequently destroyed in the flooding.

On Saturday August 27, several hours after the last regularly scheduled train left New Orleans, Amtrak ran a special train to move equipment out of the city. The train had room for several hundred passengers, and Amtrak offered these spaces to the city, but the city declined them, so the train left New Orleans at 8:30 p.m., with no passengers on board.

Here is just one of its many public relations gaffs. For rebuilding the Gulf Coast after Katrina, the federal government awarded noncompetitive contracts, apparently to its friends and political supporters, in probably violation of the law. This caused a predictable national outcry because disaster victims should have had priority for receiving such contracts and jobs.

Evaluation

British Deputy Prime Minister John Prescott linked the global warming issue to Katrina, criticizing the United States' lack of support for the Kyoto Protocol, "The horrific flood of New Orleans brings home to us the concern of leaders of countries like the Maldives, whose nations are at risk of disappearing completely. There has been resistance by the US government to Kyoto—which I believe is wrong." Ted Sluijter, press spokesman for Neeltje Jans, the public park where the Delta Works are located, said, "I don't want to sound overly critical, but it's hard to imagine that (the damage caused by Katrina) could happen in a Western country, It seemed like plans for protection and evacuation weren't really in place, and once it happened, the coordination was poor."

An article in the April 29, 2007 *Washington Post* claimed that of the $854 million offered by foreign countries, whom the article dubs "allies," to the US Government, only $40 million of the funds had been spent "for disaster victims or reconstruction" as of the date of publication (less than 5%).Additionally, a large portion of the $854 million in aid offered went uncollected, including over $400 million in oil (almost 50%).

Thinking:

1. Why many people criticized government in Hurricane Katrina? How many public relations flaws you can find in this case?
2. Analyze this case from the theory 4R Model of crisis management.
3. Please write a case study on Hurricane Katrina.

3.3.2 2011年西安世界园艺博览会

案例调研

随着经济的发展,承办国际化的活动成为各个国家和地区传播城市文化,提升自身软实力的重要途径,如奥运会、世界博览会(简称"世博会")和世界园艺博览会(简称"世园会")等。但是,由于西安位于中国内陆西部地区,地理位置和经济繁荣程度远不及北京、上海、广州等大都市。虽然西安旅游资源丰富,但公众对西安的印象仍然只停留在"六朝古都"的单一认识。这座充满活力的城市所具有的现代化、科技化并不被公众求了解,所以城市的知名度和美誉度稍逊于沿海城市。

世园会的宗旨是促进世界各国经济、文化、科学技术的交流和发展,使每一个参展国家和举办城市能向世界展示各自在各个领域所取得的成就。世园会被誉为世界经济与科学的"奥林匹克"盛会。1960在荷兰鹿特丹举行第一届世园会,1963年在德国汉堡举行。西安世园会是第41届世界园艺会,是中国第三次举办世界园艺会,前两次分别是1999年昆明世园会和2006年沈阳世园会。

公关目标

通过举行世园会改变西安历史古都的单一形象,重新塑造一个具有历史文化气息兼具现代化与科技化的新形象。同时,促进与西安与各国的国际交流,提高自身的国际地位,发展国际贸易和技术合作。促进西安经济的发展。

公关实施

2006年9月25日,西安市市委支持西安市政府申办世界园艺博览会,同意申办地址选在浐灞生态区。2007年9月4日,国际园艺生产协会最后批准2011年世界园艺博览会在西安举行。2011年西安世园会总面积为418公顷,水域面积188公顷。[①]总体结构为"两环、两轴、五组团"。其中"两环"分为主环和次环。主环为核心展区,分布室外展园和园艺景点;次环为扩展区,布置世园村和管理中心等服务设施。"两轴"指园区内的两条园艺景点,南北为主轴,东西为次轴。"五组团"分别为长安园、创意园、五洲园、科技园和体验园。四大标志建筑有长安塔、创意馆、自然馆和广运门。五大主题的园艺景点为长安花谷、五彩终南、丝路花雨、海外大观和灞上彩虹。

西安世园会以"天人长安·创意自然——城市与自然和谐共生"为主题,绿色生活追求时尚为理念,西安籍明星闫妮担任形象代言人。吉祥物和会徽为长安花、主题曲是《送你一个长安》;宣传口号为"绿色引领时尚"。

长安园和人文山水·诗意长安园与秦岭园组成自建展园,长安园以航天植物文化为内容,首次展现西安的农业科技最新成果;人文山水·诗意长安园以《诗经·国风》中秦地风光诗句和王维的《辋川别业》诗句为意境,是再现《诗经》植物的21世纪时代的新园林。西安世园会运用现代造园手段,通过堆石、塑山、理水、种植等,打造秦岭园,园内展现了陕西极具特色的"秦岭四宝"——大熊猫、金丝猴、朱鹮、羚羊等稀有动物。

为配合2011年园艺会客流量的流通,世园公交专线于2011年4月28日开通,共有10条路线贯穿于西安城内。

公关评估

西安世园会累计接待游客1572万人次,超过1200万游客接待量的预期目标。超过15万名外国游客参观了西安世园会。

西安世园会展现了绿色、时尚的新形象,人们看到了世界各地的700多种植物,各种风情的园艺和雕塑,给他们留下了深刻印象,使他们体会到一

---

① http://review.expo2011.cn/album_photos.aspx?album=14.2015年2月20日。

地方政府国际公关 | International Public Relations of Local Government

座兼具多元文化,既古典又现代的西安。一位日本游客说:"来到西安,除了看到这里的古老,还看到了它的活力和时尚。"

世园会通过园艺和场馆建设,把风姿迥异的各国文化集聚在西安,传达了中国的文化自信,也表达了西安的开放和包容,促进了中华文化和世界文化的和谐对话。闭幕后,世园会的绿色、低碳、环保理念,延伸到西安经济社会发展的各个方面,引导西安努力建设人文、生态、宜居的国际化大都市。

思考:

1. "秦岭四宝"是什么?为什么要展现"秦岭四宝"?
2. 举办赛事活动对地方政府有什么影响?地方政府举办赛事活动需要准备些什么?
3. 为本则案例写案例分析。

3.4 Simulation 情景模拟

3.4.1 Paris Hijacking[①]

Background

On January 7, 2015, at about 11:30 local time, two masked gunmen armed with assault rifles and other weapons forced their way into the offices of the French satirical weekly newspaper *Charlie Hebdo* in Paris. They fired up to 50 shots, killing 11 people and injuring 11 others, and shouted Allahu Akbar during their attack. They also killed a French National Police officer shortly after. The gunmen identified themselves as belonging to Al—Qaeda's branch in Yemen, which took responsibility for the attack. Five others were killed and another eleven were wounded in related shooting that followed in the France region.

On January 11, about 2 million people, including more than 40 world leaders, met in Paris for a rally of national unity, and 3.7 million people joined demonstrations across France. The phrase Je suis Charlie (French for "I am Charlie") was a common slogan of support at the rallies and in social media.

---

① http://www.businessinsider.com/afp-paris-hostages-survived-hidden-in-fridges-and-beneath-sinks-2015-1#ixzz3H7z7nDn. 2015年2月22日。

The remaining staff of *Charlie Hebdo* continued publication and the following issue sold out seven million copies in six languages, in contrast to its typical French-only print run of 60,000.

On January 8 over 100 demonstrations were held from 18:00 in the Netherlands at the time of the silent march in Paris, demonstrations against the shootings were held at the Place de la Republique in Paris. The phrase "I am Charlie" has come to be a common worldwide sign of solidarity against the attacks. Many demonstrators used the slogan to express solidarity with the magazine.

Media organizations carried out protests against the shootings. Le Monde Le Figaro, and other French media outlets used black banners carrying the slogan Je sues Charlie across the tops of their websites. The front page of Libération's printed version was a different black banner that stated, "Nous sommes tous Charlie" ("We are all Charlie").

Simulation:

1. According to the classification of local government public relations, what type does this case involve?
2. Background: Divide students into two groups. One group simulates the background mentioned above, and the other group of students act as the police and officials in Paris. What should they do to ease people's fear and anger in France?
   Actors: two masked gunman, several people who died and injured, some demonstrators, police and officials in Paris, etc.
3. Protest: Media organizations carried out protests against the shootings. Simulate these protests and act the role of famous journalists abroad in order to interview these people in protests. Facing panic and doubt at home and abroad, what actions should the government take to restore Paris' image?
   Actors: Protesters, journalists, government officials, etc.

3.4.2 第 x 届潍坊国际风筝节

背景

潍坊,位于中国第一大半岛山东半岛的中部,是风筝文化的发祥地,是举世闻名的世界风筝之都。早在20世纪30年代,潍坊就曾举办过风筝会。新中国成立以后,特别是改革开放以来,潍坊风筝又焕发了生机,多次应邀参加国内外风筝展览和放飞表演。1984年4月1日,在美国友人大卫·切克列的热心帮助和山东省旅游局的大力支持下,首届潍坊国际风筝会拉开帷幕。1988年4月1日,第五届潍坊国际风筝会召开主席团会议。会上,由美国西雅图风筝协会主席大卫·切克列提议,与会代表一致通过,确定潍坊市为"世界风筝之都"。1989年第六届潍坊国际风筝会期间,成立了由美国、日本、英国、意大利等16个国家和地区组织参加的"国际风筝联合会",并决定把总部设在潍坊。从此,潍坊成为世界风筝文化交流的中心。

风筝,中国北方称"纸鸢",南方称"鹞子"。"风筝"这个名字,大约始于五代(公元907—960年),据明代郎瑛《询匈录》记载,五代有位叫李邺的,在宫中作纸鸢,引线乘风为戏,在纸鸢头上系竹哨,放飞时,风入竹哨,发出像"筝"一样的声音,故名之为"风筝"。

位于潍坊市区东北15公里的杨家埠村,便是风筝的故乡。杨家埠风筝以做工考究,绘制精细,起飞高稳而闻名,分为串子类、板子类、立体类、软翅、硬翅和自由式六大系列,六十多个品种。潍坊风筝题材多样,具有浓郁的乡土风味和民间生活气息。每年4月的第三个周六举行潍坊国际风筝节,每年都有来自国际风筝联合会67个会员国的代表和全球30多个国家和地区的代表团参赛。

节庆的活动内容一般包括:举办开幕式,放飞仪式,国际风筝比赛,国内风筝大奖赛,评选风筝十绝,参观风筝博物馆,观看杨家埠民间艺术表演,参观民俗旅游村,与农民同吃、同住、同娱乐等。

"正月鹞,二月鹞,三月放只断线鹞",中国农历二月正是放风筝的好时机。因此每年4月的潍坊国际风筝节令人期待。

模拟:

1. 模拟第 x 届潍坊国际风筝节。
   角色:主办方人员、国际风筝联合会会员国代表他国参赛代表团、媒体、市民等。

形式：全班同学分为三组，每组同学分别模拟一届风筝节，设计本届风筝节主题、特色活动、媒体报道等。

2. 全班同学自由组合，分为五组，根据自己的家乡特色，设计、模拟和演绎特色赛事活动，宣传家乡形象。

Exercises
本章练习题

Gap Filling 填空题

Directions: Fill in the blanks with the correct form of the words and expressions provided.

infant	maintain	catastrophe	reduce	consecutive
hard power	distribute	officially	Brazil Cost	disseminate

1. PR of local government is based on a specific social background, and it is for the purpose of (　　) and developing relations between the government and the public, creating a good self-image through its two-way information (　　) and ensuring the citizens a stable and lasting mutual understanding of the governmental work.

2. According to Public Relations Strategy, there are also (　　) PR and soft-power PR

3. "4R" theory by Robert. Heath is (　　), readiness, response, recovery in crisis management.

4. And it went through three stages in total: (　　), development and maturation.

5. Storm surge as Luis Annas, Mississippi and Alabama cause (　　) damage.

6. According to the survey, water (　　) system in New Orleans blast pipe, fire hydrant, valve malfunction and broken pump failure, corrosion is the cause of the older section of damaged pipe.

7. The (　　) song of the tournament was "We Are One (Ole Ola)" with vocals from Pitbull, Jennifer Lopez and Claudia Leitte.

8. For fourth (　　) FIFA World Cup Finals, the coverage was provided by HBS (Host Broadcast Services), a subsidiary of Infront Sports & Media.

9. One of Brazil's main problems is what has been called (　　).

地方政府国际公关 | International Public Relations of Local Government

True or False 判断题

Directions: Read the following sentences and decide whether they are true or false.

1. Public relation aims to maintain a good image of the government and the country
2. This chapter focuses on local government actors to examine the federal government and the unitary government public relations purposes and skills in foreign public relations.
3. Local Government Public Relations property embodied in seven aspects.
4. After Hurricane Katrina, mayor of Florida and other organization actively take part in restricting infrastructure.
5. On August 22 it intensified into a hurricane, to a landing in Florida in small hurricane strength.
6. Department of health and human services to 15 areas affected by the cyclone's citizens issued will tap water to boil drinking requirements.
7. 80% of the 2014 World Cup budget is for the renovation and construction of stadiums.
8. The Brazilian federal, state and municipal governments have committed to invest a total of 50 billion for urban mobility in works aimed at the 2014 World Cup.
9. This is since Hurricane Optic in 1928, the most America hurricane death; at least 1836 people were dead.
10. There is a saying in Brazil it is possible to change wives, political parties, religion and even sexual orientation but changing teams is unacceptable.

Reading Comprehension 阅读理解

Directions: Read the following passage and choose the best answer from A, B, C and D.

Sister Cities International

Sister Cities International is a nonprofit citizen diplomacy network that creates and strengthens partnerships between communities in the United States and those in other countries, particularly through the establishment of "sister cities." More than 2000 cities, states and counties are partnered in 136 countries around the world. The organization strives to build global cooperation at the municipal level, promote cultural understanding and stimulate economic development.

The sister city idea developed from the Civic Committee. Envisioned by President Eisenhower as the "main cog" for citizen diplomacy, the sister city program grew throughout the 1950s and 1960s. The Civic Committee and the National League of Cities provided joint administrative support for the fledgling sister city movement until 1973.

A 1974 study found that many early sister city relationships formed out of the post WWII aid programs to Western Europe. The relationships that endured, however, were based on cultural or educational reasons that developed lasting friendships.

During the mid-1960s, city affiliations recognized that their diverse efforts needed coordination. In 1967, the Town Affiliation Association of the US (already popularly known as Sister Cities International) was created.

The Sister Cities program is designed as means for cultural exchange. A community of any size decides to join with a community in another nation to learn more about one another. Therefore, a sister city, county, oblast, prefecture, province, region, state, territory, town, or village relationship is a broad-based, officially approved, long-term partnership between two communities.

Sister City relationships begin for a variety of reasons. Generally sister city partnerships share similar demographics and town size. Partnerships may arise from business connections, travel, similar industries, Diasporas communities, or shared history.

The organization's mission is to "promote peace through mutual respect, understanding, and cooperation—one individual, one community at a time." Sister Cities International's stated goals are to:

Develop municipal partnerships between US cities counties, and states and similar jurisdictions in other nations.

Provide opportunities for city officials and citizens to experience and explore other cultures through long-term community partnerships.

Create an atmosphere in which economic and community development can be implemented and strengthened.

地方政府国际公关 | International Public Relations of Local Government

Stimulate environments through which communities will creatively learn, work and solve problems together through reciprocal cultural, educational, municipal, business, professional and technical exchanges and projects.

Collaborate with organizations in the United States and other countries which share similar goals.

1. Sister Cities International is a nonprofit citizen diplomacy network in ( ).
   A. UK   B. America
   C. China   D. 136 countries
2. Sister City relationship is ( ).
   A. partnership shares similar demographics and town size
   B. means not for cultural exchange
   C. to promote peace through economic respect
   D. to collaborate with organizations in the United States and other countries
3. Sister Cities International's mission is not to ( ).
   A. create an atmosphere in which community development can be implemented and strengthened
   B. develop municipal partnerships between UK cities, counties and states and similar jurisdictions in other nations
   C. provide opportunities for city officials and citizens to experience and explore other cultures
   D. collaborate with organizations in the United States and other countries which share similar goals
4. Sister Cities International strives to build global cooperation ( ), promote cultural understanding and stimulate economic development.
   A. at the municipal level   B. at the city level
   C. at the global level   D. at the state level
5. Which one is NOT correct in this passage? ( )
   A. In 1967, Sister Cities International was created.
   B. A sister city, country, oblast, prefecture, province, region, state, territory, town, or village relationship is a broad-based, officially approved, long-term partnership between two communities.

C. The sister city idea developed from the Civic Committee envisioned by President Eisenhower.

D. Sister Cities International's mission is to promote peace through mutual cooperation.

Short-Answer Questions 简答题

1. 地方政府公关经历了几个发展时期,主要代表人物有哪些? 相应的标志性著作分别是什么?
2. 危机公关的3T原则具体内容是什么?
3. 友好城市建立的基础是什么? 友好城市对城市形象公关有哪些作用?

International Public Relations of Intergovernmental Organization
政府间国际组织国际公关

Gist
内容概览

With the deepening of globalization, more and more global economic, political and ecological issues undermine national sovereignty and make the global governance important. Intergovernmental Organization (IGO), as the main body of global governance, is conducive to establishment of new international rules and regulations in the era of globalization. As an important actor in international community, IGO usually take part in global governance and promote its image by colorful public relations activities.

This chapter discusses international public relations which focus on intergovernmental organizations. Students can learn the definitions, features, classifications and methods of intergovernmental organizations' public relations from bilingual cases, including proactive image-shaping public relations and reactive crisis management public relations. Students discuss and analyze the successful experience and failed lessons, then apply what they have learned to scene simulation, which cultivates student's practical public relations.

随着全球化进程的日益深入，人类所面临的经济、政治、生态等全球问题使各国的国家主权受到不同程度的削弱，全球治理的重要性日益突出。政府间国际组织，顺应了这一世界发展的需要，成为了全球治理的主要机构，有利于在全球化时代确立新的国际规则和秩序。作为国际舞台上重要的参与者，政府间国际组织开展公关活动进而维护或宣传自身的形象已成为一种常态。

本章以政府间国际组织为公共关系行为主体,介绍了政府间国际组织的定义、属性、分类和方法。案例部分选取了有代表性的政府间国际组织公关双语案例,主要涉及主动宣传公关和危机应对公关。学生在总结经验教训的同时将学习的公关技巧和方法运用到情景模拟中,培养学生创造性解决公关危机的能力。

4.1 Basic Knowledge
基础知识

4.1.1 Definition 定义

An IGO is an organization composed primarily of sovereign states, or of other intergovernmental organizations. An IGO is established by treaty or other agreement that acts as a charter creating the group. Treaties are formed when lawful representatives (governments) of several states go through a ratification process, providing the IGO with an international legal personality.

政府间国际组织(Intergovernmental Organization)是两个及以上国家的政府通过签署符合国际法的协议而组成的国家联盟(union of states)或国家联合体(association of states),具有常设体系和组织机构,其宗旨是通过成员国合作实现共同目标。政府间组织作为国际组织的"中坚力量",在国际事务中发挥着非政府组织所无法比拟的重要作用和影响力。政府间国际组织不仅为单个成员国家的政治意愿或者是多个国家的集体意志提供了表达平台,而且还为国家之间、国家与国际社会之间关系的处理发挥着积极的作用[①]。

政府间国际组织公关是指政府间国际组织为实现国际公众对其组织的信任,并在此基础上支持其政策的目的,利用传播手段以及其他交往形式的国际活动。政府间国际组织公关不仅有助于塑造组织形象,同时,在全球治理的基本框架下,更有助于协调国际体系、国家、国际公众等之间关系,通过和平磋商等方式解决全球问题。

4.1.2 Features 属性

Intergovernmental organizations in a legal sense should be distinguished

---
① 赵麟斌,《公关理论与实务培训用书:国际公关》。北京:北京大学出版社,2013年。

政府间国际组织国际公关 | International Public Relations of Intergovernmental Organization

from simple groupings or coalitions of states, such as the G8. Such groups or associations have not been founded by a constituent document and exist only as task groups.

Intergovernmental organizations differ in function, membership and membership criteria. They have various goals and scopes, which are often outlined in the treaty or charter. Some IGOs developed to fulfill a need for a neutral forum for debate or negotiation to resolve disputes. Others developed to carry out mutual interests with unified aims to preserve peace through conflict resolution and better international relations, promoting international cooperation on issues such as environmental protection, to promote human rights or social development (education, health care), to render humanitarian aid, and to foster economic development. Some are more general in scope (the United Nations) while others may have subject-specific missions (Interpol, the International Organization for Standardization and other standards organizations).[1]

（1）政府间国际组织的属性[2]

政府间国际组织的构成有三个要素:1. 成员国之间要有合作的政治意愿,这是政府间组织能够存在的前提与基础;2. 组织之中要有一定的结构或形式,这是保证组织稳定性的条件;3. 组织要有一定的运作机制,包括组织的宗旨、权力、职能、活动方式和议事规则等等,这种运作机制可以体现组织的某种自主性。通常,组织的这三个要素体现在一定的条约、协定或章程中,这些条约、协定或章程构成了组织的基本制度。

政府间国际组织的基本特性是政府间国际组织的参与者是国家而非自然人。政府间国际组织是国家之间的组织而非凌驾于主权国家之上的世界政府;与国际会议不同,政府间国际组织设有常设机构,具有相对的持续性和稳定性;依据国家间的正式协定,拥有一定的自主权和单独意志,且具备合作职能。

（2）政府间国际组织公关的特征

政府间国际组织在有计划、有组织的活动中要寻求一个获得承认的团体的公共利益,即河流体系中"大河"与"小河"之间的休戚与共。政府间国际组织出于合作理念,将其作用渗透到国际事务的方方面面。面临危机时,政

---

[1] https://en.wikipedia.org/wiki/Intergovernmental_organization 2014年12月25日
[2] 赵麟斌,《公关理论与实务培训用书:国际公关》。北京:北京大学出版社,2013年。

府间国际组织在公共关系中彰显的是统筹全局、共担责任和联手合作的综合特征。

（1）统筹全局。公共关系中的任何组织和个人，不能完全凭借自身力量去解决生存发展中的危难问题，而主要是通过与其他组织和个人的相互供需来解决，各成员国应相互扶持与合作，树立促进各国共同发展的时代思维，在政府间国际组织的协作下更加注重交流合作、相互借鉴，更加注重互利共赢、共同发展。政府间国际组织则要从眼前和长远的角度出发，从人类生存和发展的高度，用相互联系的眼光看待和应对全球性的重大挑战和威胁。

（2）共担责任。当今世界正在发生着前所未有的历史性变革，我们所处的时代是一个充满机遇和挑战的时代，求和平、促发展、谋合作，是不可阻挡的历史潮流。政府间国际组织和国际社会有责任、有义务努力建造一个持久和平、共同繁荣的和谐世界；政府间国际组织应引导各成员国树立共同责任意识，从人类生存和发展的高度多方入手，统筹兼顾，合力化解危机；共担责任，发挥联合国及相关国际组织的作用，重视发挥科学技术作用，加强能力建设。

（3）联手合作。公关行为活动的价值和价值实现，最主要的是有效地调整公关主体与公关对象的行为活动关系，为生存发展创造适宜的公共关系状态、条件和环境。政府间国际组织是国际合作的产物，离开了成员间的合作，就不可能有政府间国际组织的存在。国际组织会议为成员国提供了一种合作体制，营造了发达国家和广大发展中国家能够为达成共识而走到一起的氛围，这样的氛围就是一种和谐的公共关系状态和环境。

4.1.3 Classification 分类

Common types of public relations of intergovernmental organizations (IGO PR) can be classified according to the actors or functions of public relations.

Worldwide or global organizations public relations, generally related to nations worldwide as long as certain criteria are met. This category includes the United Nations (UN) and its specialized agencies, the Universal Postal Union, Interpol, the World Trade Organization (WTO), the World Customs Organization (WCO), World Nature Organization (WNO) and the International Monetary Fund (IMF).

Regional organization public relations, related to members from a particular

政府间国际组织国际公关 | International Public Relations of Intergovernmental Organization

region or continent in the world. This category includes the Council of Europe (COE), European Union (EU), Energy Community, NATO, Organization for Security and Co-operation in Europe, African Union (AU), Organization of American States (OAS), Association of Southeast Asian Nations (ASEAN), Union of South American Nations, Asia Cooperation Dialogue (ACD) and Pacific Islands Forum.

Cultural, linguistic, ethnic, religious, or historical organization public relations, open to members who fit a cultural, linguistic, ethnic, religious, or historical profile. Examples include the Commonwealth of Nations, Arab League, Organization Internationale de la Francophonie, Community of Portuguese Language Countries, Latin Union, Turkic Council, International Organization of Turkic Culture, Organization of Islamic Cooperation, and Commonwealth of Independent States (CIS).

Economic organization public relations, related to economic organization. Some are dedicated to free trade, the reduction of trade barriers (the World Trade Organization) and the International Monetary Fund. Others are focused on international development. International cartels, such as OPEC, also exist. The Organization for Economic Co-operation and Development was founded as an economics-focused organization. An example of a recently formed economic IGO is The Bank of the South.

Educational organizations public relations, centered around tertiary level study. The Academy of European Law offers training in European law to lawyers, judges, barristers, solicitors, in-house counsel and academics. EUCLID (university) chartered as a university and umbrella organization dedicated to sustainable development in signatory countries and the United Nations University attempts to resolve the pressing global problems that are the concern of the United Nations, its Peoples and Member states.

Health and Population Organization public relations are based on commonly perceived health and population goals and address those challenges collectively.

关于政府间国际组织公共关系的类型,可以从以下几个维度区分[①]:

从组织成员构成的地域范围来看,可以将它划分为全球性的国际组织公

---

① 鲁巧玲,《政府间国际组织发展演变规律初探》,青岛:青岛大学国际关系专业,2005。

关和区域性的国际组织公关,此种区分可以体现一个国际组织在国际社会中的参与程度及其公关活动的影响范围。全球性国际组织的组织成员资格向全世界所有国家开放,当然,此处的"全球性"是相对意义上的,只要一个组织不以地理区域、社会制度、发展水平等因素为其组织构成要件,那么它就可以归为全球性国际组织。联合国是当今世界上最具广泛性、成员国最多的政府间国际组织,截至2006年6月底其成员国数量共计有192个,基本囊括了世界上所有的主权国家。而区域性国际组织则只包括国际社会中的某一部分国家,其成员资格受限于某一特定的地域范围,或者某一共同的军事、经济利益,或者某种共同的文化、宗教、民族背景。根据不同的地理特征,又可以将其进一步分为跨地区性(一般是洲际的)和地区性(一般来自某一大洲或限于大洲内某一局部地区)的国际组织。

依照组织宗旨目标及职能范围来划分,政府间国际组织公关又可以分为一般性国际组织公关和专门性国际组织公关。一般性国际组织的活动领域和职权范围比较广泛且具有综合性,涉及政治、经济、社会、文化等各个方面,如联合国是最为重要的一般性政府间组织,它负责全球范围内国际社会和国家之间的各个方面的合作事务;欧盟和东南亚国家联盟则分别致力于欧洲和东南亚地区范围内的国际合作。专门性国际组织则一般只针对某个专门的活动领域,主要进行金融、贸易、科技、文化、教育、卫生等专业技术性活动,比如世界贸易组织、联合国教科文组织、国际劳工组织等。

按组织职能的专业化程度可以分为一般性国际组织公关和专业性国际组织公关。实际上,某些按照其组织宗旨应该定性为一般性职能的国际组织,经常会专注于某一活动领域内的工作,比如东南亚国家联盟在以往就主要把工作精力放在成员国家之间的经济合作领域;而某些承担专门性职能的国际组织,比如世界贸易组织,它的实际活动范围可以说比较广泛,超越了经济贸易领域,例如在促进社会就业与改善劳工生活条件等方面其都有涉及,而石油输出国组织时常以石油为武器来进行国际政治、经济斗争以表达成员间的政治经济意愿,还有国际原子能机构对核能利用的监督,也通常涉及国际社会的核武器政策分歧及军事安全领域的交流与合作。国际组织之所以存在这种看似"一般不一般、专门不专门"的情况,是与国际组织职能的表现在政治、经济及其他领域的相互联系性密切相关的,而其中以政治—经济联系的表现尤为突出。

政府间国际组织国际公关 | International Public Relations of Intergovernmental Organization

4.1.4 Practice 实 施

（1）实施的缘由

利益需求

政府间国际组织是国际公共物品（International public goods）的主要提供者，弥补无政府状态国际社会单个国家行动能力不足。政府间国际组织开展公关活动体现了国际组织的国际"治理绩效"，一方面满足了成员国家对政府间国际组织提出的"利益需求"，另一方面这也构成了政府间国际组织合法性的重要基础。

价值追求

政府间国际组织是各个国家表达自己在政治、经济、社会、宗教、民族、文化等各方面的价值追求的重要国际平台，也是推行本国政治、经济、军事、外交等政策的重要工具。政府间国际组织按照组织的宗旨和目标开展公关活动，体现了成员国家间的共同的政治意愿、意识信仰等价值追求，有助于在全球范围内巩固其合法性，达成国际社会的价值共识。

规则要求

政府间国际组织成员国的"价值共识"决定了国际组织的职能权限，决定了国际组织具体的规则形式。政府间国际组织开展公关活动满足了履行政府间组织职能，遵守章程规则和实践运作程序的要求，也有利于保障政府间组织宗旨目标、活动原则等价值追求，并进一步巩固了其在国际社会行为活动的合法性。

（2）实施的战略

公关中联合结盟的力量。生产力的发展、全球化的进程，使国际合作成为必然；另一方面，政府间国际组织的形成，又为全球化问题的解决提供了平台和合作场所。今日南北贫富的巨大鸿沟以及由此产生的发达国家与发展中国家的政治歧异、观念分化、心理失衡，可能带来形形色色的恐怖主义袭击、国际金融秩序的潜在危机、强权政治和地区分立主义的巨大影响，即使国际合作和政府间国际组织面临困境，同时也给国家之间发展合作、主权国家走向政府间国际组织形式的联合提供了新的契机和动力。

组织整体目标的展望。政府间国际组织成员国之间的共同目标应该具有一致性，既然已建立了联盟，那么其长期目标就应该具有一致性，只有以整体的组织愿景为依托，各成员国才能同心协力、集中精力、共渡难关。

政府间国际组织的形象塑造。塑造组织形象是公共关系的核心，它通过整合组织资源,寻求真诚与沟通、信任与合作,系统而协调地展开公关职能,建立社会与组织的和谐关系,为组织在社会公众中全面塑造良好的形象。早期政府间国际组织的成立基于共同的利益诉求,而后需要不断塑造自己的组织形象,为各成员国谋取福祉。

(3) 实施的手段

An issue originates as an idea that has potential impact on some organization or public and may result in action that brings about increased awareness and/or reaction on the part of other organizations or public. This mutating process of IGO public relations can be described as a cycle made up of four stages: origin, mediation and amplification, organization and resolution.

Public relations practitioners of IGO understand that they are expected to play increasingly complex and involved roles in promoting the bottom line, building harmonious relations with member states, and protecting organization's interests in ways that must be sensitive to the needs of a variety of external interests.

当然,政府间国际组织通过国际事务开展公关活动也存在诸多因素的制约,有其局限性。在解决一些重大危机事件中,政府间国际组织除了向成员国提供相应的资金、技术支持外,其所支撑的影响和作用势单力薄。由于组织内部力量对比情况错综复杂,各成员国的利益存在不同程度的矛盾。当成员国之间的矛盾激化时,政府间国际组织的力量就受到影响。例如世界卫生组织在处理SARS疫情、国际货币基金组织面对欧洲主权危机、世界粮农组织应对国际粮食安全等情形中不时折射出这些政府间国际组织的无力和无奈,所以最重要的依然是各成员国从整体利益出发,通过对话和协商解决分歧和矛盾,互利合作,建立健全多边国际合作机制,整合组织的目标和诉求,才能共克时艰,达到满意的公关效果。

4.1.5 International Meeting 国际会议[①]

作为政府间跨国组织的常见活动形式,国际会议主要是指数国以上的代表为解决互相关心的国际问题,协调彼此利益,在共同讨论的基础上寻求或采取共同行动(如通过决议、达成协议、签订条约等)而举行的多边集会。

国际会议通常是围绕着特定的国际问题而进行的,它的举行往往涉及利

[①] 周安华、苗晋平,《公共关系:理论、实务与技巧(第4版)》。北京:中国人民大学出版社,2013年。

政府间国际组织国际公关 | International Public Relations of Intergovernmental Organization

害相关的国家。为了保证会议的成功,会前必须做好充分的准备。会议的准备工作一般包括会议的发起、会议召开的时间和地点的选择、会议的邀请,以及会议议程的拟定、会议文件的准备和有关的技术性问题(如与会各国代表团的座次安排、名称的使用等等)。周密的准备工作可为会议的成功奠定良好的基础。

(1) 会议的地点

国际会议的开会地点,虽然属于技术性问题,但由于其往往对会议的结果、特别是会议的气氛有相当的影响,故常为各方所关注。在19世纪,国际会议大都在主要有关的大国之一的首都举行。20世纪以来,重大国际会议时常在中立地点(如瑞士的日内瓦、奥地利的维也纳等)举行。国际会议有时也在发起国的首都或某一城市举行,也有在对解决所讨论之问题最为关心的国家举行的情况。一些定期的国际会议(如西方七国首脑经济会议)轮流在各参加国举行或在有影响的国家举行(如不结盟首脑会议)。不少情况下,举办国际会议对东道国来说意味着在一定程度上对其国际地位的肯定,甚至扩大能其国际影响。

(2) 会议的邀请

一旦会议的准备工作完成,有关方面便着手邀请工作。邀请一般由会议主办国发出,有时由非主办国的发起国发出。在发出邀请信之时,应附有一份拟议中的程序规则草案,并说明对参加会议的要求。邀请信往往要阐明举行会议的目的和希望取得的结果。会议邀请的对象,即会议的参加国,一般应包括与会议讨论问题有关的所有国家,有时也包括对所讨论之问题有兴趣的或对问题的解决可能发挥重大作用的国家。为了确保会议的圆满成功,保证其结果的公正、合理并能得到普遍承认和遵行,一切直接有关的国家都应该被邀请参加会议。但是,有时某些国家为了达到一定的目的,故意借口阻止某个与会议所讨论问题有直接关系的国家参加会议。

(3) 会议位次

双边会议位次按惯例应遵循一般的外交礼节。多边会议通常以与会国国名的英文(或法文)字母次序确定各国的位次。按传统,各国代表的席位依次交替地安排在主席的右、左两方。现在,一般是按国名字母顺序,从主席右边开始排列位次。但主席右、边第一个席位通常由抽签或协商决定。在有些情况下不同因素,如与会国之间的关系,各国代表团的人数,也影响到席位的安排。在国际和平会议中,交战双方国家的席次一般分为两个相对的集团。在一些国际组织的会议上,各国代表与主席相对而坐,各国代表的位次按抽签决定的字母顺序排列。

（4）会议组织

国际会议因其举行规模及讨论问题的不同，往往有不同的组织形式。有些会议只有全体会议（即大会），许多会议则分为全体会议和小组会议（即各委员会），有时还设立特别委员会。从理论上讲，全体会议为国际会议的最高机构。但在实践中，特别是在历史上，真正起最高机构作用的往往是由少数大国组成的某种形式的委员会。第一次全体会议具有开端的性质，其任务包括选举主席、通过议事规则、确定议程，并按需要建立相应的下属各委员会以及任命有关的官员（如各委员会主席、报告员等）。在外交实践中，国际会议根据不同的情况往往分为公开性会议和非公开性会议，有时两者兼而有之。

（5）会议结果

国际会议结束后总有一定的结果，其具体形式往往表现为会议的文件，如决议、协议、声明、宣言、条约、和约或最后文件。当然，也有的会议一无所获。会议的文件有时在会前就准备好草案，以便在会议上供各国代表讨论、修改。有时则是在会议讨论的基础上草拟的。文件草案可由一国或数国提出，也可出于与会国的共同意愿而以主席的名义提出。会议文件必须经过大会的通过方有效。对会议文件表示赞同的国家都应履行其应该承担的义务。国际会议的条约、和约一般须经各国代表签字，并得到法定数量国家批准后才能生效。

4.2 Bilingual Case Studies
双语案例

4.2.1 World Health Day Campaign[①]

Research

In the 21st century, health is determined by and contributes to broad social trends. Economies are globalizing, more and more people live and work in cities, family patterns are changing and technology is evolving rapidly. One of the biggest social transformations is population aging.

Between 2000 and 2050, the proportion of the world's population over 60

---

① http://www.who.int/en/ 2015年4月20日

政府间国际组织国际公关 | International Public Relations of Intergovernmental Organization

years will double from about 11% to 22%. The absolute number of people aged 60 years and over is expected to increase from 605 million to 2 billion over the same period.

Objective

The WHO promotes a healthy lifestyle across the lifespan of people to save lives, protect health and alleviate disability and pain in older age. Age-friendly environments and early detection of disease as well as prevention and care improve the well-being of older people. Population aging will hamper the achievement of socioeconomic and human development goals if action is not taken today.

In 2012, WHO wants to go beyond awareness-raising to elicit concrete action and positive change. The World Health Day campaign aims to engage all of society from policy makers and politicians to older people and youth to: take actions to create societies which appreciate and acknowledge older people as valued resources and enable them to participate fully; and to help protect and improve health as we age.

Target Audience

Policy-makers in governments and international organizations;
City and municipality leaders;
Health-care providers;
Civil society groups;
Researchers;
Private sector entities;
Older people, their caregivers, service providers and families;
Community leaders;
Youth and youth groups;
General public

Practice

Slogan: "Good health adds life to years"

The theme of this campaign is "Aging and Health." The official slogan for World Health Day 2012 is "Good health adds life to years." Aging is inevitable, but everyone ages differently. Even if we are young at heart, we need to maintain our physical, mental and social well-being to stay healthy and independent well into old age. Beyond our wish to add years to life, we need to add life to years.

Poster Series

WHO has designed a series of posters challenging the current stereotypes older people have to grapple with. They show older people in positive situations. The posters feature a PLAY button as seen on internet videos symbolizing the dynamism and enjoyment that older people can and should have in their lives.

Social Media

On World Health Day, social media will be used to engage people and to challenge some of the stereotypes of aging. Images and stories of older people and their valuable role in society will be made available through WHO's social media channels.

Media Outreach

Prior to World Health Day, WHO will make the following materials available for people's reference, local adaptation and media outreach:

Global news release;

Statement from the WHO director-general and Regional Directors;

Video material;

Fact sheet on aging and health;

Technical document;

Photos on aging and health for journalists to download;

Photo stories;

List of communication contacts and experts available for media interviews;

At the same time, communication and technical materials will be posted on the WHO World Health Day 2012 web site during the weeks leading up to 7 April. WHO's regional and country offices are making communications materials available on their respective web sites. WHO will link to these sites as well as to partners' sites.

Calendar of WHO Events

As a response to WHO Health Day program, 2012 is the European Year for Active Aging and Solidarity between Generations. A chance for all to reflect on how Europeans are living longer and staying healthier than ever before—and to realize the opportunities that this represents. The European Year seeks to encourage

政府间国际组织国际公关 | International Public Relations of Intergovernmental Organization

policy-makers and stakeholders to improve opportunities for active aging in general and for living independently.

On 9-22 March 2012, in Malaysia, The World Congress, co-sponsored by WHO, will focus on "Evolution: holistic aging in an age of change" and encompass all aspects of aging and health issues—from conventional and complementary medicine, to societal and policy level approaches to physical, mental and social well-being.

From 28 May to 1 June 2012, Prague, in Czech Republic, this "Aging Connects" conference hosted by the International Federation on Aging aims to have a positive impact on age-related policy and practice globally and focuses on older people and development; health and well-being; enabling environments and connected technologies.

At the same time, WHO has issued a tool to assist governments to translate aging and health knowledge into policy and practice, with a particular emphasis on age-friendly health policies and action plans. The aim is to improve health and health systems policies and outcomes which are sensitive to the needs of older people.

In the middle of 2012, WHO has launched Lancet series, which focuses on aging and health. It takes stock of the evidence on the physical and mental health status of older adults around the world and identify patterns in high-, low- and middle-income countries. It also identifies possible research gaps and point towards evidence-based innovative policy options.

In the late of 2012, WHO Bulletin series on the health of women beyond the years of reproduction has been issued. This series focuses on health issues for women that may be overlooked by the traditional focus on their reproductive role. These include cancers such as breast and cervix cancer, and mental health.

Evaluation

Many media reported this campaign and the issue aging, for example, "WHO calls for action to ensure healthy aging" "World health day observed in Nepal calling for healthy aging" "WHO sees health improvement in Laos" "Health problems of elderly linked to lifestyle" from Xinhua.com, Chinadaily.com, ifeng.com and so on.

In general, this campaign has achieved its expected results. Specifically, it

103

has raises awareness that good health across the lifespan contributes to a happy and productive older age. People become aware of ageist stereotypes and support older people in being active, resourceful and respected members of society. Governments implement innovative strategies to ensure good health for the elderly. Governments take action now to anticipate and address public health challenges related to population aging. This is particularly important in low-income and middle-income countries, which are experiencing the fastest aging.

> **Case Study 案例分析**
>
> This public relations campaign is a proactive program created by World Health Organization, an influential intergovernmental organization. It strictly implemented the public relations campaign under the framework of ROPE principles.
>
> After being aware of the severity of the aging population problem, the WHO set up clear and strategic goals, which involved specific target audiences ranging from policy makers to older people. While putting into its goals into practice, the WHO launched multiple interesting activities, such as designing slogans and posters, and meanwhile took full advantage of media for the purpose of changing people's stereotypes and promoting this campaign. In addition, with the assistance of various countries, the WHO organized a calendar of events about aging and health, including international conferences, translator tool and policy publishing. Owing to WHO's thorough plan, the campaign became far-reaching and productive. This successful PR campaign also made WHO popular all over the world.

4.2.2 马德里"3·11"事件公关[①]

案例调研

西班牙是欧盟的重要成员国,马德里遭遇连环火车爆炸案对于欧盟各国人民来说,无疑也是个晴天霹雳。欧盟必须立即采取行动应对马德里爆炸案,除了为西班牙处理爆炸案提供协助、逮捕恐怖分子,更需要非常严肃地

[①] 赵麟斌,《公关理论与实务培训用书:国际公关》。北京:北京大学出版社,2013年。

政府间国际组织国际公关 | International Public Relations of Intergovernmental Organization

对待整个欧洲的恐怖袭击威胁,维护欧洲地区的安全,从而塑造起负责任、有担当的国际组织形象。

公关实施

2004年3月19日,欧盟针对这次恐怖袭击事件召开了紧急会议,欧盟现有的15个成员国和10个准成员国的内政部长和司法部长们出席了会议并讨论如何应对恐怖袭击,并制定出相关的具体措施。这次会议是在欧盟多国家领导人参加完西班牙为"3·11"事件遇难者举行的国葬之后不到24小时内举行的。

2004年3月25日,欧盟针对这次恐怖袭击事件召开了为期两天的紧急会议,来自25个欧盟国家的国家元首或政府首脑参加了在布鲁塞尔举行的欧盟首脑会议,他们对马德里恐怖袭击事件深感震惊。恐怖主义对所有的人都构成威胁,因此欧盟只有通过团结和联合行动才能战胜恐怖主义。该会议立即通过了一项反恐声明,严厉谴责2004年3月11日在马德里发生的恐怖袭击事件,表示欧盟将采取各种有效手段在欧盟范围内打击恐怖活动,并为欧盟公民的合法权益提供安全保障。

面对这一突发危机,欧盟和欧盟各成员国都表示将依据欧盟的基本原则、《联合国宪章》和联合国安理会等1373号决议规定的义务,使用一切手段打击恐怖活动。并且欧盟决定采取具体措施提高安全保障能力,措施包括向恐怖活动受害者提供援助、加强欧盟成员国之间以及欧盟与第三国之间的安全合作、加强边界控制与文件保密工作、情报共享、切断恐怖组织的资金来源、进一步加强交通系统的安全和任命欧盟反恐协调员等,保证各国一起努力,消除恐怖袭击带给欧盟各国的恐慌,并进一步捍卫欧盟各国的安全。

欧盟委员会很快举行记者招待会,指出一些欧盟国家在执行欧盟有关安全法规方面比较迟缓,敦促这些国家尽快把欧盟的相关法律制定成本国法律,以改善欧盟整体安全环境。与此同时,欧盟负责外交与安全策略的高级代表索拉纳指出,反恐行动具有内部和外部两个层面。欧盟在打击恐怖活动时既要进行内部协调,也需要与国际社会进行密切合作,而且欧盟理事也会在这方面提高协调能力。

公关评估

这是西班牙有史以来死伤最严重的一次爆炸事件,为了悼念此次爆炸案的遇难者,西班牙政府宣布"3·11"周年纪念日为全国哀悼日;为了纪念马德里"3·11"爆炸案发生一周年,旨在探索反恐途径的"民主、反恐和安全"国际峰会2005年8月在西班牙首都马德里举行。

马德里爆炸案，提高了欧盟内部的凝聚力，促使欧盟成员国进一步团结起来，加强合作，一致铲除滋生恐怖主义的土壤。同时，欧盟统筹全局，协调目标，在各成员国及世界人民面前树立起一个负责任和真诚的国际组织形象。

Case Study 案例分析

欧盟是一个典型的区域政府间国际组织，其宗旨是促进国际和平，加强国际合作。马德里"3·11"爆炸事件是欧盟应对危机的公关。

首先，突出了国家间合作的精神，加强欧盟成员国之间以及欧盟与第三国之间的安全合作与情报共享等。欧盟国家把边境限制取消后，在欧盟15个国家之间基本上可以随便进出，欧洲反恐不是一个国家反恐，而是15个国家一起反恐。所以，这种高程度的一体化也决定了他们之间的反恐合作要比一般国家之间的合作程度要高。

其次，"3·11"危机事件一发生，欧盟也做到速度第一的原则。3月19日，欧盟针对这次恐怖袭击事件召开了紧急会议，欧盟现有的15个成员国和10个准成员国的内政部长和司法部长出席了会议并讨论如何应对恐怖袭击，并制定出了相关的具体措施。这次会议是在欧盟多数国家领导人参加完西班牙"3·11"事件遇难者举行的国葬之后不到24小时内举行的。

再次，按照现代公共关系之父艾维李的"公众要被告知"的公关原则，欧盟正确处理了其与媒体和公众之间的关系。媒体是危机爆发的途径，同时也是危机控制的关键。通过媒体与公众坦诚的沟通，表明态度，欧盟掌握了报道的主动权，控制了事态的发展，如公布马德里爆炸案的事实真相、实播国家元首出席国葬、电视屏幕转播葬礼实况等一系列公关举措。

4.3 Further Reading
拓展阅读

4.3.1 UN Oil-for-Food Scandal PR[①]

Research

The Oil-for-Food Program (OIP), administered by the United Nations in 1995 (under UN Security Council Resolution 986) was established to allow Iraq to sell oil on the world market in exchange for food, medicine, and other humanitarian needs for ordinary Iraqi citizens without allowing Iraq to boost its military capabilities.

The program was introduced by United States President Bill Clinton's administration in 1995, as a response to arguments that ordinary Iraqi citizens were inordinately affected by the international economic sanctions aimed at the demilitarisation of Saddam Hussein's Iraq, imposed in the wake of the first Gulf War. The sanctions were discontinued on 21 November 2003 after the US invasion of Iraq, and the humanitarian functions turned over to the Coalition Provisional Authority.

In January 2004, an Iraqi newspaper published a list of 270 people from some 40 countries—including UN officials, politicians and companies—it alleges that they may have profited from the illicit sale of Iraqi oil during the Oil-for-food Program. Later, US Senate investigators concluded that the Iraqi regime under Saddam Hussein made about $13.6 billion from selling oil to neighbor states keen to breach the sanctions. Billions more were allegedly earned through kickbacks and illegal surcharges on services and goods provided by companies contracted under the OFF Program, the Senate investigators found.

The UN, the organization responsible for administering the Program, was embroiled in the corruption scandal.

Objective

After the news was released, the scandal dealt a great blow to the United Nations, and threatened to discredit the whole United Nations system. With more media focusing on the issue, global attention had been drawn to the

---

① The United Nations Oil-for-food Program http://www.un.org/ 2015年4月22日

subsequent measures taken by United Nations. For the purpose of restoring the international image and regaining the global trust, United Nations should respond to doubts from the public, investigate the issue, publish the final results and prohibit such affairs from occuring again. Only by those prompt and efficient means can United Nations reduce the negative impacts of the oil-for-food scandal.

Practice

Responding to these allegations, the Secretary-General on 21 April 2004 named Paul A. Volcker, former Chairman of the Board of governors of the United States Federal Reserve System, to head an Independent Investigation Committee (IIC). In an official press interview, Anna said, "It is highly possible that there has been quite a lot of wrongdoing, but we need to investigate and see who was responsible." Later, UN handed over all relevant documentation to the IIC.

That same day, the Security Council adopted a unanimous resolution, calling on the Coalition Provisional Authority, Iraq and all other member states, including their national regulatory authorities, to cooperate fully with the probe.

The Secretary-General also issued written instructions to all UN staff to do the same, and publicly declared that those who fail to cooperate will face dismissal. On the question of outside requests for information, the UN has urged contractors working for the Oil-for-Food Program to cooperate with subpoenas from other investigations and they are in fact doing so.

In addition, Mr. Volcker has stated on a number of occasions that he is committed to cooperating with other ongoing investigations. In early January 2005, Mr. Volcker made public 58 audit reports under his purview, including 37 related to the Oil-for-Food Program, 16 related to the UN Compensation Commission and two draft reports related to the Oil-for-Food Program which were not finalized due to the outbreak of war. These reports, and an initial analysis or Briefing Paper by the IIC, are now available on the IIC website at www.iic-offp.org.

The Secretary-General immediately welcomed the release of the internal audits as part of the effort he initiated to get to the bottom of allegations surrounding the Program.

The Briefing Paper showed that there was a dynamic auditing process generated by the United Nations itself, as well as the reports of external auditors which have already been made public. All the audits, both internal and external, were conducted in accordance with internationally recognized standards.

At the same time, the IIC briefing paper identified deficiencies in the management of the Oil-for-Food Program, which it noted operated "amid acute political sensitivities in an area of the world where corruption is rife."

While awaiting the IIC's final report, the UN is already focused on issues of management and accountability, and engaged in a critical review of the way it works, which will lead to a broad overhaul of the UN's management structure and systems in order to improve performance and accountability. The lessons of the Committee's interim report, expected by early February, will be fully taken into account in that process.

In October 2005, the commission led by Paul Vilcker wrapped up its 18-month oil-for-food investigation Thursday with a final 600-page report. The document adds detail to earlier reports explaining how former Iraqi leader Saddam Hussein corrupted the humanitarian program, earning billions of dollars in illicit revenue and directing lucrative contracts to influential UN Security Council members.

Mr. Volcker said the findings of this report re-emphasize the conclusions of earlier installments that point out the failures of the United Nations. He said political differences within the world body frustrated any effective response to the manipulation and corruption of the program, grievously damaging the United Nations' reputation and credibility.

After the final Volcker report had been published, Annan, general-secretary of UN, pledged UN reforms and proposed that national authorities must act to thwart illicit deals. In press remarks, he said, "We already have proposals for reforms that will ensure that, in future, we are better equipped to handle this sort of Program." Later, in a statement, Annan said he intended to pursue reforms "with even greater vigor" to enhance oversight, transparency and accountability at the UN.

At the same time, Annan decided to take the following steps: First, set up a new UN ethics office, which will help administer new financial disclosure forms and handle other issues related to conflicts of interest. Ethics training is now required for staff at all levels of the Secretariat. Second, create a new "whistleblower" policy to provide staff with a mechanism so that they feel free to come forward with concerns with the confidence that they will be protected against retribution. Third, win approval from the General Assembly to make internal audits available to member states upon request.

Evaluation

In spite of the personal damage to Annan, longstanding attempts at reform that he has championed received a boost. A UN summit in September 2005 addressed several management reform initiatives, including reforms for: ensuring ethical conduct; strengthening internal oversight and accountability; reviewing budgetary, financial, and human resources policies; and reviewing mandates.

The scandal brought multiple impacts to UN. Initially, UN's reputation and credibility were grievously damaged. Criticism and doubts from the international society flooded to UN and its general-secretary, Annan. With a progression of prompt measures being implemented, the public came to learn the truth and their anger for the misconduct of UN began to reduce, although UN was found frauds in the management. After the final report was published, UN admitted its oversight in the oil-for-food program and subsequently adopted reform measures to prevent such affairs from happening again.

Thinking:

1. Please write a case study on UN Oil- for-Food scandal PR.
2. Why did UN, the most influential intergovernmental organization, confront many scandals? What should UN do to restore its image and earn the public support?
3. Compare the two cases, Madrid "3.11" explosion incident PR and UN Oil-for-Food scandal PR, and summarize the principle of crisis management of Intergovernmental Organizations.

4.3.2 2014 APEC 峰会公关[①]

案例调研

2014年是APEC成立25周年,也是中国时隔13年再次举办APEC会议。过去的13年,是中国快速提升经济实力的13年,更是中国逐步参与国际经济事务,并日益扮演主要角色的13年。2001年上海APEC会议时,中国的GDP还不到日本的一半,但13年后,中国已超越日本,一跃成为世界第二大经济体。因此,APEC会议重返中国,无疑让北京"年会"具有了13年前不可比拟的含金量。

公关目标

继2001年后,APEC峰会再一次来到中国。2014年北京APEC峰会,正是向世界展现中国在这13年间发生翻天覆地的变化的好时机。借助这次峰会,中国要向世界展示其积极进取的外交姿态和大国气派,同时向世界传递着中国的精神与文化,绽放充满独特魅力的亚太梦、中国梦与东方梦,实现从APEC参与者到引领者的华丽转身。

同时,随着越来越多的政府间国际组织活跃在国际舞台上,作为环太平洋地区重要的多边外交场合,APEC需要进一步发挥实质性作用,提高国际影响力和号召力,持续推动亚太地区的发展。

公关实施

"APEC"蓝

峰会期间,"APEC"蓝成为了出现在各新闻媒体的报道中的热门词汇。在2014年北京APEC会议期间,京津冀实施道路限行和污染企业停工等措施,来保证空气质量达到良好水平。2014年11月3日上午8点,北京市城六区PM2.5浓度为每立方37微克,接近一级优水平。网友形容此时天空的蓝色为"APEC蓝"。在11月10日的欢迎晚宴致辞中,习主席表示:"我希望并相信,通过不懈的努力,'APEC蓝'能保持下去。"

选址新型"国际会都",提升国际形象

从联合国第四次世界妇女大会,到世界小姐、国际小姐中国赛区总决赛、东亚商务论坛,再到如今的APEC会议,这些年一系列的国际性重要会议及活动纷纷选择在怀柔举办。怀柔实施植树造林、小流域治理、城市污水处理等"水陆空"立体生态环境治理体系,营造绿色居住环境。在APEC会址核心岛工程建设中,更注重生态环保。雁栖湖建设秉承"低碳环保、科技创新"的

---

① 《公关世界》编辑部,《APEC峰会中的公关亮点》,《公关世界》,2014年。

理念,应用七十余项世界领先的生态环保技术。诸多优质的条件基础,促使此次APEC的会址成为会议亮点。

新中装,点亮"水立方之夜"

2014年11月10号晚,璀璨的APEC之夜,水立方以APEC领导人非正式会议晚宴及文艺演出迎接贵宾,各国领导人陆续抵达水立方北门。晚会的主题就是:上善若水,同舟共济。水象征环太平洋国家因水而连、因水沟通,同时,它更象征着中国作为此次APEC东道主国家,向世界传递出的中国古代道德追求——上善若水。

在水立方的中国风文艺演出之前,所有参加APEC领导人身着"新中装",拍摄了一张具有浓郁中国韵味的全家福照片。此次APEC领导人服装是一系列展示中国人新形象的中式服装,其根为"中",其魂为"礼",其形为"新",合此三者,谓之"新中装"。这一系列服装整体上气势恢宏,仪式感强,表达了中国人"有朋自远方来,不亦乐乎"的好客之道。

别致中餐,展现中国文化

APEC会议期间,会议餐型包括茶歇、自助餐、酒会、中式桌餐和正规西餐。而中餐展现了中国文化的水饺、春卷、小笼包等,以烤鸭、糖葫芦、芸豆卷儿、驴打滚等北京特色小吃和菜品为主,全国各地的名菜也有选择,但有所改良。此外在餐桌的百态装饰上也有亮点,有手工糖粉塑萌版兵马俑手持长兵器,仰起小脸"萌"态尽显。糖前摆放的不同灯光能渲染不同的颜色,也能烘托APEC晚宴和酒会的现场气氛。除糖塑外,APEC会议期间还有糖雕、果蔬雕、面雕等制作的各种食品雕刻,体现出了中国文化和北京元素。

公关评估

美国《华盛顿邮报》2014年11月13日报道称,此次APEC会议是一次中美双赢的盛会,也是史上最好、最有成果的APEC会议。同时《中国日报》中提到,APEC会议及相关活动取得丰硕成果,实现了预期目标,各方感到满意,舆论广为赞誉。这是一次开创性的历史盛会,书写了难忘的历史新篇,留下了深刻的历史印记。

APEC成员人口总数占全球总人口的40%以上,经济产值和贸易总额分别占全球总量的56%和48%。2014年的APEC峰会落幕后,诸多外国媒体以及中国社会各界都称之为最精彩的一届APEC。北京峰会为APEC未来的发展注入了新活力,不仅各成员国之间在推进地区贸易和投资自由化方面取得了突破性进展,而且APEC峰会迎来了新转机,受到了国际社会超乎往常的关注,国际影响力进一步得到提升。

政府间国际组织国际公关 | International Public Relations of Intergovernmental Organization

思考：

1. 2014年APEC峰会受到了国际社会的一致好评，请问其实施的公关措施有什么特点？
2. 作为国际组织的主动公关，WHO 和 APEC 如何通过媒体宣传？
3. 请分析并总结国际组织的年度会议筹办方该如何开展成功的公关活动。

4.4 Simulation
情景模拟

4.4.1 IMF Scandal PR

Background

The International Monetary Fund headquartered in Washington, D.C., in the United States, of 188 countries working to foster global monetary cooperation, secure financial stability, facilitate international trade, promote high employment and sustainable economic growth and reduce poverty around the world. Formed in 1944 at the Bretton Woods Conference, it came into formal existence in 1945 with 29 member countries and the goal of reconstructing the international payment system.

In 2011, the chief of IMF, was arrested and charged with a criminal sexual act, attempted rape and unlawful imprisonment. The arrest of IMF chief on charges of sexual assault has cast doubts over the future of the IMF and its role in the European debt crisis and the global economic recovery. The affair may have a significant impact on short-term EU/IMF negotiations, particularly talks over Portuguese program and Greek debt.

Specifically, in the very short term, the scandal may have a significant effect on the current EU/IMF proceedings, particularly the negotiations regarding the Greek bailout. The chief was on his way to Europe, and was supposed to meet with Chancellor in Germany to talk about the Portuguese program and the situation in Greece. Then, he was to go on and meet in Brussels with EU finance ministers. In his place, the IMF has decided to send one of the deputy managing directors, which puts the fund at a distinct disadvantage in these discussions.

In the very short term, the scandal puts IMF at somewhat of a disadvantage vis-à-vis the EU. This disadvantage may be less in the case of Portugal because that lending arrangement has already been forged, but may be more important for Greece. The IMF is currently discussing whether to provide additional financing to Athens and is negotiating the long-term issues with regard to its debt, whether some type of restructuring or reprofiling is going to be necessary.

The arrest of IMF chief on sexual assault accusations in New York throws into disarray not only the IMF's leadership but also its central role in the financial rescue of several struggling European countries. The public commenced to worry the substantial functions of IMF played in the handling with the recent finance crisis.

Simulation:

1. Investigation: The sex scandal is not only related to the person, but has something to do with IMF. Since the affair has been reported by media, worldwide attention is drawn to the IMF. If some clues showed that the chief is not guilty, how should IMF conduct the investigation and give truth to public? Simulate the PR actions taken by IMF before, during and after the investigation in order to reduce the negative reports by the global medias resulted by the sexual scandal.
2. Press Conference: Simulate the spokesman or spokeswoman of IMF who answers the questions of some doubts and criticism on IMF's human resources and leadership in a press conference.
3. Further Actions: Personnel of a prominent and influential organization, especially leaders, always act a significant role in shaping the images of their affiliated organization. Applying lessons from this affair, what PR measures should IMF take to prevent such scandals from happening?

4.4.2 第 X 届东盟首脑会议公关

东南亚国家联盟(Association of Southeast Asian Nations),简称东盟(ASEAN)。成员国有马来西亚、印度尼西亚、泰国、菲律宾、新加坡、文莱、越南、老挝、缅甸和柬埔寨。1967年8月7—8日,印度尼西亚、泰国、新加坡、菲律宾四国外长和马来西亚副总理在曼谷举行会议,发表了《曼谷宣言》(《东南亚国家联盟成立宣言》),正式宣告东南亚国家联盟成立。

东盟的宗旨和目标是本着平等与合作精神,共同促进本地区的经济增长、社会进步和文化发展,为建立一个繁荣、和平的东南亚国家共同体奠定基础,以促进本地区的和平与稳定。

东盟主要机构有首脑会议、外长会议、常务委员会、经济部长会议、其他部长会议、秘书处、专门委员会以及民间和半官方机构。首脑会议是东盟最高决策机构,自1995年召开首次会议以来每年举行一次,已成为东盟国家商讨区域合作大计的最主要机制,主席由成员国轮流担任。

东盟首脑会议是东盟最高决策机构,会议每年举行2次,主席由成员国轮流担任。秘书处设在印度尼西亚首都雅加达。自1967年成立以来,东盟已举办26次首脑会议,就东盟发展的重大问题和发展方向做出决策。

第1届东盟首脑会议

1976年2月23日至24日,第1届东盟首脑会议在印尼巴厘岛举行。东盟5国首脑签署了《东南亚友好合作条约》和《东南亚国家联盟协调一致宣言》。

第2届东盟首脑会议

1977年8月4日至5日,第2届东盟首脑会议在马来西亚首都吉隆坡举行。会议确定东盟将扩大区域经济合作,加强同美、日、澳等国和欧共体的对话和经济联系。……

第24届东盟首脑会议

2014年5月10日,第24届东盟峰会在缅甸首都内比都开幕。来自东盟10国的领导人和代表将就加速推进东盟共同体建设、加强内联外合等事关东盟发展的议题进行讨论。本届东盟峰会的主题是"团结起来,迈向和平与繁荣的共同体"。重点议题包括如何加强内联外合,缩小发展差距,推动东盟一体化进程,尤其是在2015年建成东盟经济共同体的最后阶段所需要做的事以及2015年后东盟共同体建设需要努力的方向。

第25届东盟首脑会议

2014年11月13日,第25届东盟峰会在缅甸首都内比都落下帷幕。会议主题为"团结一致,迈向和平繁荣的共同体"。东盟领导人就推动东盟共同体建设、进一步融入地区经济一体化进程等问题交换了意见,并与包括中、日、韩在内的对话伙伴国领导人进行多场双边和多边对话,达成一系列重要共识,取得了积极成果。会议通过了《关于东盟共同体在2015年发展愿景的内比都宣言》《关于加强东盟秘书处和评估东盟机构的宣言》和《东盟2014年气候变化联合声明》。

第26届东盟首脑会议

2015年4月27日,第26届东盟峰会在马来西亚兰卡威落下帷幕。峰会主题为"我们的人民、我们的共同体、我们的愿景"。会议通过三项宣言包括《建设一个以人为本的东盟吉隆坡宣言》《"全球温和运动"兰卡威宣言》,以及进一步加强规范应对灾害和气候变化措施的宣言。东盟领导人就在今年年底前如期建成东盟共同体、制订东盟2015年后的发展愿景,以及进一步发展与外部世界关系等议题达成一系列重要共识。

东盟计划于2015年年底前建成以东盟安全共同体、东盟经济共同体和东盟社会文化共同体三大支柱为基础的东盟共同体。

模拟:

1. 策划:假如现在你是第X届东盟首脑会议的主办国负责人,为了提高此次会议的国际影响力,同时实现会议目的,请你结合基础知识部分的国际会议策划流程,并借鉴本章中APEC等会议的组织亮点,拟定此次会议实施方案。
2. 会议:请将本班同学分为会议的组织人员、参会人员、国际媒体三部分,模拟第X届东盟首脑会议情景,预测此次会议的成果,并通过会议中的首脑新闻发布会及时告知国际公众。

Exercises
本章练习题

Multiple Choices 选择题

Directions: In this part there are 5 sentences. For each sentence there are four choices marked A, B, C and D. Choose the ONE answer that best completes the sentence.

1. This following manipulating process of IGO public relations can be described as a cycle made up of four stages: ( ), mediation and amplification, organization, and resolution.

   A. implementation B. origin
   C. recognition   D. decision

政府间国际组织国际公关 | International Public Relations of Intergovernmental Organization

2. The Oil-for-Food Program (OIP), administrated by the United Nations in 1995 (under UN Security Council Resolution 986) was established to allow (　) to sell oil on the world market in exchange for food, medicine, and other humanitarian needs for ordinary citizens without allowing (　) to boost its military capabilities.

   A. Iran　　　　　　　　　B. Pakistan
   C. Iraq　　　　　　　　　D. Syria

3. Which is not included in the target audiences of World Health Day campaign launched by WHO?

   A. Civil society groups.　　　B. Researchers.
   C. Private sector entities.　　D. Journalists.

4. In 2012, WHO wants to go beyond (　) to elicit concrete action and positive change. The World Health Day campaign aims to engage all of society, from policy makers and politicians to older people and the young.

   A. imagination　　　　　　B. programming
   C. awareness-raising　　　　D. goal-setting

5. IGOs have various goals and scopes, which are often outlined in the (　) or charter. Some of them developed to fulfill a need for a neutral forum for debate or negotiation to resolve disputes.

   A. law　　　B. rules　　　C. chapter　　　D. treaty

Gap Filling 填空题

Directions: Fill in the blanks with the correct form of the words and expressions provided.

1. (　　　)是两个及以上国家的政府通过签署符合国际法的协议而组成的国家联盟(union of states)或国家联合体(association of states)。

2. 政府间国际组织是国家之间的组织而非凌驾于主权国家之上的(　　)；与国际会议不同,政府间国际组织设有(　　　),具有相对的持续性和稳定性；依据国家间的正式协定,拥有一定的自主权和单独意志,且具备合作职能。

3. 政府间国际组织是(　　　)(International public goods)的主要提供者,弥补无政府状态国际社会单个国家行动能力不足。

4. 政府间国际组织成员国的(　　　　)决定了国际组织的职能权限,决定了国际组织具体的规则形式。
5. 水象征环太平洋国家因水而连、因水沟通,同时,它更象征着中国作为此次 APEC 东道主国家,向世界传递出的中国古代道德追求——(　　　　)。
6. 在水立方的中国风文艺演出之前,所有参加 APEC 领导人身着(　　　　),拍摄了一张具有浓郁中国韵味的全家福照片。

Table Completion 表格题

国际会议类型多样,名目繁多,可以根据政府间跨国组织的议题、规模、性质等召开相应的会议。请根据基础知识理论,填写下面表格。

划分标准	国际会议类型
按会议参加国家的数量	1_____
2_____	政府间国际会议或民间国际会议
按会议所涉及问题的范围	3_____
按与会各国代表的级别	4_____

Paraphrase 释义题

Directions: Explain the following sentences in your own words.

1. Intergovernmental organizations in a legal sense should be distinguished from simple groupings or coalitions of states, such as the G8. Such groups or associations have not been founded by a constituent document and exist only as task groups.

2. Practitioners of IGO public relations understand that they are expected to play increasingly complex and involved roles in promoting the bottom line, building harmonious relations with member states, and protecting organization's interests in ways that must be sensitive to the needs of a variety of external interests.

3. On World Health Day, social media will be used to engage people and to challenge some of the stereotypes of aging. Images and stories of older people and their valuable role in society will be made available through WHO's social media channels.

Thinking 思考题：

1. 模仿WHO关于人口老龄化议题进行的国际公关活动，草拟一份WHO关于在欠发达国家减少贫困的活动策划书。
2. 搜索并阅读《国际组织人才十大核心素养》①，试写一份应聘某个国际组织的自我简历。

---

① 新华网. 国际组织人才十大核心素养. http://news.xinhuanet.com/politics/2015-01/29/c_127435546.htm.2015-10-12.

International Public Relations of Non-Governmental Organizations
非政府间国际组织国际公关

Gist
内容概览

Non-Governmental Organization (NGO) refers to the unofficial, private organizations whose members are not nations, but individuals, social groups or other civil organizations. Since the 1980s, people in various occasions increasingly mentioned NGOs rather than governmental organizations. With the advent of the globalization age, NGOs played a significant role in the international public relations. NGOs can be an object or a subject when implementing public relations activities.

This chapter discusses public relations which focus on NGOs. Some, but not all, NGOs are chosen as typical cases in this chapter in light of the variety and diversity of NGOs. Students can learn the purposes, methods, and techniques of NGO public relations from bilingual cases and further reading. Then they can apply what they have learned in simulations, which cultivates students' collaboration and creativity.

非政府组织(Non-Governmental Organizations),英文缩写NGO,是指非官方的、民间的组织,其成员不是国家,而是个人、社会团体或其他民间机构。20世纪80年代以来,人们在各种场合越来越多地提及非政府组织,而非政府组织在国际舞台上也发挥着越来越重要的作用。随着全球化程度的不断加深,非政府组织在国际公关中的重要性日益突出。非政府组织既是公关的工具和对象,也是公关的主体。

本章选取非政府间国际组织为公共关系行为主体。鉴于非政府间国际

非政府间国际组织国际公关 | International Public Relations of Non-Governmental Organizations

组织具有大小不一、特征各异的特点,本章选取了在国际上较有代表性的非政府间国际组织公关案例作为样本,使学生在案例中了解和体会不同的非政府间国际组织在具体的公关实践中确立的目标以及采用的方法和技巧。学生在分析总结案例经验的同时,把学习的公关技巧和方法运用到情景模拟中,使学生既能熟练运用所学到的知识,又能协同合作,培养学生的创新性。

5.1 Basic Knowledge
基础知识

5.1.1 Definition 定义

A Non-Governmental Organization (NGO) is an organization that is neither a part of a government nor a conventional for-profit business. Usually set up by ordinary citizens, NGOs may be funded by governments, foundations, businesses, or private persons. Some avoid formal funding altogether and are run primarily by volunteers. NGOs are a highly diverse groups of organizations engaged in a wide range of activities, and take different forms in different parts of the world. Some may have a charitable status, while others may be registered for tax exemption based on recognition of their social function. Others may be fronts for political, religious or other interest groups.

非政府组织(英语:Non-Governmental Organization,缩写:NGO)是一类不属于任何政府、不由任何国家建立的组织,通常独立于国家政府。虽然从定义上包含以营利为目的的企业,但该名词一般仅限于非商业化的、合法的、与社会文化和环境相关的倡导群体。非政府组织通常是非营利组织,他们的基金至少有一部分来源于私人捐款。由于各国文化、法律等的差异,不同国家对这个概念的指称所适用的对象范围也各不相同。美国一般称之为"非营利组织""独立组织"或"第三部门"(The Third Sector),英国称之为"志愿组织"(voluntary organization),还有许多国家则用"社团"称之。

非政府间国际组织既是国际团体也是国际机构,是具有国际性行为特征的组织,是三个或三个以上国家(或其他国际法主体)的非政府组织为实现共同的政治经济目的,依据其缔结的条约或其他正式法律文件建立的有一定规章制度的常设性机构。

The criteria to classify or sort out NGOs are various. One of the easiest ways to type NGOs is by the scope of their operations. Operations can be global, region-specific or purpose-specific. Global NGOs operate in many different countries, while region-specific NGOs operate in one area of the world, for example, a peace and conflict organization that works in the region affected by the Israeli-Palestinian conflict. Purpose-specific NGOs fundraise for many different issues and typically distribute the funds raised to smaller, regional NGOs.

按定向分类,可分为以下几类。

By orientation

"Charitable orientation" often involves a top-down authoritarian effort with little participation by the "beneficiaries." It includes NGOs with activities directed toward meeting the needs of the poor.

"Service orientation" includes NGOs with activities such as the provision of health, family planning or education services in which the programme is designed by the NGO and people are expected to participate in its implementation and in receiving the service.

"Participatory orientation" is characterized by self-help projects where local people are involved particularly in the implementation of a project by contributing cash, tools, land, materials, labour etc. In the classical community development project, participation begins with the need definition and continues into the planning and implementation stages.

"Empowering orientation" aims to help poor people develop a clearer understanding of the social, political and economic factors affecting their lives, and to strengthen their awareness of their own potential power to control their lives. There is maximum involvement of the beneficiaries with NGOs acting as facilitators.

按等级分类,可分为以下几类。

By level of operation

"Community-based organizations" (CBOs) arise out of people's own initiatives. They can be responsible for raising the consciousness of the urban poor, helping them to understand their rights in accessing needed services, and providing such services.

非政府间国际组织国际公关 | International Public Relations of Non-Governmental Organizations

"City-wide organizations" include organizations such as chambers of commerce and industry, coalitions of business, ethnic or educational groups, and associations of community organizations.

"National NGOs" include national organizations such as the YMCAs/YWCAs, professional associations and similar groups. Some have state and city branches and assist local NGOs.

"International NGOs" range from secular agencies such as Ducere Foundation and Save the Children organizations, OXFAM, CARE, Ford Foundation, and Rockefeller Foundation to religiously motivated groups. They can be responsible for funding local NGOs, institutions and projects and implementing projects.[1]

非政府间国际组织具有跨国性，主要表现在组织的目的和活动范围至少涉及两个国家，组织的成员来自于不同的国家，经费的来源和使用具有国际性。对于五花八门的非政府间国际组织，根据其不同特征，相关学者和一些国际组织给出了不同的分类。

按照规模和范围来分，可分为全球性的、地区性的和国家之间的非政府组织。以地缘经济与整治相结合，可分为北方发达国家的非政府间国际组织和南方发展中国家的非政府间国际组织，北方非政府间国际组织又可分为三类：1. 以推动可持续发展为己任；2. 着眼于救援工作；3. 致力于妇女、人权、裁军、生态和贸易等公民的倡议性活动。南方非政府间国际组织由于资金、人员、规模的局限，影响相对较小。从活动的目标来分类，非政府间国际组织可以分为发展取向的和非发展取向的。发展取向的主要包括乡村发展、扶贫、教育、卫生、儿童、环境保护等，非发展取向的非政府间国际组织主要从事人道主义救济、难民安置、和平主义运动等。

按照非政府间国际组织的工作领域，又可分为：环境保护类、体育卫生类、政治外交类、文化教育类、慈善人权类、贫困发展类等。

世界银行将非政府间国际组织分为两类：运作型非政府间国际组织（operational NGOs）和倡议性非政府间国际组织（advocacy NGOs）。前者主要的目的是设计、执行和发展有关的工程项目。后者主要的目的是捍卫和促进某一特殊事业，进而吸引更多的资金和参与者[2]。

---

[1] Lynn Lawry, "Guide to Nongovernmental Organizations for the Military," *US: Center for Disaster and Humanitarian Assistance Medicine*, 2009.http://fas.org/irp/doddir/dod/ngo-guide.pdf 2015年9月12日。

[2] 中国网.国际非政府组织：概念、分类与发展[OL].http://www.china.com.cn/node_7000058/2007-04/02/content_8047369.htm, 2015年12月6日。

5.1.2 Characteristics 特征

All positive social roles, along with criticism and problems, create space for the implementation of international public relations. Public relations could, in a sense, be considered as a catalyst or even generator of positive international NGO practice and an impediment to negative practices. NGOs should obey the following principles when implement public relations activities:

(1) Information collection and dissemination;

(2) Policy development consultation;

(3) Policy implementation;

(4) Assessment and monitoring;

(5) Advocacy for environmental justice.

All NGOs are more or less dependent on the support of the public. All are also placed in the middle of various social, political and economic trends that require high-quality management and good public relations. In today's society where the media determine what is "just," NGOs have to struggle to gain public attention among many competing interests while also overcoming indifference of this international audience. They also have to compete with various powerful opponents such as governments, multinational companies and international financial institutions that are supported by highly organized public relations. In that kind of context the transnational NGO community displays a clear hierarchy of influence and reputation. Large and powerful organizations such as the Human Rights Watch, Amnesty International, Greenpeace and Friends of the Earth have the resources and expertise to investigate the claims of local groups from distant places and give them legitimacy.

尽管非政府组织具有不同的称谓,但学者对非政府组织的非营利性和自愿性等几个特征都予以认同,莱斯特·M.萨拉蒙(Lester M. Salamon)和赫马特·K.安海尔(Helmut K. Anheier)将这些特征总结为组织性、私有性、非营利性、自治性和志愿性五个特点。[①] 综合各方观点,非政府间国际组织的公关活动具有以下特征。

(1)公益为导向

[①] 莱斯特·M.萨拉蒙等主编,贾西津、魏玉等译,《全球公民社会——非盈利部门视界》。北京:社会科学文献出版社,2002。

非政府间国际组织国际公关 | International Public Relations of Non-Governmental Organizations

非政府间国际组织公关一个显著的特征是,不以营利为目的的行为活动的公益性。这种公益性不仅对政府失灵与市场失灵是一个补充,而且,它们能够为社会尽最大的可能提供一些社会所有公众都可以使用的公共产品。

(2)真诚沟通为基础

以事实为基础是非政府间国际组织公共关系活动必须切实遵循的基本原则之一。非政府间国际组织必须为自己塑造一个诚实的形象,才能取信于公众。精诚所至,金石为开;至诚可以移山;热诚能成万事;真诚能产生最大的说服力。唯有真诚,才能赢得合作。

(3)追求美誉为目标

塑造形象是非政府间国际组织的核心问题,塑造组织形象的基本目标有两个,即知名度和美誉度。所谓知名度是指一个组织被公众知道、了解的程度以及社会影响的广度和深度。所谓美誉度是指一个组织获得公众信任、赞美的程度,以及社会影响的美、丑、好、坏。在公众中树立组织的美好形象是公共关系活动的根本目的。

(4)跨文化交际为背景

非政府间国际组织开展公关活动必定会涉及两个或多个国家,这就决定了非政府组织开展公关活动需要以跨文化交际为背景。非政府间国际组织必须该了解公关对象的文化的价值观念和信仰,了解交际对象来自何种文化模式,才能进行有效沟通,完成预期的公关目标。

5.1.3 Objective 目标

Non-governmental organizations need harmonious relationships with the public to meet their goals. They often seek to cultivate public awareness, support and involve in their activities. Foundations and charities use sophisticated public relations campaigns to raise funds and employ standard lobbying techniques with governments. Interest groups may be of political importance because of their ability to influence social and political outcomes. At times NGOs seek to mobilize public support, therefore, use various strategies to conjure funds and create awareness about the organization's aims and objectives. As a result, NGO public relations tend to engage heavily in relationship-building activities. Foundations and charities use sophisticated public relations campaigns to raise funds and employ standard lobbying techniques with governments. Interest groups may be of political importance because of their ability to influence social and political outcomes.

非政府间国际组织作为非国家行为体,日益活跃在经济全球化时代的世界舞台上。非政府间国际组织的公关活动是为增进公众的信任和支持,利用传播的手段以及各种形式的国际交往,树立组织的良好形象,协调非政府间国际组织与政府、非政府国际组织与社会,以及非政府间国际组织之间的关系而开展的。

要扩大组织的世界知名度和影响力就必须通过一系列的宣传来达到预期目标。基金会和慈善机构往往通过娴熟的公关活动筹集资金,用游说的方式从政府那里得到支持。总体而言,非政府间国际组织的公关活动受众群体较广,具有跨国性和分散性。公关活动也涉及各个领域,包括教育、农业、环境、健康、经济等,能对一国政府和公众产生较大的影响。

5.1.4 Principles 原则

The Principles of NGOs' Public Relations

(1) Practice an activity which is based on a global vision, should attaches great importance to the local characteristics, and complies with international conventions.

(2) Preserve the NGOs' reputation in order to pursue a high degree of efficiency and specialization.

(3) Understand the foreign public attitudes and economic, political and social situation of the target in order to effectively use foreign public news media.

(4) Carry out public relations activities in a locally receptive way by means of cross-cultural communications, in accordance with the foreign public language, culture, beliefs, and habits.

(1) 确立组织建立的目标,坚持组织宗旨,坚定组织信念,提升全世界人民对国际组织形象的认同,塑造组织良好国际形象;

(2) 丰富组织文化,创新组织模式,与时俱进,改进机制;

(3) 维持良性的组织经济状况,拓宽资金来源;

(4) 承担国际责任,关注致力于解决全球面临的种种问题;

(5) 审时度势,开展创意公关活动,提升组织的知名度,实现组织的公关目标。

5.1.5 Practice 实施

(1) Develop public awareness of the organization's purpose and activities. All of the trends mentioned earlier, mainly the globalization of media and the fast development of information technology make it possible to communicate globally. Delivering the message to an international public becomes easier in light of those trends, even though the problem of cultural and national differences still remains an issue.

(2) Induce individuals to use the services the nongovernmental organization provides. After the public becomes aware of the NGO's purpose, the second and closely related step is connecting with the people at whom the service is aimed. The importance of communication in informing potential users of free medical examinations, clothing, food, counseling, scholarships and other services is essential. The difficulties in transcending communication barriers are significant even without an international dimension. An example includes health and welfare agencies that need to build a communication bridge between ethnic communities. Traditional programs and communication messages fail to reach various needy publics because of cultural and linguistic differences, limited access to information, and low levels of education.

(3) Create educational materials (especially important for health-oriented agencies). Again the international factor plays a major role in the formulation of the message but the issue of "speaking the same language" is a problem for NGOs domestically as well as internationally. The main challenge is in understanding the publics with whom the NGO is communicating. For example, in the population control campaigns in many developing countries, a major achievement of public relations campaigns has been to demystify contraception and make it acceptable for public discussion of contraception in general, and specific contraceptive methods in particular.

(4) Recruit and train volunteer workers. A significant proportion of international nonprofit organizations rely on unpaid volunteers for clerical assistance, fundraising, conducting tours and even volunteer recruitment. This can create two types of problems for the manager of the nonprofit organization. First, the need for a steady inflow of volunteers means that a third public is added to

those with whom the manager must communicate. On one hand, programs must be designed to attract paid personnel, while on the other, communicators must be careful about the possible consequences of the proposed programs on existing volunteers, none of which is simplified with the international factor. Second, it is not easy to manage volunteers, because their status allows them to get away with a higher level of unreliability.

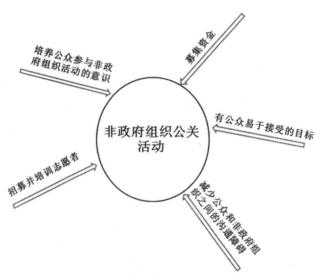

图5.1　非政府组织公关活动

(5) Obtain funds to operate the organization. The main financial resources of NGOs worldwide consist of large donations from private foundations, large individual public contributions, companies, other NGOs and government/governmental agencies. According to an estimate by Hulme and Edwards (1996), some $5.7—10 billion passes through international NGOs annually. The role of high-quality, transparent international communication strategies in obtaining these funds are crucial.[①]

非政府间国际组织既作为国际公关的对象，也作为公关的主体，在开展公关的时候有其自身特点。特别是冷战以来，非政府国际组织如雨后春笋，每年以迅猛的速度递增，以非政府组织为主的公关成为西方国家对外政策

---

① Krishnamurthy Sriramesh, Dejan Vercic, *The Global Public Relations Handbook, Revised and Expanded Edition: Theory, Research, and Practice.* London: Routledge, 2009.

非政府间国际组织国际公关 | International Public Relations of Non-Governmental Organizations

和国家安全战略的重要组成部分。同时,随着国际行为体的相互依存程度不断增加,非政府组织也被作为是公关的主体,利用国际公关实现全球治理。所以,非政府组织在开展公关活动时应具备一定的技巧。

首先,在开展国际公关时要遵循国际交往时的国际惯例、当地的法律法规,在法律的框架内进行公关活动。

其次,要尊重当地的文化和风俗习惯,力求实行本土化策略。良好的跨文化交际能力,是公关成功实施的重要保障。

最后,根据不同的组织特点,在开展国际公关时应力求有较高的参与度和创新性,符合自身的利益需求。

5.1.6 Fund Raising 募集资金

非政府间国际组织募集资金

Whether the NGOs are small or large, various NGOs need budgets to operate. The amount of budget that they need would differ from NGOs to NGOs. Unlike small NGOs, large NGOs may have annual budgets in the hundreds of millions or billions of dollars. For instance, the budget of the American Association of Retired Persons (AARP) was over US $540 million in 1999. Funding such large budgets demands significant fundraising efforts on the part of most NGOs. Major sources of NGO funding are membership dues, the sale of goods and services, grants from international institutions or national governments and private donations. Several EU-grants provide funds accessible to NGOs.

Even though the term "non-governmental organization" implies independence from governments, many NGOs depend heavily on governments for their funding. A quarter of the US$162 million income in 1998 of the famine-relief organization Oxfam was donated by the British government and the EU. The Christian relief and development organization World Vision United States collected US$55 million worth of goods in 1998 from the American government.

Government funding of NGOs is controversial, since, according to David Rieff, writing in *The New Republic*, "the whole point of humanitarian intervention was precisely that NGOs and civil society had both a right and an obligation to respond with acts of aid and solidarity to people in need or being subjected to repression or want by the forces that controlled them, whatever the governments concerned might think about the matter."① Some NGOs, such as Greenpeace do not accept funding from governments or intergovernmental organizations.

非政府组织（Non Governmental Organizations）一般简称NGO，非政府组织是当今在国际上通行的一个词，是相对政府而言，一般指非政府的、非营利的、带有志愿性的致力于公益事业的社会中介组织。20世纪80年代以来，因非政府组织在世界各国的社会经济发展中所发挥的作用越来越大，非政府组织扮演着越来越重要的角色，影响力大的非政府组织对于国家之间的关系和地区的稳定起着举足轻重的作用。然而，非政府组织由于并非由政府支持组建，其资金来源得不到保障，很多情况下必须借助公关活动推广和宣传，以此募集更多的资金，维持组织的正常运转。故募集资金也是非政府间国际组织开展公关的主要目标之一。

一般而言，非政府组织的资金来源不外乎四个渠道：民间捐赠、服务收费、政府补贴和外国援助。所有国家的非政府组织都或多或少地依赖前三种来源，但那些发展中和转型中国家的很多非政府组织还依赖于外国捐款。

民间捐赠，包括来自个人、基金会和企业的捐款，这是非政府组织独特的收入来源，也是它们与政府组织及私人营利机构相区别的标志之一。如前所述，民间捐赠不仅不是非政府组织收入的主要来源，甚至都不是第二个重要的来源。在发达国家，民间捐赠比例最高的是美国，仅占到19%。其余国家则更为有限，英、德、法、日分别仅占12%、4%、7%、1%。在民间捐赠这一类中，个人捐款最重要。个人捐款在美国占非政府部门收入总额的13.9%，在英国占6.5%，在法国占3.8%，德国占2.1%。

服务收费是非政府组织获得资金的极其重要来源。在一些国家，来自会费、收费活动和商业经营的收入超过了所有其他来源的收入，构成了非政府组织总收入的最大部分。在美、意、日三国非政府部门收入中，收费所占的比例都在一半以上。在美国，近年来的一个新趋势是非营利部门日益变得商业化起来。譬如，非营利医院纷纷兴办面向社会的健康俱乐部，非营利博物馆纷纷开办礼品店，非营利的各种社团纷纷与公司签订产品认可或促销协议，以换取对方的捐款等例子层出不穷。如果目前的这种趋势持续下去，早已高度商业化的美国非营利部门会变得更加商业化。

政府补贴是非政府组织和非营利组织资金的一项重要来源。包括直接

---

① David Rieff. New Public, https://newrepublic.com/article/75421/ng-uh-o, 2015年11月16日。

非政府间国际组织国际公关 | International Public Relations of Non-Governmental Organizations

拨款(即政府直接给予非政府组织补贴以支持它们的活动和项目)、合约(即非营利组织向有资格享受某些政府项目的人提供服务,而由公共机构支付服务费)和补偿(即向那些有资格享受政府项目并从非营利组织那里购买服务的人支付补偿费)。在发展中国家,政府拨款不会是非政府组织收入的主要来源,但在欧洲一些发达国家,非政府组织最大的一个资金来源就是政府补贴和拨款。如德国非政府组织收入的68%来自政府,法国则占到60%。相反,服务收费的比例分别为28%和34%,民间捐赠的比例分别为4%和7%。在美国,政府对于非政府组织的资助分为直接资助和间接资助两种形式。到1980年,联邦政府对非政府部门的直接资助高达410亿美元,相当于非政府部门总收入的35%。此外,州及州以下政府也资助了相关的非政府组织。除了直接资助外,联邦政府对非政府组织所得税的豁免,对私人和企业非政府捐款的减税,以及州和州以下政府对非政府组织所得税、财产税和销售税的豁免,也是一笔相当大的数目。

在广大发展中国家,政府、企业和百姓的收入还十分微薄,非政府组织在国内难以筹集到足够的资金。外国援助是发展中国家非政府组织收入的重要来源,包括来自发达国家政府机构、基金会和其他非营利组织的拨款和捐款。譬如,在1990年,发达国家的非政府组织(又称北方非政府组织Northern NGOs)就向发展中国家的非政府组织(又称南方非政府组织Southern NGOs)输送了价值72亿美元的援助,相当于第三世界国家当年收到的官方援助的13%,或当年流入这些国家总资金的2.5%。由于得到了北方非政府组织的支持,南方非政府组织在过去20年内获得了迅速的发展。

通过对非政府组织的上述四种资金来源的分析,我们发现,民间捐赠是非政府组织最好的收入来源,因为这一类支持很少或没有附带条件,可以保证非政府组织按照其目标自主地进行资金分配和参与援助活动。只有充足的资金保障,非政府间国际组织才能正常运作。由此可见,公关活动显得异常重要,一次成功的公关将会显著提高非政府组织的国际声誉,从而吸引获得更多的捐赠和补贴,使非政府间国际组织蓬勃发展。①

---

① 参考 周批改,周亚平,《国外非营利组织的资金来源及启示国外非营利组织的资金来源及启示》,《东南学术》,2004年第1期:第91—95页;毛红华,王瑞红,《非政府组织资金来源的一个保障问题》,《西昌学院学报(社会科学版)》,2006年第2期:第95—98页。

5.2 Bilingual Case Studies
双语案例

5.2.1 WWF Giant Panda Conservation PR

Background

This peaceful creature with a distinctive black and white coat is adored by the world and considered a national treasure in China. The panda also has a special significance for WWF because it has been WWF's logo since its founding in 1961.The rarest member of the bear family, pandas live mainly in bamboo forests high in the mountains of western China, where they subsist almost entirely on bamboo. They must eat from 26 to 84 pounds of it every day, a formidable task for which they use their enlarged wrist bones that function as opposable thumbs.

WWF, originally stood for "World Wildlife Fund," in 1986, changed its name to "World Wild Fund for Nature." WWF was the first international conservation organization to work in China at the Chinese government's invitation. WWF's main role in China is to assist and influence policy-level conservation decisions through information collection, demonstration of conservation approaches, communications and capacity building.

Research

Pandas play a crucial role in the bamboo forests where they roam by spreading seeds and facilitating growth of vegetation. In the Yangtze Basin where pandas live, the forests are home to a stunning array of wildlife such as dwarf blue sheep, multicolored pheasants and other endangered species, including the golden monkey, takin and crested ibis.

The panda's habitat is at the geographic and economic heart of China, home to millions of people. By making this area more sustainable, they are also helping to increase the quality of life of local populations. Pandas bring huge economic benefits to local communities through ecotourism.

Despite their exalted status and relative lack of natural predators, pandas are endangered. Severe threats from humans have left fewer than 1600 pandas in the wild, according to a 2004 survey. A census of the wild panda population

非政府间国际组织国际公关 | International Public Relations of Non-Governmental Organizations

is undertaken every 10 years.

The Pandas are facing habit loss and hunting danger at present. China's Yangtze Basin region, which holds the panda's primary habitat, is the geographic and economic heart of this booming country. Roads and railroads are increasingly fragmenting the forest, which isolates panda populations and prevents mating. Forest destruction also reduces pandas' access to the bamboo they need to survive. The Chinese government has established more than 50 panda reserves, but only around 61% of the country's panda population is protected by these reserves.

Hunting remains an ever-present threat. Poaching the animals for their fur has declined due to strict laws and greater public awareness of the panda's protected status. But hunters seeking other animals in panda habitats continue to kill pandas accidentally.

Practice

The logo of WWF emphasizes the significant role of giant panda. The inspiration for the WWF logo came from Chi-Chi: a giant panda that was living at the London Zoo in 1961, the same year WWF was created. WWF's founders were aware of the need for a strong, recognizable symbol that would overcome all language barriers. They agreed that the big, furry animal with her appealing, black-patched eyes would make an excellent choice.

The first panda sketches were done by the British environmentalist and artist, Gerald Watterson. Based on these, Sir Peter Scott, one of WWF's founders and a world-renowned conservationist and painter, drew the first logo. The design of the logo has evolved over the past four decades, but the giant panda's distinctive features remain an integral part of WWF's treasured and unmistakable symbol. Today, WWF's trademark is recognized as a universal symbol for the conservation movement.

WWF has provided some advocate to China government, such as increasing the area of panda habitat under legal protection, creating green corridors to link isolated pandas, patrolling against poaching, illegal logging and encroachment, building local capacities for nature reserve management, continuing research and monitoring.

WWF has been helping with the Chinese government's National Conservation Program for the giant panda and its habitat. Owing to this program, panda reserves now cover more than 3.8 million acres of forest.

Evaluation

The WWF has earned its fame by this kind of project. And most of people understand their mission is to stop the degradation of our planet's natural environment, and build a future in which humans live in harmony with nature. The Giant Panda Conservation has got a really good advertising effect, and WWF will get a quick and strong development.

What's more important, this project of endangered panda protection has let more people know WWF's function and mission. Every year plenty of volunteers join in WWF to protect endangered species, food, climate, water and etc. WWF has done a well job to propagate their organization, and encourage everyone become the backbone of the planet to protect giant pandas.

Case Study 案例分析

This is a proactive case by WWF (World Wildlife Fund or World Wild Fund for Nature). In this case, the WWF has a clear PR objective, which is protection of giant pandas.

Giant pandas are known by the world due to their cute image. The WWF tries to help public to realize that giant pandas are endangered and that they need the assistance of the world. WWF's logo, a panda with a slogan "WWF for a living planet," is very attractive. The public relations with government are very important. With the help of Chinese government, the WWF has realized the PR objective of protecting giant pandas by increasing the area of panda habitat under legal protection, creating green corridors to link isolated pandas, and patrolling against poaching.

Furthermore, the WWF has recruited numerous volunteers to participate in this activity, which may create a groundswell of support to protect giant pandas. This project will effectively raise public's awareness of protecting wildlife, thus make WWF more popular.

非政府间国际组织国际公关 | International Public Relations of Non-Governmental Organizations

5.2.2 国际奥委会盐湖城丑闻公关

案例调研

在美国人的眼中,盐湖城一向是个宁静的城市,它不屈不挠地申办冬奥会已有近30年的历史,1991年输给日本的长野后,1993年终于获得2002年举办冬奥会的权利。但现在这个城市却被申办2002年冬奥会过程中曝出来的种种丑闻所玷污。这起丑闻的严重性也令人始料不及,上至中国人非常熟悉的国际奥委会主席萨马兰奇,下至该组织的数十名高级官员都卷入其中。

80岁的国际奥委会的执行委员霍德勒曝出惊人内幕:在奥运会的申办和投票阶段,至少有4个城市,包括亚特兰大、长野、悉尼和盐湖城,通过贿赂等不法手段击败其他竞争者。贿赂是有组织的,至少有4个"中间人"作为在行贿与受贿方之间的"代理",一方出不菲的价钱,另一方则投支持票。有的申办国家贿金多达100万美元,最终获得主办权的国家用于这方面的"投资"高达500万美元。霍德勒还透露,在国际奥委会115名委员中,有5%到7%的委员曾要求以支持票换取钱财,上述四名"中间人"中有一位甚至是国际奥委会的成员。霍德勒没有点出这个人的姓名,但认为这个人"手眼通天",能保证"给予某个申办国家足够获胜的票数"。这一系列丑闻的曝光顿时使国际奥委会处在各方指责的"风口浪尖"上。

公关目标

危机发生后,对国际奥委会的声誉必然造成极大损害。一方面,需要一个长期的过程来恢复奥委会声誉;另一方面,为杜绝类似事件的发生,国际奥委会必须进行体制改革,用更加透明的方式进行投票,扮演一个更公正的角色。

公关实施

国际奥委会因为此次事件声誉严重受损,奥委会已经湮没在全世界的质疑当中。为了妥善解决此次事件,作为国际奥委会主席,萨马兰奇必须迅速组织内部调查,对涉事的官员进行严惩。同时,需要召开新闻发布会,向外界说明此次事件的进展状况和惩处措施。

国际奥委会主席萨马兰奇在瑞士洛桑奥林匹克博物馆举行的新闻发布会上,宣布了对涉嫌美国盐湖城丑闻的14名国际奥委会委员的处理决定。决定说,在国际奥委会调查委员会调查、证实和建议的基础上,国际奥委会执委会一致通过决定,暂时中止6名国际奥委会委员的资格,并建议由当年3

月举行的国际奥委会特别代表大会正式将他们开除。这6名委员是阿约(厄瓜多尔)、甘加(刚果)、扎因(苏丹)、基塔(马里)、姆科拉(肯尼亚)和桑坦德(智利)。执委会还决定对恩迪亚伊(科特迪瓦)、金云龙(韩国)和斯米尔诺夫(俄罗斯)3名委员继续进行调查,并对吉欣克(荷兰)提出警告。

在执委会做出决定之前,已有3名涉嫌的委员提出辞职。他们是海格曼夫人(芬兰)、阿塔拉布斯(利比亚)和西班兹(斯威士兰)。萨马兰奇对他们的辞职表示欢迎,同时希望其他涉嫌丑闻的委员主动提出辞职。此外,一名涉嫌的委员埃松巴(喀麦隆)已于1998年去世。在新闻发布会上,国际奥委会副主席、调查委员会主任庞德说,以上涉嫌的委员"既不是受贿、也不是腐败、更不是刑事犯罪",但他们违背了当初的誓言和国际奥委会的规章制度。他们有权在特别会议上做自我辩护。

萨马兰奇在会上特别强调指出,这次对涉嫌委员的处理仅仅是惩治错误行为的开始,而不是结束。国际奥委会将继续打击和根除各种错误行为,开除任何行为不端的委员。为了尽快解决这起丑闻,萨马兰奇表示将改革现行的奥运会申办机制。为了便于控制和掌握重大的决定,以后改由拥有11名执委的执委会投票来做出,而不再由近百名全体委员参与决定。他认为,经受了这场危机的考验之后,国际奥林匹克运动将更加壮大。

公关评估

在盐湖城丑闻发生后,国际奥委会迅速开展调查,对丑闻中所涉事的官员进行了严肃的处理。国际奥委会主席萨马兰奇随后在新闻发布会上也宣布了此次处理决定,果断地采取了补救措施,为今后的形象恢复提供了契机。经过此次危机之后,国际奥委会将更加成熟,国际奥委会的声誉也得到一定程度的恢复。如今,国际奥委会依然在奥林匹克精神的领导下,促进世界和平以及各国人民之间的相互了解,发展世界体育运动。《奥林匹克宪章》明文规定,国际奥委会的宗旨是:鼓励组织和发展体育运动和组织竞赛;在奥林匹克理想指导下,鼓舞体育运动的发展,促进和加强各国运动员之间的友谊。

> **Case Study 案例分析**
>
> 国际奥委会盐湖城丑闻公关是非政府国际组织的危机公关。在盐湖城丑闻危机爆发后,国际奥委会就此事迅速开展调查,体现了速度第一的原则。而国际奥委会主席萨马兰奇随后召开了新闻发布会,

向大众媒体说明了事情的来龙去脉,与外界真诚沟通,并主动承担了责任,体现了承担责任的原则。对于涉事官员,国际奥委会执行委员会一致决定终止他们的委员会委员资格,向公众承诺不会再发生类似事件,体现了态度真诚的原则。在危机公关的过程中做到了循序渐进,标本兼治,不仅就此事向世界人民道歉,而且从自身内部找原因,进行体制改革,对症下药,谋求治本,体现了标本兼治的原则。通过一系列公关措施,国际奥委会既有效地处理了危机事件,又能重新获得公众的信任,可谓一举两得。

国际奥委会作为一个非政府的民间组织,需要自筹经费以维持生存。长期以来国际奥委会资金拮据,20世纪60年代后期曾一度出现赤字。自20世纪70年代开始,随着电视转播收入的增长,情况开始好转,1975年取消了会员费。20世纪80年代中期后,萨马兰奇当选国际奥委会主席,大幅改革,引进商业赞助计划,国际奥委会获得了大量经费,国际奥委会的成员结构开始趋向合理,国际影响力也日益上升。

5.3 Further Reading
拓展阅读

5.3.1 Sanishop PR

Research

The World Toilet Organization pioneered the creation of SaniShop—a social enterprise that improves sanitation conditions globally by empowering local entrepreneurs. From 2010 to 2012, the World Toilet Organization piloted its market-based approach in two provinces in Cambodia—Kg. Speu and Kg. Chnnang, reaching more than 100000 households.

There are more people worldwide who own mobile phones than toilets. Cultural norms and lack of awareness are key obstacles in triggering behavioural change among individuals who practice open defecation. Many do not see the value in investing in a toilet. This was a neglected crisis for a very long time. All efforts by humanitarian community over the last 10 years have not produced any significant impact because not enough donor funds were available and in any case, donated toilets are often used as storerooms instead of toilets, or they are not maintained and abandoned eventually.

Objective

Based on a "social franchise" model, SaniShop involves training local masons in developing countries to build and sell toilets to their community.

By empowering individuals to develop entrepreneurial skills, the SaniShop model provides livelihoods to local masons and sales agents. In addition to job creation, masons and sales agents are trained to deliver sustainable sanitation solutions to their communities, thereby improving the sanitation conditions in villages. Our SaniShop sales agents are also trained in facilitating Community-Led Total Sanitation (CLTS) workshops.

Practice

In Cambodia, the SaniShop model is built around a local owner. The SaniShop owner is trained by the World Toilet Organization to produce low-cost toilets using steel moulds and locally sourced materials (cement, piping, ceramics and tiles). They are also trained in basic business practices. Each SaniShop also has a small number of sales agents who are trained in marketing and sales. These agents hold village discussions and go door-to-door taking orders for toilets. WTO field office in Cambodia provides all of the training over the course of two weeks; helps to negotiate bulk prices and provides on-going support for three to four months afterwards.

In late 2011, World Toilet Organization established its SaniShop model in India to increase access of rural households to safe and affordable sanitation. On the ground, they work closely with local implementing partners eKutir, a social business, based out of Odisha, and Sattva, a media and social business consulting firm based out of Bangalore.

The pilot project was set up in Odisha where eKutir had established its strong rural base. By deploying eKutir's micro-entrepreneurs to further SaniShop's mission in providing safe and affordable sanitation to the rural population, this partnership allows the World Toilet Organization and eKutir to create more livelihoods, boost health and dignity among the farming households. eKutir has been able to establish 25 micro-entrepreneurs working for the sanitation cause in three different states of India.

Evaluation

In 2012, SaniShop Cambodia tested the market in 7 provinces and has since scaled up in Kampung Chnnang where it has trained close to 60 sales people and 15 SaniShop franchisees. In 2012, the SaniShop ecosystem built 1800 toilets, and we expect that this rate of toilet construction will be financially sustainable in the future in each province.

With the establishment of SaniShop, farmers have access to low-cost and affordable toilets. As a result, households reduce their medical expenses as they do not fall sick as often and this increases their savings. With a proven track-record of impact in the pilot villages of Odisha, World Toilet Organization and eKutir are collaborating on broadening this impact to other states in India. Currently, the partnership between World Toilet Organization and eKutir aims to reach out to over 20000 households by 2014.

Thinking:

1. Based on the classification of NGOs, what type of NGO WTO (World Toilet Organization) is? What is WTO's mission and objective?
2. What experiences we can learn from the case Sanishiop?
3. Please write a case study on case Sanishop.

5.3.2 绿色和平组织"我是一棵树"公关

案例调研

绿色和平(Greenpeace)是绿色和平组织的简称,属于一个国际性的非政府组织。作为发展中大国,中国对全球环境的影响至关重要。20多年来,中国的发展举世瞩目,但环境危机却与日俱增。绿色和平相信经济发展不应以破坏环境为代价。他们立足中国,放眼全球,致力于以实际行动开拓一条绿色的发展道路。

地球上森林能吸收二氧化碳,产生氧气,固定泥土,调和气候,平衡水的循环系统,并且提供给动物及植物一个相当理想的栖息处。然而,过去四十年来,地球上近半的原始森林,约三十亿公顷面积,已被破坏;余下的只有20%未受人类打扰。而这一现象随着经济的发展,仍在恶化。

中国是森林资源缺乏的国家,人均森林占有面积在全球仅排139名。再加上中国公众的环保意识不强,在许多餐厅和饭馆都可以见到一次性筷子的身影。顾客的大量需求加速了一次性筷子的生产,加速了森林资源的消耗。在2009年,中国共生产并使用了230亿双一次性筷子。如果把中国年产的一次性筷子首尾相接,可以往返月球15次。一次性筷子的大量生产和消耗,无疑给我国本来匮乏的森林资源带来更大的压力。

公关目标

国际环保绿色和平组织希望通过举办"我是一棵树"这样的活动来吸引更多的公众参与其中,以唤起人们的森林保护意识。绿色和平希望通过该活动,呼吁公众拒绝使用一次性筷子,保护中国原本匮乏的森林资源。促成可持续发展,给我们的地球留下更多的绿地。

公关实施

"我是一棵树"活动由奥美广告构想和创作,包括所有筷子树的设计和制作,借这个活动向中国公众宣传环保意识,对一次性筷子说不,保护中国匮乏的森林资源。在过去的几个月中,奥美先后与国际环保组织绿色和平、本地艺术家徐银海和来自20多所大学的200多位志愿者合作,到餐馆搜集使用过的一次性筷子80000多双,并将他们拼接还原成了四棵高度达5米的大树。

绿色和平森林保护项目主任李艾虹表示:"这四棵大树原本应该是郁郁葱葱充满生机的,但现在却由废弃的一次性筷子拼凑而成。我们希望每个人都能坚定的向一次性筷子说不,在'举手投筷'之间保护森林。"

奥美广告北京执行创意总监陈国辉表示:"我们希望能向公众展示,这些看起来无伤大雅的一次性筷子正在耗尽中国的森林资源。我们回收了8万多双筷子,并把它们还原成大树。我们希望这次的展出能给公众带来震撼,并最终在行动上支持森林保护。"

以"麦田守望者"组合主唱萧玮为首的绿色和平员工和志愿者、筷子森林的制作者徐银海、奥美员工和大学生于12月18日在世贸天阶对公众和媒体展出了此次"我是一棵树"活动。活动中,参观者被邀请签名承诺拒绝使用一次性筷子。绿色和平为支持此项活动送出了几百双生态环保可重复利用的筷子。奥美公司还为此次活动专门制作了一个网站,邀请民众在线签名支持森林保护。每当一人在线签名,网站页面上的大树就会长出一片新的绿叶。

公关评估

通过参加此次"我是一棵树"的活动,让公众感受到了保护森林资源的重要性和紧迫感,增强了他们的绿色环保意识。活动所展出的"筷子树"给参与者带来了极大的震撼,可以使他们最终从行动上支持森林保护。利用签名的方式使环保活动更具责任感,让大众切实感受到自身的环保责任,也为这次活动增添了严肃性。网站活动的开展使更多的人能参与进来,扩大了宣传的受众层面,使本次活动更加具有推广性和实践性。经过此次活动,绿色和平保护森林的理念已深入参与者的内心,相信他们身体力行,会向更多人宣传绿色环保意识,为保护绿色地球做出自己的贡献。

思考:

1. 从国际组织分类来看,你认为绿色和平组织属于哪一类?
2. "我是一棵树"的公关活动有哪些新意?你从中学到了什么?
3. 列举你所知道的环保类国际组织的创意公关,总结经验。

5.4 Simulation 情景模拟

5.4.1 FIFA Corruption Crisis PR

FIFA is the body responsible for running world football. It has recently been dogged by accusations of corruption, particularly after awarding the 2022 World Cup to the tiny but rich and influential Gulf state of Qatar. In December 2014, Fifa chose not to release its own investigation into corruption, instead releasing an executive summary which it said exonerated the bidding process. The report's independent author, American lawyer Michael Garcia, resigned in protest.

The World Cup is the most-watched sporting event in the world, larger even than the Olympics. It generates billions of dollars in revenue from corporate sponsors, broadcasting rights and merchandising. These arrests and investigations cast doubt over the transparency and honesty for the process of allocating World Cup tournaments, electing its president and the administration of funds, including those earmarked for improving football facilities in some of Fifa's poorer members.

The FBI has been investigating Fifa for the past three years. The investigation was initially sparked by the bidding process for the Russia 2018 and Qatar 2022

World Cups, but was widened to look back at Fifa's dealings over the past 20 years. The Department of Justice's indictment says that the corruption was planned in the US, even if it was then carried out elsewhere. The use of US banks to transfer money appears to be key to the investigation. Mr. Blatter consistently denied wrongdoing while several of his close colleagues were indicted by the US. In September, he was named as the subject of a separate criminal investigation launched by Swiss prosecutors.

Swiss prosecutors have accused Mr. Blatter of criminal mismanagement or misappropriation over a TV rights deal and of a "disloyal payment" to European football Chief Michel Platini. Meanwhile, the US authorities have charged 14 defendants with racketeering, wire fraud and money laundering conspiracies. The 47-count indictment, unveiled in a US federal court in New York, said the defendants participated "in a 24-year scheme to enrich themselves through the corruption of international soccer."

Apart from Mr. Blatter, the most senior figures accused are football powerbrokers in North America, Latin America and the Caribbean. They are connected to Concacaf, the continental confederation which operates under the FIFA umbrella and is essentially in charge of football in that region. One of its key roles is helping to agree World Cup TV and sponsorship deals in the US.

Other multimillion-dollar sponsors, including Adidas, McDonald's and Budweiser's parent company, Anheuser-Busch, also issued statements saying they were in contact with FIFA. But it remains to be seen if any of them would go as far as severing ties.

Simulation:

1. FIFA has now encountered a severe crisis of confidence. FIFA wants to invite a public relations company to rebuild its image, and they have several choices. Now you are the manager of Ogilvy. What would you do if you want to win FIFA's business? Try to make a detailed plan, and the teacher will be the judge to decide whether or not to use your plan.
2. Mr. Blatter is accused of bribery. If related authorities prove that he is not guilty after the investigation, what he would say to the public? Write a statement for him to read.

非政府间国际组织国际公关 | International Public Relations of Non-Governmental Organizations

3. Some sponsors are involved in this event, and they may lose faith in FIFA. Now you must attempt to pacify these sponsors; try to simulate the scenario. The class can be divided into several groups, one acting as FIFA official, one group as the sponsors, one as the journalist and one as the judges.

5.4.2 "地球一小时"公关

"地球一小时"(Earth Hour)是世界自然基金会(WWF)应对全球气候变化所提出的一项倡议,希望家庭及商界用户关上不必要的电灯及耗电产品一小时,以此来表明他们对应对气候变化行动的支持。过量二氧化碳排放导致的气候变化目前已经极大地威胁到地球上人类的生存。公众只有通过改变全球民众对于二氧化碳排放的态度,才能减轻这一威胁对世界造成的影响。"地球一小时"在3月的最后一个星期六20:30-21:30期间熄灯。

"地球一小时"活动首次于2007年3月31日在澳大利亚的悉尼展开,一下子吸引了超过220万悉尼家庭和企业参加;随后,该活动以惊人的速度迅速席卷全球。在2008年,WWF(中国)对外联络处透露,全球已经有超过80个国家、大约1000座城市加入活动。

燃烧煤、石油和天然气等化石燃料所排放的二氧化碳和其他污染物在大气层中不断积累,包裹着地球,导致局地空气污染和全球气候变化。同时,由于目前能源生产使用方式的不可持续,化石能源也在快速耗尽中。解决全球能源危机与环境污染的办法就在我们的身边——可再生能源。能源转型,不仅仅是我们的最优选择,也是我们的唯一选择。

2015年3月28日(星期六)晚8:30,"地球一小时"活动开始。为响应全球应对气候变化的主题,今年"地球一小时"在中国将继续聚焦当前最急迫、最受关注的环境议题——雾霾,发出"能见蔚蓝"的倡议。

"能见蔚蓝,代表了我们的建议和对未来的期待。'能',意味着可再生能源能够带来改变,'蔚蓝'代表我们每个人对告别雾霾、寻回蓝天的期待。"WWF中国总干事卢思骋表示,在深化2014年"地球一小时""蓝天自造"主题的基础上,今年的"地球一小时"将聚焦于能源议题,致力于推动可再生能源的主流化应用。

化石能源的过度使用,是目前中国局地空气污染的罪魁祸首,也是导致全球气候变化最主要的原因。中国正消耗着全球约一半的煤炭。2012年,因煤炭消费的一次PM2.5、二氧化硫和氮氧化物排放量分别占中国污染物排放总量的62%、93%和70%。同时,政府间气候变化专门委员会(IPCC)于

2014年年底发布第五次气候变化评估综合报告,进一步确认了温室气体排放以及其他人类活动是自20世纪中期以来观测到的气候变暖的主要原因,二氧化碳浓度已升至过去80万年以来前所未有的水平,而使用化石燃料是二氧化碳主要来源之一。

模拟:

1. 如果你作为2015年"地球一小时"的宣传大使,你会用什么方法去宣传"地球一小时"活动。请你为"地球一小时"设计一个宣传标语并向公众介绍"地球一小时"活动。

   角色:"地球一小时"宣传大使、公众等。

2. 众所周知,仅仅有环保意识和采取实际的环保行动对世界产生的真实影响是不同的。WWF原本希望,随着人们的环保意识增强,大家能够做出环保改变,保护我们的地球。许多人做到了,但很多人仍然没有行动。自2007年发起至今,公众对"地球一小时"的平均参与率达2.7次。但有24.2%的公众表示从未参与过。如果你是WWF的推广负责人,你会怎么解决此类问题? 请做出具体的方案(广告、宣传册、签名活动等)。

3. 中国目前面临严重的环境污染问题,大气污染、水污染呈不断扩散的态势。近年来,雾霾现象更是频频发生,让老百姓怨声载道。现请你就雾霾为主题设计下一次"地球一小时"的主题活动,包括计划书、参与对象、宣传广告、公益活动等。请以小组为单位,进行模拟演练。

   角色:世界自然基金会的工作人员、政府官员、民众、记者等。

Exercises
本章练习题

Gap Filling 填空题

Directions: Fill in the blanks with the correct form of the words and expressions provided.

rely on	dependency	empower	roam	emphasize
improve	diverse	aware	difference	sophisticate

1. The World Toilet Organization pioneered the creation of SaniShop—a social enterprise that (   ) sanitation conditions globally by empowering local

非政府间国际组织国际公关 | International Public Relations of Non-Governmental Organizations

entrepreneurs.
2. A significant proportion of international nonprofit organizations (　　) unpaid volunteers for clerical assistance, fundraising, conducting tours and even volunteer recruitment.
3. Pandas play a crucial role in the bamboo forests where they (　　) by spreading seeds and facilitating growth of vegetation.
4. All NGOs are more or less (　　) on the support of the public.
5. NGOs are a highly (　　) groups of organizations engaged in a wide range of activities, and take different forms in different parts of the world.
6. "(　　) orientation" aims to help poor people develop a clearer understanding of the social, political and economic factors affecting their lives, and to strengthen their awareness of their own potential power to control their lives.
7. Develop public (　　) of the organization's purpose and activities.
8. The logo of WWF (　　) the significant role of giant panda.
9. Foundations and charities use (　　) public relations campaigns to raise funds and employ standard lobbying techniques with governments.
10. The amount of budget that they need would (　　) from NGOs to NGOs.

Multiple Choices 选择题

Directions: In this part there are 6 sentences. For each sentence there are four choices marked A, B, C and D. Choose the ONE answer that best completes the sentence.

1. Which operation does not belong to an NGO?
   A. Global　　　　　　　　　B. Region-specific
   C. Purpose-specific　　　　　D. Economy-specific
2. In late 2011, which country did World Toilet Organization establish its SaniShop model? (　)
   A. Cambodia　　B. India　　C. Bangladesh　　D. Burma
3. The local attitude toward SaniShop can be described as (　)
   A. dissatisfied　　B. welcoming　C. indifferent　　D. elusive
4. Why has the WWF taken some measures to protect pandas? (　)
   A. Because they think pandas are cute.
   B. Because the panda is their logo.

C. Because pandas are facing a loss of habitation and are endangered by hunters

D. Because the Chinese government hoped that they would do so

5. What is the purpose of Earth Hour activity? (　)

   A. To tell us we can turn off our lights together.

   B. To advise people not to waste their food.

   C. To warn people that everyone can save our earth.

   D. To suggest that people not smoke

6. NGOs can obtain funds to operate organizations in many ways except (　)

   A. by public donation　　　　　B. by issue shares

   C. by membership fees　　　　D. by foreign aid

Matching 连线题

国际奥委会	AI
世界气象组织	Oxfam
绿色和平组织	WCS
国际特赦组织	Greenpeace
世界自然基金会	The Ford Foundation
乐施会	IOC
福特基金会	WWF
国际野生生物保护学会	WMO

Table Completion 表格题

Directions: Fill these blanks with correct words or sentences.

By level of orientation

	International Committee of the Red Cross, OXFAM
Service orientation	
	WWF, IFAW, WMO
	BRAC, Mercy Corps

Paraphrase 释义题

Directions: Explain the following sentences in your own words.

1. Charitable orientation often involves a top-down authoritarian effort with little participation by the "beneficiaries." It includes NGOs with activities directed toward meeting the needs of the poor.
2. By empowering individuals to develop entrepreneurial skills, the SaniShop model provides livelihoods to local masons and sales agents. In addition to job creation, masons and sales agents are trained to deliver sustainable sanitation solutions to their communities, thereby improving the sanitation conditions in villages. Our SaniShop sales agents are also trained in facilitating Community-Led Total Sanitation (CLTS) workshops.
3. The logo of WWF emphasizes the significant role of giant panda. The inspiration for the WWF logo came from Chi-Chi: a giant panda that was living at the London Zoo in 1961, the same year WWF was created. WWF's founders were aware of the need for a strong, recognizable symbol that would overcome all language barriers. They agreed that the big, furry animal with her appealing, black-patched eyes would make an excellent choice.

Short-Answer Questions 简答题

1. 非政府间国际组织的公关涉及的领域有哪些？可以借助现实实例说明。
2. 根据本章的案例学习，你对非政府间国际组织公关有怎样的认识？能不能用自己的话总结出非政府组织公关的技巧。
3. 非政府间国际组织和政府间国际组织在进行公关活动的时候有何异同？试列表比较或选择两个案例进行分析。

Thinking 思考题

1. 非政府组织在应对危机时有哪些优势？非政府组织在危机公关时又会面临哪些困难？试做一个比较分析，梳理非政府组织公关的优势和劣势。
2. 搜索一个国际非政府组织的资金来源，根据基础知识部分的募集资金内容对比分析。
3. 请你谈谈参加或观看一次非政府组织举办的公益活动的体会。

Public Relations of Foreign Transnational Corporations
外国跨国企业国际公关

Gist
内容概览

The public relations of foreign transnational corporations (Foreign TNCs) is most widely and deeply used in international PR. Transnational corporations are economic entities which operate independently and must rely on profit to maintain their survival and development. Therefore, the dependence on the market determines that transnational corporations must gain the public trust and support and launch a series of public relations activities to guide the consumer, develop new markets and deal with crises.

This chapter discusses the public relations which focus on Foreign TNCs. Students can learn the definitions, classifications, objectives and methods of Foreign TNCs' public relations from bilingual cases and further reading. There are not only analyses, but also simulations and exercises for thinking, which help students to learn and better understand ideas and knowledge of public relations of foreign transnational corporations.

外国跨国企业国际公关是国际公关运用最广泛、最深入的领域之一。在经济领域，跨国企业作为拥有雄厚资金实力、先进生产技术和管理体系的组织，在对外拓展业务的同时，必然与母国、东道国以及国际社会发生关系，从而成为国际关系的一个重要行为体[①]。跨国企业对市场具有高度依赖性，"走出去"意味着其注定要承受包括舆论风险在内的各种考验。因此，外国

---

① 顾杰、胡伟，《对跨国公司开展公共外交的思考》，《青海社会科学》，2014年第4期，第34-40页。

外国跨国企业国际公关 | Public Relations of Foreign Transnational Corporations

跨国企业必须通过开展一系列公关活动,争取国际社会尤其是东道国的信任与支持,引导消费、开拓市场、应对危机。

本章以外企为国际公关行为主体,介绍了外企国际公关的定义、演变、目的、方法和技巧,选取了具有典型意义的外企公关双语案例,包含主动的外企形象公关和被动的危机公关,主要涉及雀巢和联邦快递公关等。拓展阅读补充了外企危机公关专题。学生在学习完本章内容后,举一反三,更好地掌握外企公关理念及相关知识的运用。

6.1 Basic Knowledge
基础知识

Globalization has resulted in many businesses setting up or buying operations in other countries. Companies that operate in several countries are called multinational corporations (MNCs) or transnational corporations (TNCs). They are increasingly becoming the main players in international public relations.

The majority of TNCs come from MEDCs (More Economically Developed Country) such as the US and UK.

外国跨国企业是一个独立运作的经济实体,以赢利维持自己的生存与发展。外国跨国企业是国家形象的重要载体,也是国际公关的行为主体。

进入21世纪以后,这一类非国家行为主体陆续出现在国际舞台,他们参与国际活动,制定国际游戏规则,承担国际义务,推动和加深各主权国家在政治、经济和文化上的相互依存,日益成为当代国际公共关系领域中最为活跃的因素之一。①

The role of TNCs in the global economy has increased considerably during the second half of the twentieth century. Their activities have grown at a much faster pace than world output, and during the 1990s the stock of foreign direct investment (FDI) has almost quadrupled, from $1.7 trillion in 1990 to $6.6 trillion in 2001. UNCTAD estimates that today there are about 64000 TNCs, with about 840000 foreign affiliates. These affiliates account for about 54 million employees, but the economic importance of international production is even higher when non-equity relationships such as subcontracting and licensing

---

① 黄河,《跨国公司的公共外交决策》,《公共外交季刊》,2011年第2期,第21-26页。

are considered.

What TNCs do (or do not do) affects the lives of a substantial share of the world's population. This impact can take many forms: for instance, the dissemination of new technologies and management practices changes production methods and performances of domestic industries; extractive activities can change the lives of local communities and local affiliates of TNCs can be agents of cultural change in host societies. Because of their size and capacity to transcend national boundaries, TNCs have traditionally been a reason for concern on the part of important social and political groups, notably trade unions and socialist, traditionalist and nationalist parties. The governments of recently de-colonized countries perceived TNCs as potential or actual agents of a neo-colonialist project aiming at exploiting national resources without adequate compensation and at interfering in the political process of the newly independent states.

During the 1990s, the economic and political significance of TNCs has brought them once again into the spotlight of public attention. Anti-corporate activism has become a mass movement again, with campaigners forming networks at the same global level as the activities of the TNCs they target. This is a serious challenge for TNCs, since it may trigger a reversal of the trend towards a business-friendly political climate that has dominated policy-making in developed and developing countries since the early 1980s. At the heart of this challenge is the issue of accountability. Because of their often huge economic clout and their capacity for global mobility, corporations are widely perceived as capable of evading public control and getting away with behavior that harms employees, consumers, vulnerable communities or the environment.

In this regard, it is necessary and significant for foreign TNCs to develop public relations and relieve such concerns.

随着投资的加深,外国跨国企业面临着机遇和挑战并存的海外投资环境,开展国际公关是克服种种误解、偏见和不信任的重要途径。国际公关是一种基本战略工具,用以建立全球品牌,在国际上取得成功并从中盈利。跨国企业的国际公关不仅可以为企业自身带来经济效益,也有助于塑造良好

外国跨国企业国际公关 | Public Relations of Foreign Transnational Corporations

的企业形象。①

6.1.1 Definition 定 义

In American English the word corporation is most often used to describe large business corporations. In British English and in the Commonwealth countries, the term company is more widely used to describe the same sort of entity while the word corporation encompasses all incorporated entities. In American English, the word company can include entities such as partnerships that would not be referred to as companies in British English as they are not a separate legal entity.

Originally, corporation is set up merely for commercial purposes, and they pursue interests and profits to a large extent.

Public relations of Foreign TNCs is, simply-stated, the practice of managing the spread of information between corporation and the public, also the art and science of building relationships between a corporation and its key audiences. And it can have many different platforms including internal and external functions: Internal functions can range from employing social media, such as a blog, to an internal newsletter highlighting employee affairs; external PR for companies can be vaster and include numerous messages to the public.

外国跨国企业国际公关是跨国企业与公众之间信息传播与管理的实践，同时也是构建与主要客体良好关系的一种艺术与科学，其是广义的公关活动在具体领域的应用。

6.1.2 Types of Company 分 类

Company has many types due to different standards and laws in different countries, and the various types of registered companies according to British company law *Companies Act 2006*② are:

(1) Limited and unlimited companies

(2) Private and public companies

(3) Companies limited by guarantee and having share capital

---

① 赵启正，《跨国经营公共外交十讲》。北京：新世界出版社，2014年1月。
② 2006年11月，英国议会通过了历史上最长的一部成文法，即《2006年公司法》，该法案中对企业明确进行了分类。

(4) Community interest companies

In the US, since it's a federal system, most company law issues retained by the states. Thus company law can vary substantially from state to state. Commonly, types of company are as follows:

(1) Sole proprietorship

(2) General partnership(GP)

(3) Limited partnership (LP)

(4) Corporation

(5) Limited liability company(LLC)

(6) Limited liability partnership(LLP)

在我国,企业有不同的分类标准,根据不同标准,企业主要分为以下几类:

(1)以投资人的出资方式和责任形式分为:个人独资企业、合资企业、公司制企业;

(2)以投资者的地区不同分为:内资企业、外资企业和港、澳、台商投资企业;

(3)按所有制结构可分为:全民所有制企业、集体所有制企业、私营企业和外资企业;

(4)按股东对公司所负责不同分为:无限责任公司、有限责任公司、股份有限公司。

企业的分类有很多,本书采取按"引进来"和"走出去"的标准将企业分为外国的跨国企业和中国的跨国企业。

6.1.3 Objectives 目标

Corporation's objectives are measurable. They effectively describe the actions required to accomplish a task.

Finance

Clear financial objectives to emphasize the financial targets of the corporation must be set. Objectives should be ambitious but also measurable and realistic. An example of a financial objective could be growth in corporation revenues and earnings. Another financial objective could focus on increasing capital and investments, such as attracting new shareholders and investors by improving credit worthiness and cash flow.

外国跨国企业国际公关 | Public Relations of Foreign Transnational Corporations

Sales and Marketing

Sales and marketing objectives help companies measure their position against industry competitors. These objectives tend to focus on ways an organization can surpass the competition in market share, product quality and brand recognition. An example of a marketing objective could be to lower costs in respect to competitor pricing to attract a new class of buyers, or to introduce a new product line to appeal to a broader demographic.

Human Resources

To operate effectively, organizations need competent employees. Human resources objectives cover organizational structure and employee relations matters. They also cover the employee training and development goals of the organization.

Customer Service

These objectives attempt to measure customer satisfaction with costs and overall quality of a product or service. A customer service objective could be to reduce delivery and distribution time of products and services. Another could be to reduce the number and frequency of customer returns and complaints, or to improve the response time of client inquiries.

企业的经营目标主要是为了追求利益最大化,但随着全球经济互动不断深化,市场竞争日益加剧,企业的经营目标由单一转向多元,其中既有经济目标又有非经济目标,既有主要目标,又有从属目标。它们之间相互联系,形成一个目标体系。其主要内容包括财务、销售、人事和顾客四方面。

企业经营目标主要有三大理念:

(1) 市场营销的理念从4P转向4C。自从20世纪中叶杰罗姆·麦卡锡①提出市场营销的4P组合即产品、价格、渠道、促销(Product, Price, Place, Promotion)以来,该模式主导了全球商业活动几十年。20世纪末,市场营销理念发生根本变化,由4P转向4C即客户需要、客户成本、客户便利和客户沟通(Consumer, Cost, Convenient, Communication),企业经营彻底由生产者导向转变为消费者导向。

(2) 深度为客户服务。为满足不同顾客的需要,企业广泛采用柔性生产

---

① Jerome McCarthy,美国密西根州立大学教授,20世纪著名的营销学大师。他于1960年在其第一版《基础营销学》中,第一次提出了著名的"4P"营销组合经典模型。

系统,企业生产策略由以往提供大批量标准化产品转向发展个性化服务。

(3) 企业不断增加投入以满足客户需要。近年来企业不惜投资建立客户关系管理系统CRM①,及时了解客户的需求;实施流程再造,降低成本,缩短供货周期,对客户要求立即做出反应。

Objectives of PR

The corporations use marketing public relations (MPR) to convey information about the products they manufacture or services they provide to potential customers to support their direct sales efforts. Typically, they are supporting sales in the short run, i.e., to boost immediate revenue, and the long run, i.e., to establish and burnish their brand name for a strong, ongoing market. Also, the corporations use public-relations vehicles to reach legislators and other politicians, seeking favorable tax, regulatory and other treatment. And they may use public relations to portray themselves as enlightened employers, in support of human-resources recruiting programs.

Besides, transnational corporation are usually compelled to respond to global competition and to interest groups who can band together across borders and apply pressure in a given country or globally. The main function of its PR activities is to connect with the public using means such as press releases, social media, products and events to facilitate the building and managing relationships. In a word, public relations of Foreign TNCs are mainly designed to protect and defend the corporation facing a public challenge to its reputation and its core interests. It is the perception of an unpredictable event that threatens important expectancies of stakeholders and can seriously impact an organization's performance and generate negative outcomes, or, it combats crises and lessens the actual damages inflicted.

企业公共关系有三大功能——关系协调、信息传播、形象管理。具体而言,本章所探讨的外国跨国企业国际公关目的主要为:

提高产品质量,满足公众需求;

协调各方关系,便于业务开拓;

重视社会责任,塑造良好形象;

---

① Customer Relationship Management,客户关系管理。其核心思想是:客户是企业的一项重要资产,客户关怀是CRM的中心,客户关怀的目的是与所选客户建立长期和有效的业务关系,在与客户的每一个"接触点"上都更加接近客户、了解客户,最大限度地增加利润和利润占有率。

外国跨国企业国际公关 | Public Relations of Foreign Transnational Corporations

应对突发危机,重塑企业信誉。

6.1.4 Evolution of PR for Foreign TNCs 演变

企业公共关系的演变是随着企业自身的发展而进行的。结合外国跨国企业的发展,我们将外国跨国企业国际公关的演变划分为以下几个阶段:

(1) 16、17世纪:几乎空白的公共关系

"跨国公司"一词是在第二次世界大战后才广为各国所使用,但这种由某一国家的企业到其他国家投资、生产与销售的跨国经营活动,则可以追溯到16、17世纪。在这一时期,有些特许贸易公司,已具有跨国公司的雏形,例如,活跃在东南亚地区的英国东印度公司。这类公司具有三大特点:①负有殖民地的政治使命;②经营目的在于开发国外的自然资源,满足母国的工业生产和市场需求;③投资行业多为农、矿业,例如,印度、斯里兰卡的茶园、古巴的糖业、东南亚的橡胶园,马来西亚和刚果的锡矿等。这类跨国公司具有掠夺性,其所实施的公关措施几乎为零。①

(2) 19世纪末—20世纪初:公共关系活动多表现为广告宣传

这一阶段出现了真正具备现代跨国公司组织的工业企业,很多著名的跨国公司都在这一时期相继成立。例如:英荷合股的联合利华公司、英荷皇家石油壳牌公司、德国的西门子电气等。这一时期的跨国经营活动具有两个特点:①国外资源开发及经济作物的生产仍然占很大比重,但制造业的对外投资开始蓬勃发展;②跨国公司开始逐渐脱去"政治使命"的外衣,以企业本身利益为主要经营目的。

跨国公司在东道国与母国政府的管理下成为有形与无形稀缺资源的跨国界的配置者,甚至是垄断者,为了保持这种优势,跨国公司逐渐意识到开展公关活动的重要性,并为此投入大量资金,突出表现为广告宣传。

(3) 20世纪80年代以来:公关战略——"本土化""信息化""科学化"

20世纪80年代以后,世界政治经济格局发生了巨大变化:从敌对走向缓和,从冲突走向对话,国际经济朝着一体化方向发展。在这种相对和平的环境中,跨国经营活动获得新的发展,公共关系蓬勃发展,公关战略主要表现为"本土化""信息化""科学化"。

"本土化"——各行业的跨国公司为抢夺国际市场,重新组合国际格局,

---

① 谢岷,《跨国公司的发展及其基本概念——跨国公司经营与管理讲座第一讲》,《国际贸易》,1989年第1期,第48-51页。

展开了激烈的竞争。东道国某些企业与跨国公司优势相差不远,东道国着手打造自己的品牌企业,因此,本土化成了跨国公司发展的重要战略,服务于企业整体公关活动的实施。IBM、丰田、联合利华、摩托罗拉、爱立信、柯达、诺基亚等都在中国实施本土化战略。

具体说来,本土化战略就是经营管理本地化、研发中心本地化、采用本地化营销策略、实施本地化管理、聘请本地经理、人力资源本土化,也就是本地采购、本地研发、本地生产、本地销售以及任用本地的销售及管理人员。

跨国公司本土化可以克服各国、各民族文化、传统、习惯的不同,在全球范围内帮助树立母国的话语霸权,提高消费者认同度,还可以降低因交通、区位、时差产生的成本,避免母国技术人员和管理人员到东道国工作所面临的语言文化障碍和"国外生活津贴"。本土化也可以直接增加东道国的就业岗位,缓解其就业压力。

"信息化"——跨国公司通过世界各地的分支机构编织起了一个信息网络,并通过这个网络指挥经营全球的业务。有人曾计算过,日本的大型综合商社能够在2秒钟内了解非洲某个角落的商业情报。信息化使得企业充分对市场做出反应,制定相应的公关措施。

"科学化"——由职业公共关系专家和各类公关专业人员组成的公关公司日益兴起,跨国公司纷纷与公关公司合作,进行公共关系咨询或委托其开展公共关系活动。这类公关专家涉猎人际关系、公共传播、传播管理、组织行为、市场营销等诸多领域,并拥有自己独特的知识体系,掌握大量的知识,包括政治学、社会学、传播学、心理学、管理学等理论原理,又包括RACE工作法、项目管理、流程管理、MI评估方法等技术方法,还包括媒介关系、公关调查等专业技能。在他们指导下制定的跨国公司公关活动科学、客观,具有前瞻性。

6.1.5 Methods 方法

Public relations of Foreign TNCs should not merely be reactionary; it should also consist of preventative measures and preparation in anticipation of potential crises, and the building and maintenance of the corporation's image. Additionally, it is also simultaneous strategic communications and actions with home, host and transnational public, thus practitioners must take pre-emptive steps to ensure their voices are heard in cross-national conflicts or transnational crises, particularly through the cultivation of relevant media representatives, both at home and in host countries.

外国跨国企业国际公关活动的开展也可以从以下四个层次进行。

（1）统一形象：一个面孔、一种声音、注意强烈品牌形象。

（2）一致声音：前后一致的声音和面孔，对不同受众（顾客、同行、供应商等）采取相应信息。

（3）好听众：采取双向传播，通过免费电话号码、调查、商展等获取反馈，注重长期联系。

（4）世界级公民：关注广阔的社会，尤其是东道国的经济、政治及社会文化；建设自身环保、健全的企业文化。

外国跨国企业在实施公关活动时需转变国际理念，从单向的"对外宣称"走向双向的"国际传播"。同时充分考虑东道国受众的需要，以"国外受众语言"向外国民众说"企业故事"，同时高度重视媒体的力量，借助境外媒体积极引导国际舆论，从被动走向主动。①

6.1.6 Corporate Social Responsibility 企业社会责任

（1）企业社会责任的定义

企业社会责任（Corporate Social Responsibility，简称CSR）是指企业在创造利润、对股东承担法律责任的同时，还要承担对员工、消费者、社区和环境的责任，企业的社会责任要求企业必须超越把利润作为唯一目标的传统理念，强调要在生产过程中对人的价值的关注，强调对环境、对消费者、对社会的贡献。

（2）企业社会责任的发展

这是一个相对年轻、含义甚广，且不断变化的概念。

① 19世纪末20世纪初，西方开始出现足以抗衡国家经济体的超大型跨国公司，其所有权与管理权分离。对短期利益的追求，让它们在全球范围内无限制地使用资源。整个人类社会因此曝露在前所未有的系统性风险之下，许多负面影响显现出来。

② 从20世纪初期的劳工与人权问题暴发，到后来的环保主义运动、消费者权益运动，都是对这些社会风险的强烈回应。学者Oliver Sheldon 于1924

---

① 赵启正，雷蔚真，《中国公共外交发展报告（2015）》，北京：社会科学文献出版社，2015。

年首次提出"公司社会责任",而后的几十年中,不断有学者尝试进行明确定义。直到 Carroll Archie 提出"四层金字塔模型"①,John Elkington 提出"三重底线理论",分别从程度和领域两个范畴,回答了"企业有哪些社会责任"。②

③ 2000年,联合国前任秘书长科菲·安南倡议的"全球契约"正式启动,涵盖了人权、劳工标准、环境保护及反腐败等方面的十项基本原则。③

④ 全球报告倡议组织(Global Reporting Initiative, GRI)发布的GRI《可持续发展报告指南》和国际标准组织发布的ISO26000《社会责任实施指南》,都详细介绍了"企业社会责任"指向的"利益相关方",以及具体需要履行哪些责任。

(3)企业社会责任的内容

企业作为一种组织形态,所有经营行为在受外部社会作用的同时,也势必造成影响,作为影响的主体,企业应该承担起相应的责任。CSR包含了经济发展、反腐败、员工、外部劳工、社区、环境等不同议题。

(4)怎样担当企业责任

CSR报告

首先,CSR报告发布对于部分企业来说,已经是一个必要动作;还有一些来自供应链上的要求,也即客户对其供应商企业是否披露CSR信息做出规定;还有来自行业的要求,尤其是高社会与环境风险的行业,如化工、能源采矿、直销等。一般来看,CSR报告由公关、品牌牵头,关注点在于传播性。

企业公益

企业公益在CSR的框架内,企业有责任通过回馈并帮助其所在的社区实现共同繁荣,同时有利于其可持续经营。

在一个"什么样的企业具有社会责任感"的公众调研中,排名前三的结论:产品好、对员工好、做公益。"产品好""对员工好"对企业来说是应有之义,"做公益"就显得很重要。2015年初,《哈佛商业评论》上发表的文章,卡斯图里·兰加等作者在调查了哈佛商学院CSR高管教育项目的142位管理者后指出,将目前的CSR活动划分为三条战线的话,仍有48%的企业处于第一战线,也即"慈善"。

---

① Carroll 的金字塔模型,将CSR分为"经济责任""法律责任""伦理责任""慈善责任"。
② 其中,"三重底线理论"提出企业在经济、环境和狭义社会,这三个领域应承担的责任,是目前CSR实践的主要指导方针。
③ 联合国全球契约 http://csr.mofcom.gov.cn/article/policies/intl/201405/20140500597802.shtml 2015年12月30日。

外国跨国企业国际公关 | Public Relations of Foreign Transnational Corporations

以社会公益为切入点,开展CSR活动,有助于企业管理层获得社会问题的视角;同时,对于不同利益相关方来说,社会公益的可参与性较强。

(5)企业担当社会责任实施技巧

① 帮助平民英雄

目标受众为被现实生活中的需求和共同社会挑战联系在一起的个体,能够满足于即时提高销量的有创意的服务。

案例 强生公司通过其网站发起了为"背奶妈妈"进行的活动,提供申领"临时哺乳室"告示牌及上海写字楼哺乳室数字地图的服务,凭借该项活动,强生的零售业绩跳涨。

② 改变生活

这无关一个产品或者服务的功用,而是其如何将生活变得更为健康安全,如何更为环保,更易佩戴、使用或更物美价廉。

案例 印度农村的卫生标准低,每年腹泻夺去110万儿童的生命。卫宝把在大壶节上食用的印度煎饼标出了"hot"标志,并附上提示"你是否用卫宝洗手了?"作为更大活动中的一部分,带有水池和肥皂的信息亭将这条提示进行强化,将卫宝在印度市场的份额推向新高。

③ 触及心灵

揭示能够建立情感联系的人文真理,一个高尚的目标能够产生真实持久的文化转变。

案例 宝洁公司进行的护舒宝like a Girl活动指出了潜在的严重影响自信的因素,给予各地女孩力量。这一活动获得了数量巨大的评论、分享、点赞,也成为品牌业务增长的有力手段。

④ 赋予新用途

循环共享经济为品牌创造有意义的、创新的角色,并提供了新的利润来源。

案例 巴塔哥尼亚公司提倡消费者购买旧产品,并在其在线商城和ebay上销售二手服装,将整个销售额提高了近三分之一。①

---

① 施颖妍,《用共同影响力改变世界》,《国际公关》,2015年第64期,第74页。

6.2 Bilingual Case Studies
双语案例

6.2.1 Nestle : The Baby Killer?[①]

Background

Nestle Corporation, founded in 1867 by Henri Nestle, headquarters in Vevey, Switzerland. Nestle is the world's largest food manufacturer with more than 500 plants worldwide, and is also the world's leading Nutrition, Health and Wellness company. Their mission of "Good Food, Good Life" is to provide consumers with the best tasting, most nutritious choices in a wide range of food and beverage categories and eating occasions, from morning to night. Quality and safety is Nestle's code of conduct and Nestle has been enjoying the subsequent development and success over the years.

Research

However, in the 1970s and 1980s, the corporation encountered unprecedented PR crises. At that time, Nestle advocated bottle feeding baby in the Third World and regarded the breast-feeding as "primitive and inconvenient," also, the cause of reduced lactation, which subverted the people's conventional awareness. However, that milk powder was too expensive for the popularity of the Third World countries led to an increasing infant mortality rate in the Third World.

Early in the 1970s, people began to feel uneasy about the increasing promotion and sale of infant milk formula via Nestle in the developing countries, especially in the Third World, for evidence shows that western multinationals' milk formula lead to malnutrition. This has been reported in the media, but there is no response.

In 1974, War on Want, a campaign to make world poverty an urgent social and political issue, one of the major Third World aid agencies in Britain today, published "The Baby Killer," a report on infant malnutrition and the promotion of artificial feeding in the Third World. Bern Third World Action Group

---

[①] Mike Muller, "A War on Want Investigation into the Promotion and Sale of Powdered Baby Milks in the Third World," March 1974, Published and printed by *War on Want*.

外国跨国企业国际公关 | Public Relations of Foreign Transnational Corporations

translated "The Baby Killer" and published it in Switzerland with the title Nestle tötet Babies (Nestle Kills Babies).

On July 7, 1977, a boycott was launched in the United States by INFACT (Infant Formula Action Coalition) to protest against Nestle's unethical marketing. In 1978, Nestle boycott spread to Australia, Canada and New Zealand. And it expanded into Europe in the early 1980s. It was prompted by concern about Nestle's "aggressive marketing" of breast milk substitutes, particularly in less economically developed countries, largely among the poor. In 1983, Nestle boycott spread to Finland and Norway, bringing the total to 10 countries. Boycott in North America intensified.

Groups such as the International Baby Food Action Network (IBFAN) and Save the Children claimed that the promotion of infant formula over breastfeeding had led to health problems and deaths among infants in less economically developed countries. IBFAN claimed that Nestle distributed free formula samples to hospitals and maternity wards; after leaving the hospital, the formula was no longer free, but because the supplementation has interfered with lactation, the family must continue to buy the formula. IBFAN also alleged that Nestle used "humanitarian aid" to create markets, did not label its products in a language appropriate to the countries where they were sold, and offered gifts and sponsorship to influence health workers to promote its products.

Objective

Doctors, campaigning organizations, and the media were all accusing Nestle of killing babies. The worldwide boycott, to some extent, the scandal, greatly threatened Nestlé's marketing and its reputation. Subsequently, it triggered the dramatic financial loss due to lost sales, and crisis of confidence. For Nestle had a 40-percent market share for breast milk substitutes (BMS) in developing countries, with a profits margin of as much as 50 percent. As consumers may be torn between joining and not joining a boycott, Nestle may be torn between cost considerations and customers' ethical demands and the financial effects of both of them.

To reduce losses and save the situation, Nestle took actions.

Practice

Stage 1

At the first stage, Nestlé's PR method was very tough and reactive. It hired public relations specialists and kept a low profile stance, but lacked sincerity. When the infant formula issue was firstly proposed, Nestle mistook it for merely a nutritional health issue to be addressed, and ignored the demands of consumers, thus the company just provided a number of scientific and related data analysis.

The moment "The Baby Killer" was published, Nestle attempted to sue the group which translated "The Baby Killer for libel". After a two-year trial, the court found in favor of Nestle because they could not be held responsible for the infant deaths in terms of criminal law. Because the defendants were only fined 300 Swiss Francs (just over US $400, adjusted for inflation), and Judge Jürg Sollberger commented that Nestle "must modify its publicity methods fundamentally," *TIME* magazine declared this a "moral victory" for the defendants.

Apart from that, Nestle straightforwardly denied the allegations from advocacy groups like IBFAN. Nestle attributed the increasing infant mortality rate to consumers' improper use, and evaded its responsibility.

Stage 2

Later, with protests intensifying, Nestle came to realize that it required a better coordination of new international public affairs means to handle the relationship among different parties. A 10-people panel was established. Then, early in 1981, the company founded Nestle Nutrition Coordination Center in Washington, which was a company rather than a transactional office. Its purpose was to coordinate a series of nutrition research activities in North America and collect the information on how the company improved nutrition research project for all mothers and children in Third World, and then, to spread it in the Western Hemisphere. In addition, it also handled the boycott.

Nestle provided a detailed reference report stating that the company has taken a series of measures, such as cooperation with the countries concerned, to comply with laws and regulations in these countries; to fulfill "distribution of breast milk substitutes recommended guidelines," via the World Health Organization under the premise of respecting national sovereignty.

外国跨国企业国际公关 | Public Relations of Foreign Transnational Corporations

On February 12, 1982, two important figures in Nestle, new Chief Executive Officer and Executive Dr. Helmut and Vice President Carl flied to Dayton, Hawaii, and held dialogues with the United States Jointly Methodist Church Baby Milk Task Force. The success of the talks served to establish a good relationship between the two sides at the highest level, and ensured the Association that Nestle's statement was supported by the executives of the company.

Also, the relationship between Nestle and the media changed, Nestle took the initiative to contact *Washington Post*. Nestle had an attempt to cooperate with the Drug Management Team, and ensured compliance with its provisions.

In 1981, The 34th World Health Assembly (WHA) adopted Resolution WHA34.22 which included the International Code of Marketing of Breast-milk Substitutes as a "minimum requirement" to be adopted "in its entirety." WHA called on the WHO Director General to make a report in even years. 118 nations voted. In January, 1984, Nestle agreed to implement the International Code in developing countries. In October, monitoring has shown that Nestle has stopped some of its more blatant malpractice. *Washington Post*, the most powerful support of the boycott, claimed that Nestle has overcome its previous issue, and it was the time to talk about other issues. Finally, Nestle boycott was suspended.

Evaluation

Throughout the whole crisis, Nestlé's attitudes have shifted from reactive to proactive. At first, Nestle did not respond positively to social concerns and be accountable to the community, also, lack a dynamic and two-way communication mechanism with media. Therefore, it suffered a direct economic loss of up to $40 million and became the target of public criticism.

With crisis spreading and intensifying, Nestle came to realize the significance and adopted appropriate and positive action: communicate with the government and the media; collect scientific data and analysis; play a leading role and create a new standard of corporate behavior for the entire business community. In the end, it prevented the further spread of the crisis.

> **Case Study 案例分析**
>
> This is a crisis management PR case. A foreign transnational company, like Nestle, may encounter unexpected crises led by misguided marketing, product problems, cultural conflicts, etc. Therefore, crisis management is very important for foreign transnational companies.
>
> In this case, Nestle's crisis arose from a lot of boycott and protests against Nestle evoked by a report named Nestle Kills Babies. To solve this crisis, Nestle took lots of measures. In the first stage of this case, Nestle used scientific and legal means to prosecute many attacks on its products and it succeeded. But it lost support and trust from consumers, and presented an image of prevarication and irresponsibility, which directly led to an over 10-year crisis and more violent attacks from media. Then, they came to realize that they should try to establish a humane, responsible and trusted image. And effective methods like coordinating nutrition research activities, collecting the information on how to improve nutrition research project in Third World, and providing detailed reference reports, holding dialogues with related authoritative agencies, contacting the media, etc. were adopted. With sincerity and consistent work, they've won trust from consumers, media and the authorities finally.

6.2.2 联邦快递公关

案例调研

联邦快递(Fed Ex Corp.)成立于1971年,经过40多年的发展,已跻身全球快递业巨头,为全球的顾客和企业提供涵盖运输、电子商务和商业运作等一系列的服务。它能够调度一个由近48000辆地面交通工具、656架飞机和53500个投递点组成的全球网络系统,在全球超过220个国家和地区提供当天、隔夜或预定时间的文件、包裹和货物的航空快递服务。联邦快递屡次获选为全球最受尊崇和信任的雇主。

联邦快递于1984年进入中国,30多年来,联邦快递发展迅速:当初的每周两次变为现在每周有11个班机进出中国,是拥有直飞中国航班数目最多的国际快递公司;快递服务城市1996年只有60个,现在发展到220个城市,

外国跨国企业国际公关 | Public Relations of Foreign Transnational Corporations

联邦快递是第一个在中国设立洲际转运中心的跨国货运巨头。

联邦快递是怎样让中国人民接受一个陌生的洋公司,在中国顺利、迅速发展的呢？这不仅是因为其拥有优质的航空快递服务,还得益于联邦快递在华的一系列政府、民间层面的公关活动。

公关实施

（1）"熊猫快递"下的政府公关

"我们在任何国家公共事务的角色都在向当地政府表明:我们的立场为什么最符合你们的利益。"美国另一快递企业UPS在政府公关准则手册中这样写道,这一原则也成为众多外企政府公关核心之一。联邦快递在华业务的开展过程中进行了一系列政府公关活动。

2000年5月,联邦快递为中国2000年特奥世纪行项目捐款50万元人民币。同年,从中国运送"添添"和"美香"两只大熊猫到美国华盛顿的斯密桑宁国家动物园。2003年4月7日,它又资助中美两国政府间关于动物保护以及研究计划,用喷饰一新的麦道-11型专机"联邦熊猫快递号",无偿将来自上海的四岁雄性大熊猫"乐乐"和来自北京的两岁雌性大熊猫"丫丫"从北京运送到美国田纳西州的孟菲斯动物园落户。两只大熊猫将在美国生活十年,成就了熊猫作为"外交大使"的名气。

之后,联邦快递又与中国各级政府合作,分别将中国大熊猫"甜甜""阳光"运抵苏格兰,"欢欢"和"圆仔"运抵法国。2013年3月,随着熊猫"大毛"运抵加拿大,"联邦熊猫快递号"已进行了六次飞行。

"熊猫快递"的顺利到达,使人们认识到联邦快递在提供可靠速递服务方面所处的全球领导地位。这一行动同时引起了大量的高质量的媒体报道和社会的广泛关注,提升了联邦快递富有亲和力的良好企业公民形象。以2003年运送"乐乐"和"丫丫"赴美为例,共有73家中国报纸和商业类刊物刊登了有关此项活动的报道。在所有的新闻报道中,有70%提到了联邦快递传播的关键信息,有超过30%在文章标题中提到了联邦快递的名字。与此同时,26家主要的新闻网站向公众介绍了联邦快递运送大熊猫的全过程。在媒体报道中,有大量的联邦快递"联邦熊猫快递号"的图片与文字一同发表。图片在视觉方面对读者的冲击,使联邦快递的形象更加深入人心。

联邦快递通过"熊猫专列"成功地开展了与中国政府的合作,除此之外,2009年9月,联邦快递向中国民用航空总局直属院校——中国民航大学捐赠了一架波音727飞机。中国物流与采购联合会副会长戴定一表示,联邦快递向民航总局直属的大学进行捐赠,是一种政府公关行为,有助于联邦快递在

165

中国管理部门和教育部门建立一个良好的关系,为未来持续在华投资、拓展市场创造好的环境。

2012年7月18日,FedEx首席运营官兼国际业务总裁邓博华进京与国家邮政局局长马军胜就联邦快递公司在华业务发展问题交换了意见。邓博华还在7月16日与广东省副省长刘志庚在广州会面,就进一步推动广东物流业发展深入交流。邓博华频频与政府官员会面,也被看做是为其下一步发展国内快递业务铺路。

(2)公益营销模式——打造良好的品牌形象,提升企业知名度

联邦快递在中国的发展过程中,一直热衷于公益慈善事业,联邦快递于1996年和1997年先后两次赞助"心连心"国际组织,义务为中国四川的贫困地区运送药物。它还曾多次在中国遭受水灾和地震等灾害时挺身而出,为灾区运送救灾物资和医疗设备。

一开始联邦快递的公益活动,就更多地集中在与运输有关的领域。比如协助国际合作组织,为中国的灾区运送救灾物资,还作为非营利性的国际组织奥比斯的全球主要航空运输赞助商,奥比斯运作着世界上仅有的一家"眼科飞机医院",为发展中国家治疗可避免性盲眼病。

最近几年,联邦快递在中国的公益活动又拓展到了更多的领域,形式也越来越丰富,而且更加关注青少年一代。自2007年起,联邦快递携手非营利性组织——"牵手中国"开展了一系列包括以"科学""羽毛球""摄影"为主题的志愿者活动。超过1500名来自全国的联邦快递志愿者为外来务工子女提供各类补充教育的机会,累计服务时间超过6000小时。2013年4月14日,联邦快递与"牵手中国",在全国五大城市启动"牵手中国读书行"公益项目,来自联邦快递的志愿者们与外来务工子女结伴,参加在上海、苏州、北京、广州和深圳举办的主题活动,其中包括"真实图书馆""大学学府游览""职场体验"和"志愿者分享会"。联邦快递于2013年荣获"牵手中国"所颁发的"2012最具活力公司志愿者团队"称号。

联邦快递和其公益伙伴供同行开展的"儿童安全步行"教育活动于2012年已经走入第八个年头,惠及全国25个大中型城市中的270多万名儿童。此外,还向云南省青少年发展基金会捐赠50台电脑及相关书籍,以帮助云南边远贫困地区的电脑教育发展;向北京市农民工子弟救助会(CMC)捐赠57台电脑,推动当地开展千余名民工子弟的电脑启蒙教育;2013年,向中国听力医学发展基金会捐赠100万人民币,开展"贫困听障儿童救助行动",救助中国西部来自低收入家庭的听障学生,迄今共有48名贫困听障儿童已经从

外国跨国企业国际公关 | Public Relations of Foreign Transnational Corporations

中受益。2014年,联邦快递与非营利组织"太阳村"联合发起"暖意爱心,'邦'您传递"大型公益活动,向全国18所高校的大学生发起各类爱心捐赠物的收集令,并将这些物品送到"太阳村"里需要帮助的孩子手中。

联邦华人高级副总裁陈嘉良认为,公益事业与公司业务发展并不冲突,因此,公益事业是作为联邦快递发展整体策略的一个组成部分,通过战略性投入公司的人力、资源和网络等来支持我们所服务的社区,从而提高公司在主要受众中的企业声誉。所以自1984年进入中国市场以来,联邦快递一直在寻找能够反映公司价值观的各种社会公益活动,主动承担社会责任,为企业树立良好的品牌形象,同时也扩大在中国的品牌知名度。

公关评估

美国企业的发展史上,联邦快递公司是几个发展最快的公司之一,是企业开拓进取、敢于创新精神的代表。1979年12月的《幸福》杂志称联邦快递公司是"20世纪70年代最成功的十大企业"之一。《邓氏商业月刊》称联邦快递公司是"1981年管理最佳的5家公司"之一。联邦快递公司还被誉为"美国100家工作条件最佳的公司"之一。1990年,联邦快递公司因服务完善获得了极负盛名的"马尔科姆·鲍得里奇奖",联邦快递公司是美国历史上第一个获得这项大奖的服务性企业。2014年3月联邦快递日前在《财富》杂志公布的一项调查中,入选"全球最受尊敬公司"榜单,列第8位,并且位居运输行业首位。联邦快递公司以其利润10%的巨额资金用在推销活动上,在广告宣传、公关活动、塑造企业形象中投入了大量的人力、物力、财力,终于在社会公众面前成功地树立起一个崭新的企业形象。不仅赢得了社会公众的认可,为公司引来了源源不断的投资,还开发了更为广阔的快递服务市场。[①]

Case Study 案例分析

联邦快递公关属于主动型国际公关,其措施充满亮点:首先,联邦快递运用其先进的运输系统,与中国政府合作承担熊猫运输任务,借助政府平台与熊猫外交得到了媒体大规模的报道,使其品牌与良好形象深入人心;其次,联邦快递积极承担企业社会责任,开展多种公益活动:运送救灾物资,关注青年教育,捐资救助听障儿童……在这些活动中传达企业价值观。

企业直接投身于公益活动或慈善事业是企业社会责任感的体

---

① 来自联邦快递中国官网:http://www.fedex.com/cn/ 2015年10月20日

> 现。联邦快递通过多种公益活动成功地塑造了其富有责任感的企业形象,是一场"润物细无声"的国际公关。

6.3 Further Reading
拓展阅读

6.3.1 Shell and Its Environmental Issues[①]

Background

Royal Dutch Shell, commonly known as Shell, is an Anglo-Dutch multinational oil and gas company headquartered in the Netherlands and incorporated in the United Kingdom. The Shell Group is over 100 years old and is one of the six oil and gas "supermajors." It is principally involved in the exploration, production, refining and marketing of oil and gas products, and also has a substantial chemicals business and a stand-alone division developing renewable energy sources.

Research

Like most major multinational petrochemical giants, Shell has been criticized for its pollution worldwide with the increasing concerns for global environmental protection. For example, Shell has suffered great shocks from the environmental NGOs, especially the Greenpeace.

In October, 2014, the toy maker, Lego, announced that they will not renew its current multimillion pound deal contract with Shell to end the partnership that dates to the 1960s after coming under sustained pressure from Greenpeace.

Greenpeace, protesting about the oil giant's plans to drill in the Arctic, had targeted the world's biggest toy maker with a YouTube video entitled "Everything is not awesome" that attracted nearly 6 million views for its depiction of a pristine Arctic, built from 120kg of Lego, being covered in oil.

Objective

Environmental issues have given rise to the continuous protests against

---

① Danny Moss, Barbara DeSanto Routledge. *Public Relations Cases: International Perspectives* (2 edition). London: Routledge, 2010.

Shell, what's worse; it may distract the Group from its normal operations.

Therefore, Shell has been launching its PR campaign from different aspects: on the one hand, to maintain its business, core interest and confidence of shareholders and the public; on the other hand, to rebuild an image of responsibility and environmental-protection and gain broader understanding and acceptance of their exploration activities.

Practice

Shell has recognized the significance of consulting, informing and communicating better with the public. It needs not only to change some of its policies and practice, but also to be seen to do so and its PR strategy was comprehensive. First of all, in terms of the recent video by Greenpeace, Shell announced a "pause" in the time-line of the project in early 2013 and, in January 2014, the corporation announced the extension of the suspension of its drilling program in the Arctic.

Then for the first time in the Group's history, a global reputation management program to "build, maintain and defend Shell's capital" was set, and the group identified a series of desired responses from seven key audiences.

Investors: I'd put my last dollar into Shell.

Customers: I'd go out of my way to buy Shell.

Government: Our desired partner.

Employees and potential employees: I'm proud to work for Shell. I'd love to work for Shell if I could.

The media: I'll give Shell the benefit of the doubt.

NGOs/activists: If someone has to do it, better it be Shell.

The general public: You can be sure of Shell.

Second, a benchmark phase of tracking research was conducted among global special publics covering six key target groups: the investment community; NGOs and IGOs; the media; government and politicians; corporate peers; academics and business gurus. And the research also identified the main criteria by which each sub-group evaluated and rated major corporations:

Integrity;

Commitment to sustainable development;

Well managed;

Transparent and accountable;

Financial success.[①]

To reach the target audience of special public around the world in the most efficient and cost-effective way, the media schedule was made up of international magazines and newspapers including *Time*, *Newsweek*, *National Geographic*, *The Wall Street Journal* and *The Economist*.

Third, a full press pack was prepared. The press conference is fronted by both the communications team from Shell Center and the author of the "Shell Report" to make an overt link to Shell's sustainable development programme.

Fourth, the shell.com website is recognized from the start as a crucial tool of education, engagement and dialogue. All communications used the shell.com address to drive people to the website. The microsite allowed users to move into the main shell.com site, join a discussion forum about the issues or email Shell Center directly. A team of issues experts was set up to help handle any queries arising from the advertising.

Fifth, Shell publishes its annual report and other special reports to publicize its sustainable development strategy and the efforts they've made. Experts and scientists are invited to make it more convincing.[②]

Meanwhile, a number of activities with striking and simple slogans have been launched by Shell to interact with the public and deliver its core value, such as the let's go programme, which have become a hit in the media. On the shell.com website, there is a feature on let's go, illustrating some touching pictures as the below one.

Following the picture Shell writes "LET'S KEEP THE LIGHTS ON WHEN SHE'S YOUR AGE." "What sort of world will this little girl grow up in? Many experts agree that it will be a considerably more energy-hungry one. There are already seven billion people on our planet. And the forecast is that there will be around two billion more by 2050. So if we're going to keep the lights on for her, we will need to look at every possible energy source. At Shell

---

① Danny Moss, Barbara DeSanto Routledge. *Public Relations Cases: International Perspectives* (2 edition). London: Routledge, 2010.

②《壳牌2013年可持续发展报告》英文完整版(Royal Dutch Shell plc Sustainability Report 2013) http://reports.shell.com/sustainability-report/2013/servicepages/welcome.html 2015年2月20日

外国跨国企业国际公关 | Public Relations of Foreign Transnational Corporations

we're exploring a broad mix of energies. We're making our fuels and lubricants more advanced and more efficient than before. With our partner in Brazil, we're also producing ethanol, a biofuel made from renewable sugar cane. And we're delivering natural gas to more countries than any other energy company. When used to generate electricity, natural gas emits around half the CO_2 of coal. Let's broaden the world's energy mix." it adds.

Through let's go, Shell informs the public that their exploration of oil and gas is for the better living of mankind and they've tried and seek many advanced methods to make it sustainable and friendly to the environment.

Evaluation

The continuous comprehensive efforts and measures serve to maintain Shell's share price, the price of oil and investor's confidence in the long run. Furthermore, they help the public better understand and accept Shell's exploration of oil and gas, which greatly soothe the protests and misunderstanding and also, is a lasting prevention of Greenpeace's further action.

Thinking:

1. Petrochemical enterprises are usually protested by environmental organzitions and environmentalists. What experiences can you learn from Shell and Its Environmental Issues?
2. PR is very important when a company go out in a new market. What experiences can you learn from FedEx's PR in China?
3. Please write a case study on case Shell and its environmental issues.

6.3.2 "速成鸡"事件公关

案例调研

肯德基(Kentucky Fried Chicken),通常简称为KFC,是来自美国的著名连锁快餐厅,由哈兰·山德士上校于1952年创建。主要出售炸鸡、汉堡、薯条、汽水等西式快餐食品。肯德基属于百胜餐饮集团。百胜集团是世界上最大的餐饮集团,在全球100多个国家和地区拥有超过3.3万家连锁店和84万名员工。旗下拥有肯德基、必胜客等世界知名餐饮品牌。①

---

① 参见中国质量网,www.cqn.com.cn。

2012年11月23日,媒体曝光了山西粟海集团养殖的一只鸡从孵出到端上餐桌,只需要45天,是用饲料和药物喂养的,而粟海集团正是肯德基的大供货商。早在2012年2月,粟海集团将家禽养殖工业化的消息就已经见诸报端。报道称,仅在养殖的一个阶段11天中,就有多达11种药物喂给肉鸡。而喂食药物的原因是,肉鸡被放在狭小的空间高密度地喂养,并且在45天的喂养周期中,甚至不会清理养殖场。只有通过不断地喂药才能提高鸡的抗病能力,只要45天内,鸡不发病,就能顺利地被拉走屠宰,并且流入市场被人食用。

人类长期食用含有激素的速成鸡等其他肉制食品,即使含量甚微,但由于其作用极强,亦会明显影响机体的激素平衡,而且有致癌危险,可造成幼儿发育异常。速成鸡触动了中国公众在食品安全领域的敏感神经,成为消费者关注焦点。

公关目标

"速成鸡"事件使得很多消费者转而选择其他快餐品牌,重创了肯德基在华销售业绩。2012年,百胜集团中国区营业收入68.98亿美元,占比50.6%,中国区营收仍占百胜集团营收的一半以上。受速成鸡事件影响,百胜2012年全年业绩报告称,在12月的最后两星期,肯德基在中国的同店销售额出现了百胜形容的"大幅下跌"。在全球范围内,四季度百胜的同店销售增长为5%,美国是3%,但是中国为—6%。

该事件也让高速扩张的百胜集团在中国遭遇前所未有的信誉危机,其旗下各个品牌业绩继续巨幅下滑。数据显示,2013年1月份百胜餐饮店同店销售额下降37%,其中肯德基同店销售额下降41%,必胜客同店销售额下降15%。

肯德基在中国的遭遇也严重影响了百胜的股价,致使其股价从2012年11月29日的74.47美元跌至同年12月21日的63.5美元。这也导致多位美国投资者以百胜集团进行虚假和误导性陈述违反联邦证券法为由,将百胜及其部分高管和董事上诉至加州中央区法院。而在中国,上海雷曼律师事务所跨国诉讼律师郝俊波也在征集中国的投资者以起诉百胜索赔。

为了挽回肯德基在消费者中的形象,重塑投资者信心,百胜餐饮和旗下的肯德基展开了一系列公关活动。

公关实施

整个公关过程中,百胜餐饮充分利用了微博这一新媒体。"速成鸡"一经披露,肯德基官方微博做出回应称:"肯德基一贯重视食品安全,要求所有鸡

外国跨国企业国际公关 | Public Relations of Foreign Transnational Corporations

肉供应商都严格实施完整的食品安全管理措施,并对其产品进行抽检。山西粟海集团在肯德基鸡肉原料供应体系中属于较小的区域性供应商,仅占鸡肉采购量的1%左右。过往食品安全记录正常。根据媒体报道内容,肯德基将进行调查,加强检验,并根据调查情况做相应处理。"但肯德基仅在微博做出回应,央视记者打电话给相关负责人没有得到任何回答。

随后,百胜方面虽一再发表声明澄清此事,先是称国家相关法律、法规没有规定要求企业上报自检结果和向社会披露自检结果,后又将责任推向供应商,被指"推卸责任"。

在舆论和业绩的压力下,针对速成鸡安全问题,百胜中国事业部主席苏敬轼于2013年1月代表肯德基在其官方微博上发布了《致广大消费者的公开信》道歉,承认自检流程可操作性欠佳、公司内部沟通不到位、供应商调整速度不够迅速、检测结果没有主动通报政府。同时,在上海市动物无害化处理中心,中国百胜将上海食品药品监督管理局抽检中发现的疑似检出金刚烷胺的相关批次鸡肉原料进行了销毁。

同时,百胜餐饮从源头抓起,消除食品安全隐患,并邀请行业专家及消费者作见证。2013年2月25日,百胜中国餐饮集团召开"雷霆行动"发布会,称将联合所有25家供应商,加速淘汰具有潜在风险的上千个鸡舍,并且承诺,未来还将进一步处理老旧、条件差和规模小的鸡舍。7月25日,在宣布开展"雷霆行动"第5个月,百胜中国宣布"雷霆行动"结束,并称肯德基"淘汰了5000余栋具有潜在风险的鸡舍,取消了3家供应商资格,所有的鸡肉供应商已经全面实施百胜最新的供应商自检和抽检的标准及流程"。其中国事业部主席、首席执行官苏敬轼表示,"雷霆行动已完成使命,百胜通过此次行动快速有效地从根本上排除了主要风险因素,提高了鸡肉安全系数。根据这半年内两次对所有鸡肉供应商的药残抽查全部合格的结果来看,违规用药风险已经基本可控。现在所有鸡肉供应商都越做越好"。①

在发布会上"肯德基探秘之旅"同时启动,向广大消费者开放肯德基后厨、供应商养鸡场等,邀请大家一起来探"秘",了解肯德基如何帮大家把好食品安全关。除媒体到场外,肯德基还邀请到中国畜牧业协会、中国烹饪协会等多家行业协会的领导及政府官员到场。

最后,为了挽回迅速远离的消费者,百胜餐饮打出了"优惠牌""形象宣传牌"。以往每年要涨价一次的肯德基做出"破天荒"的降价促销:消费满10元

---

① 来自肯德基中国官网新闻中心,http://www.kfc.com.cn/kfccda/news.aspx

送一份饮料或小甜点；在70多个城市280余家电视台投放"放心鸡肉主题广告片"，覆盖全国4400余家肯德基餐厅的"放心鸡肉餐盘"、垫纸、海报等，还制作了动画版MTV"白羽鸡欢乐颂"。肯德基通过不同渠道和方法帮助大家了解全世界人民都在吃的"白羽鸡"。

公关评估

2012年末的"速成鸡"事件是自1987年肯德基进入中国以来在华的遭遇的最大危机。事件刚刚爆发时，肯德基相关负责人并没有采取积极的措施来应对，反而推卸责任，造成业绩的大量下滑，信誉受损。随后进行的一系列公关措施在一定程度上向中国政府表示自己正在积极整改，另一方面改善了这一负面事件在中国消费者心中的形象。

思考题：

1. "速成鸡"事件中肯德基采取了哪些公关实施措施？
2. 造成"抵制雀巢"运动维持长达数年的原因有哪些？
3. 企业的危机来源有哪些原因？

6.4 Simulation 情景模拟

6.4.1 "BP Oil Spill" Issue

Background

On 20 April, 2010, in the Gulf of Mexico on the BP-operated Macondo Prospect, BP oil spilled, which claimed eleven lives and is considered the largest accidental marine oil spill in the history of the petroleum industry, an estimated 8% to 31% larger in volume than the previously largest, the Ixtoc I oil spill. Following the explosion and sinking of the Deepwater Horizon oil rig, a sea-floor oil gusher flowed for 87 days, until it was capped on 15 July, 2010. The US Government estimated the total discharge at 4.9 million barrels. After several failed efforts to contain the flow, the well was declared sealed on 19 September, 2010. Some reports indicate the well site continues to leak.

A massive response ensued to protect beaches, wetlands and estuaries from the spreading oil utilizing skimmer ships, floating booms, controlled burns and

1.84 million US gallons of Corexit oil dispersant. Due to the months-long spill, along with adverse effects from the response and cleanup activities, extensive damage to marine and wildlife habitats and fishing and tourism industries were reported. In Louisiana, 4.6 million pounds of oily material was removed from the beaches in 2013, over double the amount collected in 2012. Oil cleanup crews worked four days a week on 55 miles of Louisiana shoreline throughout 2013.

Oil continued to be found as far from the Macondo site as the waters off the Florida Panhandle and Tampa Bay, where scientists said the oil and dispersant mixture is embedded in the sand. In 2013 it was reported that dolphins and other marine life continued to die in record numbers with infant dolphins dying at six times the normal rate. One study released in 2014 reported that tuna and amberjack that were exposed to oil from the spill developed deformities of the heart and other organs that would be expected to be fatal or at least life-shortening and another study found that cardiotoxicity might have been widespread in animal life exposed to the spill.

The corresponding consequences are from different aspects, whether in environment, economy, or health, definitely, it will ultimately threaten BP's public relations with governments, local residents, environmental organizations, media, etc.

Simulation

1. Imagine you are the CEO of BP and you have to deal with such a disastrous oil spill; what PR actions will you take?
   Actor: CEO of BP, and so on.
2. You are the PR expert, and your team have abundant experiences in terms of environmental issues. Will you seek cooperation with other environmental organizations? If so, what are the advantages? If not, please present your reasons or considerations.
   Actor: PR expert, PR team, some environmental organization.
3. Interview: On 15 January, 2015, it was reported that BP was to cut 200 jobs and 100 contractors following a review of its North Sea operations. The company has been downsizing since the oil spill. Meanwhile, BP faces a fine

of up to $13.7 billion. Imagine you are the spokesman of BP, how will you respond to the questions on the issues which are negative to the image of BP.

Actors: Spokesman for BP, the reporters, the journalists and so on.

6.4.2 宜家：为大众创造美好的生活①

背景

1943年成立于瑞典的宜家,迄今为止已有72年的历史,是全球最大的家居用品零售商。宜家的发展壮大过程中,有一系列成功的公关活动值得借鉴:

(1) 百人网友留宿宜家

2012年1月,面对Facebook上多达10万的网友加入"我想要在宜家留宿"的公共群,宜家选择了大方接纳——在上万人中,挑选了一百位幸运儿来宜家家居留宿。

当晚8点,这一百位网友冲进了宜家商场,选择合适自己的床和床上用品,商场免费提供包括眼罩、毛巾、拖鞋在内的各种生活用品。而晚上的时光,也全然不会无聊,因为贴心的宜家还准备了甜点美食、美甲服务、影音娱乐等项目,甚至还有名人讲述的睡前故事以及关于睡眠和挑选床具的知识。

在留宿活动前天,宜家又将留宿地点搬到了巴黎的地铁站,如果你下了火车,找不到过夜的地方,就可以来到地铁站的宜家临时暂住点。从1月9日至1月13日,乘客们可以观看五位小伙在巴黎地铁站的真人秀,看看在这样有限的空间内,这五位小伙是如何在宜家家居里生活的,而在宜家法国Facebook上的粉丝也将有机会得到留宿一晚的机会。

(2) 宜家基金会

宜家这样大型的跨国企业,在发展壮大的同时,从不曾忘记通过自身的努力工作来回报社会,这也就是IKEA Foundation(宜家基金会)建立的初衷。

宜家基金会帮助的人群包括在自然灾害和战争中的妇女和儿童等。而且,为了更好地对这些受灾群体实施救助,宜家不仅设有专门的团队从事慈善工作,还有一些国际性的合作伙伴,包括联合国儿童基金会、英国救助儿童基金会、世界自然基金会以及联合国难民署。

宜家基金会的捐助工作也主要是通过他们来实施,一般都是他们负责寻找和发现需要帮助和扶持的项目,然后宜家基金会通过他们进行慈善捐助,

---

① 王竹君,《宜家:为大众创造美好的生活》,《国际公关》,2015年第5期,第70-71页。

外国跨国企业国际公关 | Public Relations of Foreign Transnational Corporations

捐助的类别包括资金和物品等,主要是取决于当地的需求。在整个慈善的过程中,每一位宜家员工都会通过所属工作参与其中。比如每年固定的毛绒玩具活动。在每年12月到第二年的1月,全球的宜家商场都会参与,在长达6到8个星期的时间内,每卖出一个毛绒玩具,就向联合国儿童基金会和英国救助儿童基金会捐款1欧元。

模拟:

宜家"LOVE IS NOW——爱无界"发布会

2016年春节前夕,针对中国市场,宜家开展了主题为"LOVE IS NOW——爱无界"的系列公关活动。其中,"LOVE IS NOW——爱无界"微电影发布就是重要一环。根据本书相关理论知识,完成下面的情景模拟。

1. 你有幸进入"LOVE IS NOW"策划团队,请结合宜家经营理念及相关背景,为微电影拍摄内容出谋划策。以小组为单位(4-6人),构思微电影的主题、人物、故事情节等,创意成果以PPT、短片或表演等形式展现。
2. 最终,你的团队成功制作出时长15分钟的爱无界微电影。在微电影发布前期,请你为发布会拟一份公关策划(可涉及活动主题、策划思路、活动、媒体等)。

Exercises
本章练习题

Gap Filling 填空题

Directions: Fill in the blanks with the correct form of the words and expressions provided.

evade	compel	retain	recruit	term
trigger	economic	convey	disaster	consult

1. In the US, since it's a federal system, most company law issues are (   ) by the states.
2. They may use public relations to portray themselves as enlightened employers, in support of human-resources (   ) programs.
3. The corporations use marketing public relations to (   ) information about

177

the products they manufacture or services they provide to potential customers to support their direct sales efforts.

4. In British English and in the Commonwealth countries, the (   ) company is more widely used to describe the same sort of entity while the word corporation encompasses all incorporated entities.

5. It was prompted by concern about Nestlé's "aggressive marketing" of breast milk substitutes, particularly in less (   ) developed countries, largely among the poor.

6. Subsequently, it (   ) the dramatic financial loss due to lost sales, and crisis of confidence.

7. Nestle attributed the increasing infant mortality rate to consumers' improper use, and (   ) its responsibility.

8. Early in the 1990s, after exhaustive scientific analysis and wide (   ) with experts, Shell proposed to sink the oil storage platform in deep water in the Atlantic, rather than attempt a potentially more environmentally damaging salvage operation.

9. Facing such (   ) crisis, Shell took immediate actions. Firstly, Shell did not proceed with its plans for sinking the vessel.

10. Transnational corporation are usually (   ) to respond to global competition and to interest groups who can band together across borders and apply pressure in a given country or globally.

Multiple Choices 选择题

Directions: In this part there are 5 sentences. For each sentence there are four choices marked A, B, C and D. Choose the answers that best complete the sentence.

1. At the moment "The Baby Killer" was published, Nestle attempted to sue the group which translated "The Baby Killer for libel." What does "the group" refer to here?

    A. War on Want

    B. Bern Third World Action Group

    C. Infant Formula Action Coalition

    D. International Baby Food Action Network

外国跨国企业国际公关 | Public Relations of Foreign Transnational Corporations

2. The following are various types of company, which are in the British company law?
   A. Limited and unlimited companies
   B. Private and public companies
   C. Limited liability partnership
   D. Community interest companies
3. Which of the targets is not included in the objectives of a company?
   A. Financial
   B. Sales and marketing
   C. Customer service
   D. Environmental protection
4. Which is not included in 4C principle?
   A. Competition   B. Cost
   C. Convenient   D. Communication
5. Shell has launched its PR campaign from different aspects, ____, instead.
   A. launching the media schedule made up of international magazines and newspapers
   B. publishing its annual report and other special reports to publicize its sustainable development strategy and the efforts it has made
   C. setting a global reputation management programme
   D. apologizing to the public

Table Completion 表格题

对比"速成鸡"与"Nestle"案例,完成下列表格。

	Nestle	速成鸡
危机		
措施一		
措施二		
(措施三)		
效果		
评估		
反思		

Short-Answer Questions 简答题

1. 结合前几章的学习,请总结外企公关的大概步骤。
2. 外企公关实施过程中的影响因素有哪些?
3. 对外企公关效果的评估应从哪几个方面考虑? 分别是哪些,请简单阐述。

Paraphrase 释义题

Directions: Explain the following sentences in your own words.

1. Public relations of Foreign TNCs should not merely be reactionary; it should also consist of preventative measures and preparation in anticipation of potential crises, and the building and maintenance of the corporation's image.
2. At that time, Nestle advocated bottle feeding baby in the Third World and regarded the breast-feeding as "primitive and inconvenient," also, the cause of reduced lactation, which subverted the people's conventional awareness.
3. As consumers may be torn between joining and not joining a boycott, Nestle may be torn between cost considerations and customers' ethical demands and the financial effects of both of them.
4. It is principally involved in the exploration, production, refining and marketing of oil and gas products, and also has a substantial chemicals business and a stand-alone division developing renewable energy sources.

Thinking 思考题

1. 谈谈你印象最深刻的一次外企危机,以及当时外企采取的相应公关措施。对此,你有什么评价或感想。
2. 结合联邦快递等案例,思考中国企业进行海外经营时怎样更好地塑造自身形象? 这些企业可能遇到的危机有哪些,应该怎样防范或应对?

International Public Relations of China Transnational Corporation
中国跨国企业国际公关

Gist
内容概览

With the rising of China, the number of China Transnational Corporation (CTC) is increasing year by year, but the challenges faced by CTCs are also rising. These challenges come from politics, economics, culture, techniques and so on. How to integrate into target nations in the complex environment and achieve their PR objective is the task faced by China Transnational Corporations.

This chapter starts with the definition of China's transnational corporate public relations activities, and then introduces the features, challenges and practices of PR in an attempt to clarify the parameters of the discipline. The bilingual case studies and further reading include cases of Haier, Sany, Alibaba and so on. The simulation will ask students to solve the problems by using what they learned in this chapter. After learning this chapter, students are required to get the theories and practical skills of public relations of China Transnational Corporation.

随着中国实力的增强,中国企业到海外投资的数量正在逐年增加。但是中国跨国企业走出去所面临的挑战也在不断攀升,主要存在四类挑战:政治挑战、经济挑战、文化挑战、技术挑战[1],因此,面对复杂的投资环境,如何更好地融入目标国,如何掌握自身海外形象的话语权,这迫切需要具有专业性

---

[1] 于桂琴,《中国企业跨国并购政治、法律风险分析与防范对策》,《企业发展论坛经济界》,2008年第3期,第65-68页。

与国际视野的中国跨国企业公关团队去协助解决。

本章以中国跨国企业国际公关为行为主体,理论部分介绍中国跨国企业国际公关特性、挑战以及不同产业中国企业的海外公关措施。案例部分将理论与实际案例结合分析"大白兔"甲醛危机等不同行业的经典案例,情景模拟再现经典案例,在辅助问题与特定情境下引导学生自己思考如何运用中国跨国企业国际化的公关方式进行分析,解决"融进去"并塑造自我品牌的问题。学习完本章后,学生应更加清楚明晰地掌握中国跨国企业国际公关的理论和技巧。

7.1 Basic Knowledge
基础知识

7.1.1 Definition 定义

Public relations is a distinctive management function which helps establish and maintain mutual communication, understanding, acceptance and co-operation between an organization and its public; It involves the management of problems or issues; helps management to stay informed about and responsive to public opinion; defines and emphasizes the responsibility of management to serve the public interest; helps organizations effectively utilize change, serving as an early warning system to help anticipate trends; and uses research and ethical communication techniques as its principal tools.

International public relations of China Multinational Company with vision and skills, is that predict and solve problems and crisis in the process of "going out" with the help of professional PR team. China Multinational Company set up its brand, and obtains good economic benefit and social benefit as a whole by shouldering corporate responsibility, communicating with local people through various media and realizes localization.

"企业公关是企业通过各种努力,了解公众的态度和要求,并使企业的政策和做法赢得公众的理解、好感和支持的各种行为总和。"[①]中国的跨国组织指中国经济、技术实力雄厚的大中型企业在中国企业国有化大战略的引导下,从全球战略出发安排自己的经营活动,在世界范围内寻求市场和合理的

---

① 李文斐、段建军,《企业公关策划.》。武汉:华中科技大学出版社,2011。

中国跨国企业国际公关 | International Public Relations of China Transnational Corporation

生产布局,定点专业生产,定点销售,以实现利润最大化。

因此,中国的跨国企业国际公关,是指拥有国际化视野和技能的中国跨国公关团队对中国企业在"走出去"过程中遇到的融入问题和品牌问题进行专业策划与解决。中国跨国企业品牌海外的本土化主要通过各种传播媒介,树立自身的企业责任,同时与当地文化相融合,以唤起人们的好感和兴趣,以获得良好的经济效益和社会整体效益。

7.1.2 Features 属性

According to the definition we can summarize the attributes of China's corporate public relationship strategy: openness, timeliness, participation, multiplicity, compatibility. These characters are connected with the goal of China's corporation public relationship, with its profitability and transnational. The following is the goal of China's corporate public relations strategy:①

- Improving the company or brand image
- A higher and better media profile
- Changing the attitudes of target audiences
- Improving relationships with the community
- Increasing market share
- Influencing government policy at local, national or international level
- Improving communications with investors and their advisers
- Improving industrial relations.

Openness is access to information. Timeliness is providing information when needed. The emergence of online communication has increased the pressure to deliver information quickly.

基于企业公关的定义,本节将从主体、客体和公关的原则方面分析企业公关的属性。主要分为复杂性、多变性和人员的专业性、协调性、透明性、客体的多元性五个方面。

(1)多变性和人员的专业性。多变性,主要体现在作为中国跨国企业国际化公关团队应该在事先进入时,收集并分析国外跨国公司公关的成功案例和失败案例,将可能存在的危机点进行归类,同时总结塑造自我品牌的基

---

① Alison Theaker, *The Public Relations Handbook*. Bodmin,: Great Britain by MPG Books Ltd, 2004, P148.

本规律。对于专业性,既要有国际化的视野,又要了解融入国政治层面的政策动向,又要了解社会层面地方的文化、习俗。

(2) 复杂性。中国企业走出去不仅面临着融入国的宏观政策,还应了解不同政体制度下地方政府和民众的态度;同时在适用法律方面,既要关切到中央政府层面的宪法,要关切到地方的法律法规,如在联邦制度下联邦与州之间对外资的管理、劳工的适用都会有些许差别。因此中国跨国企业国际化公关具有一定的复杂性。

(3) 透明性。企业危机管理也具有公共关系的一般原则,即公开性。当企业由于产品质量或媒体失误报道损害企业形象时,企业应在第一时间告知公众真相,解释事件发生的来龙去脉,将被动公关转为主动公关。企业真诚的态度能在一定程度赢得公众的再度支持。

(4) 客体多元性。企业在公共关系学中既涉及企业的利益,又涉及公共利益与个人利益,而公共利益的实现与维护又依赖于政府,因此,企业公关的客体包括政府、企业和个人。企业输出的产品通过消费渠道流通到市场,为公众提供便利。但是企业的利益导向在法治不健全的社会易于导致企业生产危害公众利益的产品。如国内的"三鹿奶粉"事件和欧洲"马肉风波"事件等。因此,无论是公关营销还是企业危机公关,中国企业都应该处理好政府、企业、个人三者之间的关系。

(5) 协调性。企业公关的参与性主要体现在主体通过媒介向客体传播信息的过程。是主体与客体之间双向的、平衡的、互动的一种关系。客体即政府和个人只有参与到企业策划活动中,才能了解企业服务的质量,感受企业秉承的企业文化。从而对企业的服务产生信任,并对其产生偏好。

7.1.3 Classification 分类

This part introduces several classifications of public relations in an attempt to clarify the parameters of the field. First, based on the right of corporate possession, public relations is divided into State-owned enterprises and private enterprises. Second, according to particular investment environment, it will be viewed as either a domestic public relations or an international public relationship; the public relations activities of large enterprises and micro-enterprises is based on a corporation's power. With the emergence of the internet public relations has now also been divided into new media technology and traditional media. Lastly, both crisis management and image shape will be also mentioned.

中国跨国企业国际公关 | International Public Relations of China Transnational Corporation

（1）根据中国跨国企业国际化的基本形式可分为五类：中国外贸（中国企业在海外的直接投资、合同项目和劳工出口服务、跨境并购、中国企业海外上市。"中国外贸额从1978年的206亿美元增加到2001年的5098亿美元"[①]；中国合同项目在180多个国家和地区得以实施；中国拥有近2000个合格企业可以实施海外合同项目和劳工合作项目；中国海外并购项目最近几年才开始起步。

（2）从中国跨国企业所述产业性质划分，可分第一产业跨国公关，第二产业跨国公关和第三产业跨国公关。在中国企业国际一体化战略实施前，中国的跨国公关主要是处理第一产业出口问题，同时以出口外贸和输送劳动力为主，所以公关涉及的主要问题为价格的协定与合约的签署。改革开放之后逐渐转向工业领域，如首钢在海外的并购等。进入21世纪后则以第三产业为主，如电子产品和电子商务等。

（3）依据企业的性质，可将中国企业分为国有企业公关与私营企业公关。国有企业是有国家控股的企业。股权分散在国务院国资委、地方国资委、财政部以及地方财政厅（局）等部门。私营企业主要有自然人或非国家法人出资成立的企业。由于国营企业的法人为国家，即政府，因此，国有企业公关主要是由政府主导，私营企业公关则主要是由个人领导下的团队组织。政府的权威性和合法性决定了国有企业公关比私营企业公关更有效率。

（4）依据投资国界的不同，可将中国企业划分为国内公关和国际公关。随着全球化和市场化的发展，国际市场成为中国企业走出去的前沿阵地。国内企业公关所涉及的客体主要是政府、其他企业以及个人三方关系；中国企业的国际公关则既涉及中国政府，又涉及他国政府、企业和个人，同时，企业公关成功与否在一定程度上依赖于四者关系的协调，协调性的基础又在于对本土文化的理解。所以，国内企业公关与国际企业公关相比，更易于制定出具有协调性和参与性的公关策略。

（5）依据中国企业实力的差异性，可将企业分为大型企业公关、中小型企业公关、微型企业公关。国家工业和信息化部、国家统计局、国家发展改革委员会以及财政部根据企业从业人员、营业收入、资产总额等指标将中小型企业分为中、小、微型企业。不同类型的企业所拥有的资金和资源具有很大差异。大、中、小、微型企业的公关能力与它们的经济实力成正比。大中

---

① 〔法〕拉尔松、〔中〕赵纯均编著，《中国跨国企业研究》。北京：机械工业出版社，2009年，第64页。

型企业在树立企业形象、应对企业危机等方面优于小微型企业,后者更易于被前者收购失去原有的市场份额。

7.1.4 Evolution 演变

The evolution of public relations is recounted to give context to the profession. Three stages of public relations development are explained, with historical and current situation. This part will take consideration economic politics into process of the evolution.

China's corporation public relationship experience three stage: infancy and early exploration period and development stage. Compared with Western countries, China's Corporate Communications started late, so we still need to learn and form our own style for better solving oversea crisis and shaping responsibility image.

中国企业公关主要经历了三个发展阶段:萌芽期、初期探索期、发展期三个阶段。

(1)萌芽期(20世纪80年代—20世纪90年代)

试行阶段的特点是中央的大力控制和企业只能得到批准的有限数量的海外投资项目。最早确立的中国海外投资规定是1979年8月国务院制定的15项经济改革措施。加之,中国正处改革开放初期,市场经济处于起步阶段。中国私营企业较少,国有企业占市场的主导地位,此阶段的中国跨国企业国际公关主要由政府引导,利用有限的报纸、电视等传统公关方式与公众和市场其他行为体进行沟通。随着海外投资环境的反馈情况,中国跨国企业国际公关在发展过程中建立公关部门,集中处理与政府、同行企业、公众的关系。但萌芽时期的企业公关并没有系统的理论与具备公关素质的人才。

(2)初期探索期(20世纪90年代—21世纪初期)

在这个阶段,中国海外直接投资的管理从检查审批单个申请转变成为标准审批流程,建立了基础的中国对外投资管理系统。新规定明确规定了海外投资的先决条件,并明确指出海外投资的权利不仅仅局限于一部分企业。1984—1991年,中国海外投资显著增长,每年可达2亿美元,同时,平均每个企业的投资额也增加到了140万美元。

加之,随着全国市场经济的发展与内陆开放力度的加大,中国企业如雨后春笋般涌现。在国家倡导中国企业国际一体化的大战略形势下,中国跨

中国跨国企业国际公关 | International Public Relations of China Transnational Corporation

国企业逐渐增多,行业由原料市场和劳动力市场转向轻工业市场。但是,由于中国企业自身的技术、经济实力有限,企业产品质量与发达国家的跨国企业相比较差,从而导致企业形象受损。基于以上状况,企业公关在结合西方公关体系、新闻传播理论的基础上提出强力公关理论,即社会组织为了塑造良好的组织形象,全面构造软力量,通过对组织形象的策划、塑造、传播、维护和对组织机构凝聚力、文化力、传播力、协调力的整合,从而影响社会公众,调整社会关系的科学与艺术。

（3）发展阶段（21世纪初期—至今）

为了鼓励发展更快的轻工业、纺织、家电行业开展海外投资,国务院发出公告,鼓励企业在海外建立原材料加工和组装企业。国务院还对这些国际项目启用了单独的审批过程。此外,随着全球化、科学技术的发展以及中国实力的增强,中国跨国企业国际公关逐渐趋于完善,一方面企业公关更加注重公关的步骤、方案的设计以及公关部门人员的素质、企业内部公关的协调。另一方面,企业公关的渠道更加多元化,更加注重互联网技术的运用。目前国内学术界对于企业公关的研究主要分析国内企业危机处理与形象塑造。危机处理方面关注企业社会责任感,形象塑造方面注重从慈善事业、大型活动赞助两方面打造企业的品牌效应。

7.1.5 Practice 实施

A corporation's sociopolitical environment can affect its profitability, growth, and, in extreme cases, its very survival. As corporations develop their markets and become more global, they also subject themselves to the laws and agreements of other governments and international bodies. Profit maximization guides business behavior in the competitive marketplace; similarly, the quest to attain preeminent power is the motivation behind a corporation's dealings with others.

Thus research, strategic planning, effective selection of communication tools and evaluations of implementation are core elements of all successful public relations, whether in developing countries or developed countries. Effective actors also develop strategic plans grounded in their research, which leads to targeted objectives that, in best practice, serve the interests of all publics involved. Communication is then developed and carried out according to a well thought-out plan, rather than a haphazard one. The crisis cases in this book demonstrate how to reactively respond to unexpected and uncontrolled events in complex circumstances; effective practitioners are thinking ahead about how to turn reactive, relatively short-term challenges into proactive, long-term communication.

(1) 实施的基础

企业公关是在了解企业内部信息与外部信息的基础上进行的,内部信息包括员工对企业的认知感与归属感,企业股东对产品或服务的评估与建议,公司的管理水平以及公司各部门之间的亲疏关系;外部信息包括企业所占有的市场份额,社会公众对企业及产品的评价。调查分析企业内、外部信息是企业公关的前提,因此认识企业自身的地位,分析企业的优劣态势是成功确立公关目标的基础,唯有此,企业在选择品牌公关、形象公关、营销公关等公关案例中才能取得预期效果。

(2) 实施的目标

追求经济利益最大化是企业的目标和生存的基础,品牌公关、形象公关、营销公关则是企业利益实现的载体。中国跨国企业国际公关的第一个目标是"融进去",与政府民众建立友善关系,保证中国跨国企业自身的稳固发展。第二个目标则是品牌公关、形象公关、营销公关,在尊重和融合东道国的文化和品位偏好的基础上,选择适合当地形式的多种多样的媒介或团体活动,提升自身的知名度,占有更多的市场份额,提高企业的利润率。

(3) 实施的方法

中国跨国企业国际公关实施步骤。

第一,要通过问卷调查了解社会公众的偏好,目标群体。根据前两项选择恰当的公关媒介,同时在公关策划过程中结合产品特性制定企业宣传方案。比如海尔由早期濒临破产的局面转变为在海外投资的首批中国企业,在此过程中,海尔根据自身的优劣分析,通过积极学习海外的先进技术,收购、合并海外企业扩大自身市场份额,是其海外公关的一大亮点。

第二,企业在危机管理中的公关策略则是指调查损害企业形象原因,了解政府、社会公众、媒体的态度,在了解各方立场后,中国企业可与当地第三方机构合作策划危机公关方案,合理利用第三方机构的资源、信誉、人脉帮助海外中国企业渡过危机。综合各方反应制定重塑企业形象的策划方案。

第三,同时中国跨国企业的国际公关应注重与中国在东道国的大使馆与领事馆保持密切联系。同时积极与国内的对外投资事务相关的办公室沟通交流。东道国的国内稳定性与政府机构的运作形式,中国的大使馆作为中国的海外政府代表具有比较全面的认识。中国跨国企业国际化的公关团队在制定相关策略,举办影响活动,应该在他们给出建议的基础上进行策划。

7.1.6 PR Advertising 公关广告

公共关系广告,是指经济单位通过购买大众宣传媒介使用权的方式,向大众宣传企业组织信誉、树立企业组织形象的一种广告形式。

公共关系广告分为实力广告、观念广告、信誉广告、声势广告、商标广告、祝贺广告、歉意广告、谢意广告、声明广告、响应广告、公益广告、创意广告等12种。下面主要解释前9种。

实力广告是指用广告的形式向公众展示组织机构的实力,作为企业来讲,主要是展示生产、技术、设备和人才等方面的实力。

观念广告是指向社会传播管理哲学、价值观念、传统风格和组织精神的广告。

信誉广告是指一种宣传组织的信誉和良好形象的最直接的公关广告形式。声势广告主要是以宣传组织的大型活动为内容。

商标广告是指以宣传产品的商标为主要内容的公共关系广告。祝贺广告是以向社会各类公众贺喜为主要内容的。

歉意广告是用来承认错误、消除误解和表示歉意,以取得公众谅解的广告。谢意广告是用来对公众或合作者的支持表示感谢的广告。

声明广告又称解释性广告,是一种表明组织对某些事件的立场、态度的广告。包括两种情况:一是对组织不利的事件,二是就本组织和社会上出现的重大事件表明态度以体现组织形象。

公共关系广告的创意与策划应该兼顾企业处境以及所针对的目标对象:政府、社区居民、雇员、供应商、消费者、经销商、舆论领袖等,这些是企业的基本公众,其中每一种都有自身的特点,如消费者公众数量多、分布广,而企业的供应商和经销商可能只有若干家,相对集中。每个企业需要根据自身的处境和发展需要来确定广告对象,使企业的公共关系广告更好地发挥作用。

广告定位和广告主题也是公共关系广告考虑的重要因素。广告定位主要关注企业实力与公众心理,广告主题要在新、绝、深、美四个方面下工夫。

主要的广告媒介分为报纸媒介、杂志媒介、广播媒介、电视媒介和互联网。每一种报纸的普及性、吸引力、反复性、时效性、制作水平和购买费用都有所不同,企业在选择广告媒介时应该针对广告的对象评估后进行选择。[①]

[①] 周安华、苗晋平,《公共关系:理论、实务与技巧(第4版)》。北京:中国人民大学出版社,2013年。

7.2 Bilingual Case Studies
双语案例

7.2.1 Haier Branding Strategy

Research

In 1920s China, a small factory opened in Qingdao, Shandong province, to manufacture refrigerators. Though the Qingdao factory survived for more than sixty years, by the early 1980s, poor management and heavy debt nearly forced it to declare bankruptcy. At the same time, the opening of the Chinese economy to the international market saw an influx of foreign companies seeking investment opportunities. One such company was Liebherr Haushaltergäte (Liebherr), a leading German appliance maker. Liebherr saw a burgeoning market for appliances, and proposed a partnership with the Qingdao factory, in which Liebherr's technology and manufacturing know-how would be sold to the factory. In 1984, Qingdao Refrigerator Co. Ltd. was born out of this partnership. However, technology alone was not enough to rescue the company. That same year, CEO Zhang Ruimin, then the assistant manager of Qingdao city's household appliance division, arrived, bringing with him management techniques adopted from Japan and the West, with a focus on building a strong brand name founded on quality products.

Mr. Zhang's techniques were successful, and by 1991 the company had turned a considerable profit and diversified into other household appliances such as freezers, microwaves and air conditioners. Recognizing that the company's name was no longer synonymous with its products and had a poor reputation from its prior history, Mr. Ruimin decided to take a new name. The company adopted an abbreviation of the phonetic spelling of Liebherr—written as Lieberhaier—to become the Haier Group Corporation (Haier). This name change marked the birth of a new brand name and the revitalization of the company's image.

Objective

Haier knew that its brand was its most valuable resource, with brand image at the core of its business identity and strategy, therefore its early branding strategy was to build a strong, leading national brand name. When its position in China was profitable and secure, Haier embarked on a global branding strategy. This strategy aims to position the company as a local brand in different world markets in conjunction with enhanced product competitiveness and strong corporate operations.

Practice

Because the company endeavors to build a global brand, trademarks are also an essential aspect of its public relations. Haier's trademark is very innovative and attractive. In 1980s, the first trademark is cartoon figure Haier brothers, Qingdao form China and Lieberhaier from German, two lovely and vigorous boys means the bright future of cooperation between China and German. The 212 episodes of cartoon *Haier Brothers* in 1995 also made Haier popular in Chinese families.

Throughout the 1990s, the company realized its vision, and made multiple acquisitions to diversify its product portfolio and the company brand quickly become ubiquitous throughout China.

Haier's slogan is also very simple and catchy. For example, "Haier, sincere forever" "Haier, one world one family" "Haier, live your life with my wisdom" and so on.

Haier's trademark is a part of its intellectual property strategy. As such, Haier has registered a trademark for its company name under the international Madrid system. It has also made trademark registrations for its name in the United States with the United States Patent and Trademark Office (USPTO) and in Europe with the Trademark and Designs Registration Office of the European Union (OHIM).

Since the company's restructuring in the early 1980s, innovating new quality products has been of central importance to its goal of building a globally recognized brand name. Haier and its subsidiary companies constantly focus on innovating new products through research and development (R&D). One such technology the company's R&D efforts developed is its "Safe Care" technology, which it applies to appliances such as water heaters. Safe Care monitors wiring and electrical components of the appliance and gives a warning should any electricity leakage pose a risk to the consumer.

This technology was introduced at the 66th International Electro technical Commission Conference in 2002, and products equipped with Safe Care went on sale in 2006. This is just one example of Haier's innovative capabilities through its R&D efforts. The R&D department is also responsible for developing all of the computer software that runs its products such as Safe Care, and this is an essential part of the company's R&D strategy.

Haier's innovation and expansion has led it to be the owner of over 6000 atents and over 500 software copyrights worldwide. To maintain its competitive edge, the company ensures that it secures protection for all of its intellectual property (IP). Haier is an avid user of the Patent Cooperation Treaty (PCT) system, and has made over twenty PCT applications.

With three-step strategy of "go out, go in, and go up," Haier has enjoyed international success, and opened its North American headquarters in New York.

Haier designs, produces and markets its products through its global network and business framework. As of 2010, Haier had fifteen industrial complexes, thirty overseas production factories and bases, eight design centers and over 58000 sales agents worldwide.

In the domestic market, Haier focuses on four leading product categories: refrigerators, refrigerating cabinets, air conditioners and washing machines. Haier also has a significant consumer electronics division.

The success of Haier in such niche markets has allowed its brand name to become well known, which encouraged the company to target the higher-end full size refrigerator market in the United States. To do so, the company built its first manufacturing plant in the United States in Camden, South Carolina in 1999. In line with the company's goal of making its brand name "local" in international markets, this initiative was a resounding success. Haier has since undertaken similar initiatives in other markets such as the European Union and the Middle East.

The company focuses on localizing the design, manufacturing and sales processes, so it can truly become a "local" brand. The company is close to achieving its goal in important markets such as the United States and Europe, in which it has local production facilities. Its products are available in twelve of the top fifteen chain stores in Europe and in ten of the leading chain stores in the

United States.

Evaluation

Capitalizing on its new management and brand, Haier transformed itself into the second largest home appliance company in the world, and the number one such company in China. By 2010, Haier designed, manufactured and marketed over 15000 products in 96 categories sold in over 100 countries throughout the world.

Haier's focus on building a strong brand has brought it from the brink of bankruptcy to one of the most successful appliance companies in the world. By 2010 the company had over 50,000 worldwide employees. It enjoyed an annual growth rate of 68% between 1984 and 2005, with revenue in 2005 totaling 103.4 billion Chinese Renminbi (RMB). The company enjoys a 40% market share for household appliances in China and has successfully entered difficult markets such as the United States, and it is now the world's number two refrigerator manufacturer, only second to Whirlpool. Despite the economic slump in 2008, Haier profits increased nearly 20% that year and enjoyed net profits of RMB 768 million. In 2004, Haier acquired a controlling stake in Haier-CCT Holdings, a joint venture which was listed on the Hong Kong Stock Exchange that same year. Haier's international success and well known brand name led to the company becoming an official sponsor for the 2008 Beijing Olympic Games.

Key to any company's success is its brand, and strong brands allow a company to not only grow domestically but also internationally. Haier rode the wave of its strong domestic brand to enter new markets and expand into a fast growing multinational corporation. In March 2009, the *Financial Times* recognized Haier's success when it ranked among the Top 10 Chinese World-class Brands. In 2015, Xinhua.net recognized Haier "spearheads new model of innovation." Through protecting its IP and brand names with trademarks, Haier has built up a powerful asset that has transformed the company and brought global recognition for its brand and products.

Case Study 案例分析

This is a proactive PR case of Haier Group Corporation. The branding strategy brought the dying company back to life. Now Haier is one of the most successful appliance companies in the world.

Investigation and analysis on a company's internal and external information is the precondition for transnational corporation public relations. When Haier faced the bankruptcy, the company realized its current situation, cooperated with Lieberhaier and made multiple acquisitions to diversify its product portfolio, changed its name to Haier. Haier, a new name marked the birth of a new brand and the revitalization of a small company's image.

In Haier's branding strategy, products, logo, slogan and localization are very important. Innovating new products through research and development, improving products' quality is the core of the company. The catchy logo and slogan also made the brand popular. Moreover, Haier focuses on localizing the design, manufacturing and sales processes, so it can truly become a "local" brand in important markets such as the United States and Europe.

7.2.2 "大白兔"甲醛危机公关

案例背景

"大白兔"奶糖,伴随了几代人的成长,并且作为糖果行业的"驰名商标",被国人所熟知。据统计,目前"大白兔"奶糖累计国内销售达146亿元,并远销50个国家和地区。"大白兔"奶糖的事业在蓬勃发展的时期却被曝光含有甲醛(一种对人体具有极大伤害的毒性气体,其35%~40%的水溶液通称福尔马林),一时间"大白兔"被推到了风口浪尖。

2007年7月16日,冠生园集团国际贸易公司接到菲律宾经销商来电称:菲律宾食品药品局(BFAD)对中国进口的部分食品进行检验,"大白兔"奶糖被检含有福尔马林。

案例调研

这一突如其来的"灾难"使得"大白兔"奶糖的销售陷于被动之中。以上消息当天经菲律宾GMA电视新闻网公布,多家媒体转载。在菲律宾"大白兔"遭到了禁售,而香港惠康连锁超市则将"大白兔"奶糖下架,美国、新加坡、澳门、香港等地的媒体都做了报道,对"大白兔"品牌造成了巨大损害。

公关目标

彻查"大白兔"奶糖的质量,对失实报道予以纠正,维护"大白兔"奶糖的品牌形象,减轻外国公众对"大白兔"的不信任,利用权威机构的检测化解公众的质疑。赢得当地社会机构的支持,一起共同化解危机。

公关实施

面临"甲醛风波",一时间"大白兔"奶糖处于完全被动之中,甚至可能大难临头。7月16日,上海冠生园在得到了有关"大白兔奶糖被检含甲醛"的消息后,在第一时间内采取了积极主动的应对策略。在得到菲方检验结果的当日,冠生园连夜对"大白兔"奶糖组织内部检测,并在冠生园(集团)有限公司网站上公告检测结果。同时,将产品送到国际公认的权威检测机构SGS进行权威检测认定。另外,还积极通过经销商向菲律宾食品药品检测机构索取检测报告和产品实样。通过这一系列的积极应对行为,冠生园集团显示了自己的积极态度和坚定信心。

对于很多因产品质量而发生的危机事件,权威部门的权威检测与权威认证,是能够及时化解危机的一把利剑。而对于这起源于国际市场的食品质量检查风波来说,能不能得到国际权威认证的支持,是这起风波事件能否化解的决定性因素。显然,此时冠生园方面也意识到了权威认证的必要性,所以在得到"大白兔被疑含甲醛"消息的当天,就将样品送到了国际公认的权威检测机构SGS(通标标准技术服务有限公司上海分公司),并在19日上午10点得到了SGS关于"大白兔不含甲醛"的权威认证结果。这无疑给此次危机事件的应对提供了权威的证据。

对于突发性危机事件来说,媒体与舆论的主动权可以直接左右事件的发展。对于这起源于国际市场、通过各大媒体传播而来的"大白兔风波",冠生园能不能随着事件的发展而把握媒体的主动权,是关系此风波能否及时化解,并直接影响"大白兔"国际市场销售与品牌形象的关键点之一。

在"大白兔"这起意外风波的始终,冠生园都牢牢把握住了媒体主动权。在16日冠生园连夜对"大白兔"奶糖进行内部检测之后,即在冠生园(集团)有限公司网站上公告检测结果。18日,"大白兔"奶糖的生产企业——上海冠生园食品有限公司也已刊登了有关声明。这无疑在事件初期传达了冠生园的基本立场,防止了有关媒体对这起风波的盲目猜疑,从而避免了可能会出现的事件恶化。

面临危机事件时,当事企业的积极、主动的应对固然重要,但是能不能得到有关外部社会资源的强大支持,是直接影响到事件应对效率的外部因素。如果能得到有关部门的大力支持,当事企业就可以避免孤军奋战,与之进行协同作战,从而在最短的时间内化解危机。在这次"大白兔"风波事件中,自16日有关媒体对事件进行报道开始,上海质量技术监督部门就密切关注此事。并着手对此事进行调查,对相关信息进行核实;并称一旦得出结果将立即向社会公布。

公关评估

在上海冠生园的积极应对与各有关部门的大力支持下,"大白兔"风波在短期内得以化解,从而避免了不必要的国际市场销售损失与不利的品牌影响。

因为冠生园妥善处理了此次危机,相关媒体也正面报道了此次事件,向公众传达出积极的信号。媒体对冠生园更多的不是质疑,而是赞扬在"大白兔"奶糖危机发生后,冠生园采取的一系列措施帮助"大白兔"平稳度过了此次危机,赢回了国际声誉。

虽然发生在国外,但是国内民众也担心国内的产品会出现类似问题。不过,由于做好了质量检测报告,向广大群众澄清这一事实,并未发生民众恐慌,"大白兔"产品依然保持了良好的销量,群众也能够安心购买。

总的来看,经过上海冠生园的积极应对与各有关部门的大力配合,这起"大白兔"风波得以成功破解,由此可以看出企业在面临各类意外危机时,正确的应对策略是及时处理危机事件的关键所在。在这起事件中,权威机构的权威认证、权威检测结果与对媒体的主动权,可谓是冠生园积极应对这次"大白兔"风波的"双枪"。

Case Study 案例分析

这是一起成功的中国企业危机公关案例。在这起危机事件中,冠生园作为公关主体积极策划、实施公关活动,公关对象主要涉及菲律宾公众、媒体等。

在"大白兔"发生甲醛风波后,上海冠生园迅速开展了一系列的公关活动,包括送检内部机构、国际权威机构,得到了权威认可,随后牢牢把握住了媒体主动权,让媒体的宣传更有正面效应,为"大白兔"澄清此次事件。公司积极与菲律宾方面沟通,妥善地解决了此次危机,

> 巩固了"大白兔"的海外市场,挽回了声誉。
>
> 　　值得提及的是,在危机发生后,上海冠生园并不仅仅只关注国外公关,而且对国内公众也进行了相应的宣传,做好了国内国外两手准备,最后转危为安,成功化解了此次危机。

7.3 Further Reading
拓展阅读

7.3.1 Sany Group Sued Barak Obama

Research

Founded in 1989, Sany Group Co. Ltd is one of the leading enterprises of global equipment manufacturing industry in China. Adhering to the future goals of "to build a first-class enterprise, to foster first-class talents, and to make first-class contribution to humanity," Sany Group created the industry leading brand "SANY." It shortlisted as the "Global top 500 enterprises in market value" released by the *Financial Times* in the July of 2011, also being the only ranking Chinese engineering machinery enterprise. Sany Group is an equipment manufacture that mainly focuses on construction machines. It mainly produces concrete machinery, road machinery, hydraulic excavators, piling machinery, hoisting machinery, wind turbine, port machinery, oil equipment, high precision digital control machine tool and so on. Among them, concrete machinery, hydraulic excavators, piling machinery, crawling crane, mobile port machinery, and road machinery are the best in China. Excavating machinery broke the long-term monopoly state of foreign brands, and realized the first rank in China's marketing share. In 2002, Sany Heavy Industry acquired the German company Putzmeister, which was the global No.1 brand on concrete machinery. This event totally changed the competition state in industry field.

The case originated from a presidential order issued by Obama on September 28, 2012 which, on the grounds of "national security," ordered a stop to the Butter Creek wind power project launched by Chinese-owned, US-based company Ralls, and its backer Sany Group.

According to the Obama administration, the low ridge where the wind power project was located fell within the restricted area of a military base used for bombing practice. However, Sany argued their permit had been issued two years ago, and accused Obama of denying Ralls their ownership of property endowed by the US constitution.

Sany attract worldwide attention at the end of September 2014 by taking Barack Obama to court. Sany is disputing the president's ruling against four Oregon wind farms it had purchased in the US under its subsidiary called Ralls Corp.

Sany already filed a complaint against Obama and the Committee on Foreign Investment in the United States at a District Court in Washington, claiming that the president's order of preventing it from owning the Oregon wind farms exceeded its constitutional rights and failed to provide detailed evidence.

Objective

Sany Group stressed that the company is determined in its judiciary procedure against US president Barack Obama. Sany must persist in the lawsuit to the end and will appeal to the circuit court or the supreme court of the United States if necessary. Sany want to maintain its legitimate rights and interests in the United States.

Practice

According to a court order, Count IV of the amended complaint will not be dismissed. It alleges that the president's "order regarding the acquisition of four US wind farm project companies by Ralls Corporation" on Sept. 28, 2012 violates the due process clause of the fifth amendment to the United States Constitution by depriving Ralls of property without providing adequate opportunity to be heard or an adequate explanation of the reasons for the decision.

Ralls argues that Obama exceeded his power by dictating the terms of the sale, allowing the government to inspect all aspects of its operations and failing to treat the company equally as required under the law.

Chinese businesses' efforts to acquire American assets have raised national security concerns among US lawmakers. But the US Court of Appeals for the

District of Columbia Circuit on Tuesday ruled that the Barack Obama administration failed to follow appropriate legal procedures when it issued a presidential order to stop Ralls' projects in 2012.

The court, saying Ralls' rights were violated, called on the White House to tell the company what evidence the president relied on.

At issue are the Butter Creek wind farm projects in north-central Oregon. The Committee on Foreign Investment in the US, a government body, concluded that the Chinese company's ownership of the facilities could pose a threat to a nearby US naval training base. The committee drew up the order and obtained the president's signature.

The committee is generally strict about foreign investment in US companies. While the court ruling may not change the ultimate outcome for Sany, the group's successful challenge of a president-endorsed committee order could lead to a more open review process.

Evaluation

This lawsuit has attracted great concerns all over of the world. *The Wall Street Journal* reviewed this case: "In a lawsuit against the White House on Tuesday, a Chinese company has achieved unprecedented success, which may shake the US government on national security grounds to non-public review foreign acquisition.

BBC news analyzed this case, and believed this decision could prompt CFIUS to review foreign enterprises investment more transparently.

The three-judge panel has ruled "the presidential order deprived Ralls of significant property interests," constituting a clear constitutional violation. The appeals court sent the case back to the lower courts, and has ordered that Ralls be provided the unclassified evidence the president relied on and be given an opportunity to respond to it.

In mid-September a new survey by the Pew Research Center showed that while most Americans saw US relations with China as "generally good," they also saw China as posing the greatest danger to the US. The majority of those surveyed viewed China as a competitor of the US, rather than as an enemy or partner.

Zhang Guoqing (an expert on the study of the United States): from the perspective of discourse, Sany defeated Obama not only win more opportunities for Sany Group into the US market, but also help more Chinese enterprises blaze a new trail especially to investment in America.

Thinking:

1. What have you learned from the case "Sany Group Sued Barak Obama"?
2. When faced with the formaldehyde crisis, what did White Rabbit Cream Candy do to save its image? Did it work? Please explain it explicitly.
3. List some IPR skills you can use to change crisis to campaign of a brand for a transnational company.

7.3.2 阿里巴巴美国IPO上市公关

案例调研

美国时间2014年9月19日上午,阿里巴巴正式在纽交所挂牌交易,股票代码为BABA。截至当天收盘,阿里巴巴股价暴涨25.89美元报93.89美元,较发行价68美元上涨38.07%,市值达2314.39亿美元,超越Facebook成为仅次于谷歌的第二大互联网公司。

9月19日北京时间21时30分,阿里正式敲钟开市。因为交易量庞大,阿里创美股10年来开盘时间最长纪录。直到北京时间23时50分之后才出炉开盘价。开盘92.7美元,较发行价68美元高开36.3%。阿里巴巴集团市值达到2383.32亿美元,至此,阿里巴巴执行主席马云的身家超过200亿美元,超过王健林和马化腾,成为中国新首富。

据阿里巴巴招股书披露,马云占阿里巴巴8.9%的股份,以开盘价92.7美元计算,他在阿里巴巴的股份价值超过200亿美元,加上他的其他财富,他的身家可能达到王健林的近2倍。据国际货币基金组织公布的2013年世界各国GDP排行榜,阿里巴巴总市值2314.39亿美元这个数字,居第44位伊拉克及43位巴基斯坦之间,阿里之富可匹敌全球100多个国家。

公关目标

阿里巴巴作为一家中国企业,如果需要在美国上市,就必须使公司更加透明化、国际化,这样才能向美国证券交易所提出IPO申请。对于传统的中国企业来讲,财务不透明、管理体制中国化等问题将会阻碍在美国上市。为此,必须要向美国政府和美国证券机构进行公关,同时,需要借助美国的主流媒体,从舆论的角度影响政府的态度,使阿里巴巴在美国成功上市。

公关实施

阿里IPO顺利进行,首先要归功于其过去3年雇佣了关键角色游说美国政府。对政府的重视,是阿里巴巴公关成功的关键所在。阿里巴巴拥有一个政治游说公司,该公司的头目包括里根总统内阁中的人事主管、前美国贸易代表办事处总顾问、前美国财政部负责国际交流和政府沟通的主管。

其实,阿里巴巴为在美国上市早就做好了铺垫。在上市之前,阿里巴巴悄然上线了一家网站——11main.com。尽管11 main没有正式开始运营,只是在页面上写着"Opening Soon"。虽没有很多细节方面的信息,但可以明确知道,这是一家面向海外市场的电商网站,而且很可能是针对个人消费者的。

阿里巴巴官方也证实,11 main是由阿里集团在美国的全资子公司Vendio和Auctiva联合推出的新网站。有相关的科技媒体报道称,它将是一个本地卖家在线上卖商品的市场。虽然该网站正式上线之后的运营模式不得而知,包括将会引入哪些卖家、运营方式以及商业模式。《华尔街日报》则报道称:"来自时装和珠宝等行业的部分商家将在该网站上出售高质量产品。"在这之前阿里巴巴在美国已经有"国际版淘宝"速卖通(Aliexpress)和天猫淘宝的海外版运营。从阿里巴巴最近的一系列动作中不难发现,阿里对海外市场的兴趣越来越浓了,为在美国的成功上市做好了铺垫。

此外,阿里巴巴注重拓展美国市场。2013年8月,阿里巴巴就7500万美元收购了美国物流服务商Shop Runner小部分股份,两个月后又继续领投了该公司的新一轮融资。随后的10月,美国移动创业公司Quixey亦获得阿里巴巴领投的5000万美元融资。再加上1stdibs,阿里巴巴每次的投资出手都算得上阔绰,而且都有着战略投资的意味。

然而,这并不意味着阿里巴巴美国公关的结束。在纳斯达克敲钟仪式上,阿里展现了世界公司的典范,吸引了全球的目光。正式敲响阿里上市钟声的是八位来自阿里巴巴生态系统的参与者:曾经的奥运冠军,现在拥有一家淘宝店的劳丽诗;从阿里巴巴旗下论坛上成长起来的云客服;90后大学生黄碧姬;淘宝模特(淘女郎),同时担任自闭症儿童教师的何宁宁;致力于带动家乡电商发展的农民店主王志强;以电商带动汶川震后恢复的海归创业者王淑娟;拥有"淘宝博物馆"的十年用户乔丽;边送快递边为贫困地区收集旧衣旧书,建立两座乡村图书馆的快递员窦立国;以及来自美国、通过天猫将车厘子卖到中国的农场主Peter Verbrugg。

而在细数历次登上纽交所或纳斯达克的敲钟人,即使请来声势浩大的亲友团,也都从来没有过公司创始人或高管不露面的情景。作为一家公司在上市过程中最重要的环节,阿里巴巴选择用"全球最独特"的敲钟方式,让媒体的闪光灯中对准阿里的"生态圈"而不是马云个人。

公关评估

从阿里自身角度出发,阿里巴巴的成功依然沿袭其固有的公关模式。阿里巴巴在美国上市依靠了其强大的公关团队,依靠其成熟的公关体系,从马云到一个普通的公关人员,形成了一个整体的团队。遇到大事的时候,子公司的公关部都统一到集团作战,平日里也是彼此协同合作,他们是一个作战整体,公关执行力强。

阿里巴巴还沿用了政府与媒体两手抓的策略,借助当地的政治游说公司,解除了上市的政治阻碍。在中国,阿里巴巴几乎与国内的主流媒体都保持了高度密切的联系,国内报刊媒体对这一事件高度关注。虽然在美国上市情形有所不同,但是借助美国当地报纸杂志的报道,让更多的美国公众了解到什么是阿里巴巴,扩大了其品牌效应,塑造了良好的国际形象。

国内媒体如网易新闻、新浪新闻等对阿里巴巴美国上市高度关注,报道了阿里巴巴上市的进程,称阿里上市后股价一路飙升,成为仅次于谷歌的全球第二大互联网公司。

国外媒体也集中报道了阿里巴巴上市。《华尔街日报》随后报道称,阿里巴巴IPO首日股票大涨,使这家公司的估值超越了竞争对手,但要维持这样的估值,依靠的是增长率和利润率。阿里巴巴的估值面临着市场的严厉检验,为达到分析师的预期,其营收在接下来的几年里需要创造30%至35%的年增长率,这也正是整个电子商务行业的预期增长率。

《纽约时报》则给阿里巴巴的首日表现予以肯定,报道称,中国互联网巨头周五的IPO没有让大家失望,这场众人期待已久的盛事使今年上市的所有企业都相形见绌。该报援引纽交所的Ethridge观点认为,如果阿里巴巴的股票在接下来的日子里表现良好,将有更多的公司受其鼓舞而考虑上市,国外的,特别是中国公司将会效仿阿里巴巴。

思考:

1. 阿里巴巴在美国上市有什么重要意义?从阿里巴巴的公关中你学到了什么技巧?
2. 海尔的品牌战略是什么?它是如何一步一步走向成功的?
3. 新品牌在实施全球战略中可运用怎样的公关技巧?

中国跨国企业国际公关 | International Public Relations of China Transnational Corporation

7.4 Simulation
情景模拟

7.4.1 WeChat PR

Background

WeChat, or Weixin, a mobile text and voice messaging communication service developed by Tencent in China, risks losing its luster as users complain about bombardment by deceptive ads and excessive information.

The situation came to the public's attention when a business account put fake ads on "Moments," one of the major functions embedded in WeChat, which allows users to upload photos and share their daily life via texts.

On Monday, authorities in southwest China's Chongqing Municipality busted a case in which a "travel agency" account told its followers on WeChat to "Like" its ads to win a free trip to Hong Kong and Macao, which was later proved to be deceptive.

Similar cases were reported in provinces of Guangdong, Sichuan, Shaanxi and Jiangsu, with unscrupulous businesspeople trying to lure customers with coveted promotions, but later breaking their promises.

WeChat, developed by Internet giant Tencent, allows people to send texts, photos, videos and voice messages over mobile phones. The application has earned a legion of fans in China thanks to its convenience, reaching 600 million users since its debut in 2011.Along with fake ads, information overload on the app is forcing some users to escape the flood of daily annoyances.

Wei Kang, a white-collar worker in Beijing, said that he receives "tons of messages" from his colleagues in WeChat's chat groups, even on weekends.

Wei said that he spends about an hour daily replying to messages from his colleagues, and has to check WeChat every few minutes because messages from his boss might be among the sea of notifications.

"I feel like I have been kidnapped by WeChat," Wei said, jokingly.

Wei is not the only one bombarded by the app. Early in February, Huang Zhen, a professor from Central University of Finance and Economics, caused a buzz on the Internet when he announced that he would abandon all WeChat chat groups and "try to find some inner peace."

A survey in March by a newspaper in Shanghai showed that 66.67 percent of respondents had feelings of being "kidnapped" by WeChat, but most chose to put up with the barrage of messages and information.

The "Moments" section on WeChat, for instance, has waned in popularity as it has become a place for people to either share ads or "Chicken Soup for the Soul" type articles.

"My WeChat 'Moments' are basically spammed by these every single day, which is quite annoying," a WeChat user screen-named "HXfengai" told Xinhua.

As urgency for change mounts, WeChat teams need to adjust their product design and services to break the bottleneck and retain users, said Zhang Yi, CEO of iiMedia Research. WeChat development teams should step up efforts to consider feedback from users and try to understand what they truly need at the moment.

Simulation

1. As officials of Tencent, how would you respond to explain the cause of the information bombardment, and what measures would you take to make up for the damaged image of Tencent?
2. If you were managing this crisis, what's your strategy for Tencent? Try to make a detailed plan, and elaborate your reasons. Make a convincing statement to the audience.
3. As overseas users are increasing every year, do you have any suggestions for Tencent to avoid this kind of crisis? Formulate your own plans to solve this crisis if it occurs abroad.

7.4.2 华为芭蕾舞鞋广告

一只脚穿着舞鞋优雅光鲜,旁边的另一只脚却赤裸并伤痕累累,显得有些触目惊心。这幅构图对比鲜明、充满冲击力的画面,是美国摄影艺术家亨利·路特威勒的摄影作品:芭蕾脚。近期它刊登在《人民日报》上,则是作为华为的广告用图,图中的广告语是:"我们的人生,痛,并快乐着。"

先了解一下"芭蕾脚"的具体来历。如众所知,芭蕾舞是一门高贵典雅的艺术,它庄重而优美,令人陶醉。但同时,对芭蕾舞者来说,这也是一门艰辛

中国跨国企业国际公关 | International Public Relations of China Transnational Corporation

的艺术,绝非轻易就能掌控。而路特威勒是一位非常了解芭蕾舞的摄影师,他一辈子都热爱芭蕾,花了近30年时间拍摄芭蕾舞照片。在他看来,芭蕾舞"不仅仅是舞蹈",更"表达了人类情感的各种形态:爱、绝望、热情、希望,还有最重要的是,快乐"。路特威勒专门花了4年时间,用镜头跟踪记录纽约芭蕾舞团成员的工作与生活,从台前到幕后,从排练到演出,点点滴滴都不错过,最终精选照片形成《芭蕾舞》一书刊出,"芭蕾脚"就是其中的一张重要作品。路特威勒表示,"对于那些不了解芭蕾舞的人来说,这本书所呈现的,就是芭蕾舞的极致美丽与背后的汗水。"

再看一下华为的灵魂,华为总裁任正非在最近一次达沃斯论坛上发言时,是怎么提到"芭蕾脚"的:

"……我们除了比别人少喝咖啡,多干点儿活,其实我们不比别人有什么长处。就是因为我们起步太晚,我们成长的年限太短,积累的东西太少,我们得比别人多吃苦一点,所以我们这有一只是芭蕾脚,一只很烂的脚,我觉得就是华为的人,痛并快乐着,华为就是那么一只烂脚,不给社会表现出来我们这只脚还挺好,我们的广告在全球大规模的做,刚刚开始启动,就来解释我们走向了社会,走向了这个东西……"

两相对比,就能够看出华为与"芭蕾脚"的共通之处,这是对"付出与收获"之反差最为直白的表达:你看到了最好的我,但你怎知我为此曾经付出多少伤痛……

由此看出,"芭蕾脚"其实依旧承袭了华为多年来所宣扬的"华为精神",也就是艰苦奋斗,也就是吃得苦中苦方有甜上甜,也就是不经历风雨哪得见彩虹……"芭蕾脚"背后的华为相信,一切美好有序事物的背后,总有努力与付出,华为不相信不劳而获与天上掉馅饼。

模拟:

1. 从广告分类的角度来看,这则广告属于什么类型的广告? 如果你是消费者,看到这则广告后有什么想法吗?
2. 华为光鲜表明的背后承载了众多员工艰辛的付出,让我们看到了一个不一样的华为。但是有人指出,华为牺牲了员工部分权益,不是一个好企业。现在你作为华为的公关负责人,需要向外界进行一次形象公关,该如何设计? 请分组进行演练,一组代表华为公司,一组代表公众,另一组代表媒体记者,华为公司就以上问题开展公关活动。

3. 华为"芭蕾脚"广告承袭了华为多年来所宣扬的"华为精神",即一切美好有序事物的背后,总有努力与付出。你认为这则广告做到了新、绝、深、美吗? 如果你是广告的设计者,还有更好的建议吗?

Exercises
本章练习题

Gap Filling 填空题

1. China's corporation public relationship experience three stage: _____, _____ and _____.
2. At the same time, the opening of the Chinese economy to the international market saw an influx of foreign companies _____ investment opportunities.
3. To _____ its competitive edge, the company ensures that it secures protection for all of its intellectual property (IP).
4. With its position in China profitable and secure, Haier _____ on a global branding strategy.
5. Alibaba group want to use advertisement strategy to _____ its brand and popularity.
6. We then ran an online marketing program _____ Mercedes Benz to deliver targeted advertisements to a much larger set of potential customers with similar attributes without disclosing personally identifiable information.

True or False 判断题

Directions: Read the following sentences and decide whether they are true or false.

1. 中国跨国企业国际公关的4种基本形式:国际合同项目和劳工出口服务、中国在海外的直接投资、跨境并购、中国企业海外上市。
2. 中国的跨国企业国际公关,是指拥有国际化视野和技能的中国跨国公关团队对中国企业在"走出去"过程中遇到的融入问题和品牌问题进行专业策划与解决。
3. 企业在公共关系学中既涉及企业的利益,又涉及公共利益,而公共利益的实现与维护又依赖于政府。

中国跨国企业国际公关 | International Public Relations of China Transnational Corporation

4. 中国跨国企业国际公关在发展阶段，更加注重公关的步骤、方案的设计以及部门公关人员的素质，企业内部公关的协调。
5. 中国跨国企业国际公关的外部信息包括企业所占有的市场份额，社会公众对企业及产品的评价。

Matching 连线题

请把下列发展阶段、时间与中国企业每演变特点相连。

萌芽期	21世纪中期	报纸电视有限公关资源
初期探索期	21世纪初期	品牌意识和营销意识
发展期	20世纪70年代	公关专业化，工具多元化

Paraphrase 释义题

Directions: Explain the following sentences in your own words.

1. WeChat, developed by Internet giant Tencent, allows people to send texts, photos, videos and voice messages over mobile phones. The application has earned a legion of fans in China thanks to its convenience, reaching 600 million users since its debut in 2011.
2. Haier knew that its brand was its most valuable resource, with brand image at the core of its business identity and strategy, therefore its early branding strategy was to build a strong, leading national brand name.
3. Sany Group stressed that the company is determined in its judiciary procedure against U.S. president Barack Obama. Sany must persist in the lawsuit to the end and will appeal to the circuit court or the supreme court of the United States if necessary.
4. China's corporation public relationship experience three stage: infancy and early exploration period and development stage. Compared with Western countries, China's Corporate Communications started late, so we remain need to learn and form our own style for better solving oversea crisis and shaping responsibility image.

Thinking 思考题

1. 中国企业"走出去"中面临哪些公关风险？如何预防和化解这些公关危机？
2. 如何利用公关广告做好新品上市公关？
3. 搜索和分享一则中国企业公关案例。

International Public Relations of Public Figures
公众人物国际公关

Gist
内容概览

The rapid development of economic life and the complexity of social relations have determined that the members in society are unable to avoid a crisis that may occur at any time, especially those celebrities who have a good public reputation, positive social influence, or a certain organizational background. Because of their special social identity and general public concerns, they have to have a rapid and effective coping strategies and skills. Because public figures have this extraordinary influence in society, we usually regard them as special social organizations. For example, government officials, social activists, and stars in other fields can more easily attract the attention from the media and the public. In addition, they all have a vested interest in preserving the image of the organization which they represent.

Because of the indisputable social influence of public figures, we have selected plenty of PR cases involving public figures to illustrate their PR team's design, process and theories in this chapter to make students more clear about the PR of public figures and the differences between them and the general public in PR activities. Through our exercises, students can apply what they've mastered in this chapter.

经济生活的高速发展及社会关系的复杂化决定了社会成员都无法避免随时可能发生的危机事件。而具有较高公众知名度、积极社会影响力以及一定组织背景的名人因为其特殊的身份以及普遍的舆论关注性,不仅需要在危机发生之时有比普通人物更为快速有效的应对策略及技巧以应对危机造成的影响与破坏,更需要在危机未发生之前就做好相关的公关工作。由于公众人物所拥有的这种普通人物不具备的特殊社会影响力,我们通常把他们看做一类特殊的社会组织来看待。比如政府官员、社会活动家、明星等,他们的言行举止广受媒体和大众的关注并影响着人们的生活,且代表着其所属组织的形象。

正是由于公众人物有如此特殊的影响力,本章选取公众人物为国际公关主体,介绍了社会公众人物的定义、公关的目的、基础和实施的理论,选取了有代表性的中外公众人物公关案例,拓展阅读补充了名人慈善公关专题,让学生学习公众人物作为个体与普通公众在公关活动设计和处理上的不同及其原因,掌握公众人物公共关系的理论和实践技巧。

8.1 Basic Knowledge 基础知识

8.1.1 Definition 定义

Public figures, in another word, are celebrities of our society. They are a group of people who have the power to exert their influence on the general public through their opinions, individual lives and other actions. Some are part of political, business, scientific, educational, cultural circles, while others mostly come from the world of art, film and television, sports, or other public figures.

Society usually expects more from public figures, so they need to do more to maintain their public image. In turn, the society needs the special influence of this group to promote positive values. Therefore, whether the public figure is active or passive, they all need PR practice and experience to maintain a good reputation. Sometimes it's also their social responsibility. Appropriate public relations can not only make the celebrities who are suffering crisis turn "danger" to "safety." Sometimes there may even be opportunities to get higher "reputation." However, if celebrities carry out inappropriate public relations work, or take an inactive attitude towards public relations, there's a high chance that not only their situations be further deteriorated, but also produce a "chain reaction," resulting in image crisis of the region, industry and even the nation to which they belong. Therefore, normally, social public figures consciously carry out a plan to gain more public and public opinion support initiatively, which is called public relations.

公众人物:"所谓名人,是指那些对公众舆论和社会生活具有较大的影响力和号召力的有名望的社会人士,如政界的政府官员、工商界的要人、科学界、教育界、文化界的权威、艺术、影视、体育界的明星、舆论界的领袖以及社会活动家等等。"又称社会性人物。一般来说,个人是无法成为社会组织的,但社会公众人物与一般的个体不同,他们往往身份特殊、社会声誉很高,社会影响也很大。

公共人物公关:正是因为公众对他们的期望比一般人高,如何争取更多公众的理解与支持是决定他们能否发展的必要条件,也决定了他们对社会的影响方式和程度。因此,他们需要不断进行丰富的公关活动和策划以维系并延续其在社会当中的影响力,或扩大与改善其在社会大众中的声誉和美誉度。恰如其分的公关工作不仅能使名人的形象在危急时刻转"危"为"安",还有可能获得一次提升"美誉度"的机会;而开展不当的公关工作,甚至是"事不关己""无所作为"的公关态度不仅使名人形象进一步恶化,还有可能产生"连锁反应",造成其所在的地区、行业甚至整个国家的形象危机。由此,社会公众人物有意识地去主动开展这类活动以争取更多公众与舆论支持的行为就叫做公共人物公关。

8.1.2 Features 属性

Public figures' PR is one branch of the whole subject of public relations. However, based on its special situation of simultaneously being affected by personal factors and sharing high social influence, it has several distinct natures.

First of all, there are three common traits that most celebrities own when carrying out public relations:

(1) Altitude

As public figures, it is necessary to have a high degree of recognition in the following two points: responsibility and obligation. Though they are still individuals, they are different from others. Public figures own more social resources than ordinary people, so naturally they should assume more social responsibility. Every move of public figure may produces large responses from the society, and may has a direct influence on the public affairs. Therefore, public figures must understand and accept ethical and behavioral standards more than ordinary people. Furthermore, meeting media supervision is also one of their duties.

(2) Attitude

Public figures must have a positive attitude whenever they carry out public relations, especially when they confront with a crisis. It's natural that people will forgive a child who makes mistakes, but will never forgive a child who does not know the wrong.

(3) Style

Staying humble, never forgetting who they are and never ever getting dizzy with success is always a golden principle. If god wants a man to die, he will make him crazy first.

根据名人公关的以上三个特点,我们可以得出名人公关所具有的属性。

(1) 公众性。公众性是名人公关的基本特性,它首先表现为名人为公众所熟知,在社会上具有一定的知名度。

(2) 主动性。这往往是由于名人所享有的高声望决定的,他们不希望自己因为形象塑造不佳的问题而遭遇臭名昭著的境遇,因此,他们往往主动出击积极维护自己已经获得的好名声。

(3) 具有一定的商业或政治价值。名人因备受媒体与公众的关注,对公众产生了影响,在公众中具有较高的知名度,这些知名度使他们能经常成为公共关系传播中的信息传递者。

8.1.3 Classification 分类

(1) 按公法的角度分为:

政治性公众人物 Political Public 和 社会性公众人物 Social Public,何种分类是用以对公共官员的特殊要求为标准而做的划分。政治性公众人物由于其特殊的组织性,关注内容往往在公共事务和业务能力等方面,公关开展方式通常是以政治宣传进行形象塑造;社会性公众人物关注内容往往在于某种商业利益和个人形象,公关活动开展方式更加丰富多样。

(2) 按国别的角度分为:

国内公众人物 Domestic Public 和国际公众人物 International Public,这是从公众人物的影响范围分类的。由于这两者的差别在于影响范围,所以国内公众人物的影响力一旦达到了一定程度,也就演变成为国际公众人物,相

公众人物国际公关 | International Public Relations of Public Figures

应地,随着其影响范围扩大,其受舆论和公众约束的程度也就加深了。

(3) 按行为人主观意愿的角度分为:

自愿性公众人物 Voluntary Public 和非自愿性公众人物 Involuntary Public,自愿性公众人物是指在主观上追求或放任自己成为公众人物并在客观上成为公众人物的人。例如体育明星、影视明星、高级官员等人物,在主观上具有希望或放任自己被一般社会公众所熟知,在客观上已经为公众熟知,具有一定的知名度。

非自愿性公众人物,往往指没有追求或放任出名或成为社会公众关注的结果的主观意图,而是由于具有新闻价值的重大事件的发生,经过新闻媒介的传播而成为公众熟知的与这件事件有联系或牵连的人。非自愿公众人物还可以具体划分为附属性公众人物、偶然性公众人物和转化性公众人物。

该种分类的意义在于,为自愿性公众人物和非自愿性公众人物的名誉权保护的区别对待提供依据。这种区分也已成为法制健全国家处理名誉权、隐私权与新闻舆论监督权、公众知情权关系的一个重要原则。

(4) 按时间属性分为:

完全的公众人物 Complete Public 和有限的公众人物 Limitative Public。有些公众人物的影响仅限于某个具体的时段,或是在某个事件发生的阶段,不具有延续性和连贯性,我们称这类公关主体为有限的公众人物,比如运动员在一届奥运会上的高分使得该国民众对这一事件保持兴奋,但在比赛结束后的一段时间,这种影响力和范围会迅速减退。

(5) 按产生影响的不同阶段分为:

潜在公众人物 Potential Public 和既成公众人物 Accomplished Public。在对象并未对社会产生既成的实质性的影响,并未被公众广为知晓的阶段,该对象只是潜在公众人物,具备使其随时向既成公众人物过渡的各种因子。潜在公众人物的关注度可能并没有既成公众人物,所以公关吸引力有限,需要外界或内部的推动力才可能实现转变。

8.1.4 Evolution 演变

In previous chapters, we mentioned several times that public relations can be basically divided into two types: active PR and passive PR. This kind of classification is in accordance with the different purposes, phases and levels of public relations. As public figures' PR is one type of PR, it still meets this classification principle. Thus:

Phase 1

Active PR. Before a crisis happens, sophisticated celebrities usually have a good awareness of the importance of a long-term plan of PR. They try to set up PR consciousness and use various means to establish good social image for certain purposes. This is for nipping in the bud of some possible crisis as a result that people make mistakes no matter how careful they are. Since they share high reputation, their mistakes may be enlarged so that both they and their organizations will suffer irreversible effects. Therefore, celebrities in this phase will try to shape their image as much as possible to mitigate the passive effect of possible crisis.

Phase 2

Passive PR. When unfortunately, crisis occurs, regardless of any kind of active PR previously, their PR will be changed to passive PR because of immeasurable public opinion power. At this point, PR will experience the following specific stages of evolution.

（1）突发期

突发期危机应对的绝佳时期，这一时期危机往往还沉浮于水下，没有扩散，及时的处理有可能将造成的损失减小到零。

（2）扩散期

扩散期时的危机开始酝酿形成更大的灾难，此时的积极反应，遏制危机，往往成本较低，效果也较理想。

（3）爆发期

到了爆发期，危机会衍生出次生危机，形成"涟漪效应"。此时处理和平息危机的成本呈几何倍数地增长，情形就难以收拾了。

公众人物作为一种社会文化符号，具有整体象征性和代表性。尤其是一些官员和企业领导人所代表的不仅仅是其个人，而是政府和企业，只有他们成功处理个人危机事件，他们所具有的符号象征性，才不会轻易导致"个人信任危机"转化为"组织信任危机"。当危机事件发生在公众人物身上时，他就不能只考虑个人的得与失，而是要以组织整体利益为重，及时进行形象修复，以免组织形象受损。受到传统思维或者是个人媒介素养的影响，国内的公众人物在个人危机时刻，经常采取欺骗或逃避媒体的手段，不仅不能及时修复受损的个人形象，反而会适得其反。社会公众人物是接触媒体最频繁也是媒体最关注的群体，而在这些人身上，突显了媒介素养的缺失。

公众人物国际公关 | International Public Relations of Public Figures

8.1.5 Practice 实施

近年来,危及名人形象的负面新闻频频发生。而这些事件的主角也蒙受了巨大的舆论压力,各方评论不一,个人形象在瞬间经受着严峻的考验。在这种强大的舆论压力之下,名人该如何与传媒打交道,采取何种方式与公众进行沟通,维持和重塑正面形象,是名人危机公关管理必修的一个科目。

First of all, timely and detailed information for media to publish truths is important. In this stage, public figures must do a good job on information output. Major media in the crisis can guide the main public opinion and disclose wrong and purposive information through their strong agenda setting function. Thus, any rejective action to media is not desirable. Spokesman of public figures need to pay attention that no sentence like "No comment" should be sent out. What is right is to express positive attitudes and actions to solve problems and give words like "We attach serious concerns on this issue."

组织内的公众人物新闻发言人要勇于承担对危机当事人的管理和教育责任,不要极力划清自己与危机当事人的界限,这样可以给公众责任感和信任感。同时也要强调事件和个人的特殊性,以免公众对组织中其他人形象的连带受损。在当事人方便的情况下,可以请当事人出席新闻发布会,增加信源的可信度。总之,在对外信息输出过程中,要变媒体主动为组织主动。新闻发言人要时刻把握"反应快速、态度明朗、强调行动"这三条基本原则,主动配合媒体,最大限度地满足媒体和公众的知情权,防止流言的滋长,维护组织形象。

其次,做好舆情的收集和分析,保障组织外部的信息输入。随着传播技术手段的日益进步,特别是电脑和网络的普及使用,传播模式的双向互动成为了可能。网络以其传播速度快、受众覆盖面广、信息海量等特点成为当今人们获取信息和反馈信息的主要渠道之一。各类网站中的论坛成了网民发表言论、交换意见的主要阵地。所以,作为公众人物的新闻发言人,可以依靠如乐思网络舆情监测系统这样的舆情监测软件及时了解受众对事件的关注角度和关注重心,在新闻发布会上,可以针对这些热点问题详细解答。

(1) 树立公众人物的社会责任意识。

(2) 强化公众人物的组织观念意识和形象修复意识;作为个体的人必须从事社会活动和社会交往,并依存于社会,所谓"形象修复"是个人危机事件处理的一种自救行为。

(3) 随着社会经济、文化的发展和大众传媒影响力的日益增强,"社会公众人物"成为了各大媒体和广大受众最关注的社会群体之一。对公众人物的正面报道,可以增加他们在社会中的知名度和影响力,取得公众人物、媒体与受众三者得益的传播效果。但当个人危机事件发生在公众人物身上,很多人选择的却是逃避或欺骗媒体,不能满足受众的知情权,履行作为公众人物的社会责任。其结果不仅使自己在社会中的形象受到损害,也影响了个人所在组织机构的社会形象。

8.1.6 Public Speech 公关演讲

演讲作为人类社会不可缺少的一种传递信息的手段,早就为人们所重视。在历史上,许多人凭着自己非凡的演讲才能,将自己的主张传播给广大民众,左右人们的思想和行动,影响历史发展的进程。今天,在社会交往日益频繁,信息交流日益广泛的情况下,公众人物的演讲显得越来越重要,掌握公关演讲的技巧对于公关工作的开展也会起到事半功倍的效果。

演讲是一种就某个问题向公众发表见解、主张,以感化听众、教育听众的特殊的说话方式。作为一种特殊的说话方式,演讲具有以下几个特点:

第一,演讲必须面对公众。因此演讲者必须考虑听众的心理,准确地理解公众,并运用各种手段,控制听众的心理变化,满足听众的心理需要,是听众理解和接受演讲的内容。第二,演讲要有中心、有条理,结构要比较完整。为了达到演讲的目的,必须有一个中心论点,并围绕这论点有层次、有条理地开展。第三,演讲是一种有说服力、感染力和鼓动性的说话形式。演讲者面对着众多的听众,要使其接受演讲的内容,从而影响人的行为,就必须采用丰富、典型的材料,通过严密的逻辑论证,用富有说服力、感染力和鼓动性的艺术化的口语,打动听众。

演讲的准备

在选题时应当注意以下几点:要适合听众的要求;要适合自己的身份和特点;要适合当时的场合;要根据时间长短选题。题目确定后,紧接着就要投入演讲稿的写作工作。经验丰富的演讲者往往只写出提纲,但多数演讲者,特别是经验不足者,准备演讲稿是必要的,这个创作过程往往包括以下几个方面:搜集和整理资料;布局谋篇;起草演讲;修改润色。在演讲稿写完以后,有必要进行一下试讲。通过试讲可以理清思路,增强记忆;还可以对词句进行进一步的技术处理。实际上就是整个演讲准备工作的总检查。

演讲稿的写作

演讲稿一般包括开场、中间和结尾三部分。

演讲者上台后要给听众留下好的第一印象,开场需注意以下两点:美好的形象风度和得体有趣的开场白。

演讲的中间部分是演讲的中心和主体。再次,要运用各种手段,围绕演讲题目进行充分的论述和说明。这里有几种方法:加强逻辑力量、适当举例、出示实物。

演讲的结尾要顺理成章,深刻精彩,有许多方法:用呼吁式的语言结尾;总结式结尾;用赞颂的语言结尾;首尾呼应;提出问题,引人思考;引用著名诗词结尾。

演讲过程中还有许多技巧,如能够战胜怯场的自我暗示法、呼吸松弛法、心境调节法、排除刺激法、集中注意法、回避目光法等等,还有使演讲者摆脱窘境的技巧,如冻结冰点、想想讲题、超前减速、见好就收、拖延时间等等,此外,杰出的演讲者更会灵活巧妙地运用幽默来调节气氛,还会随机应变应对突发状况,这些都是要靠勤奋练习来培养的,如能够娴熟掌握并运用,会使公众人物在进行形象塑造以及思想传播的过程中如虎添翼。①

8.2 Bilingual Case Studies
双语案例

8.2.1 Putin's Hard-Man Image

Research

300 years ago, Emperor Peter built the St. Petersburg, which opened the vision of Russia to the west world and to a powerful opportunity. This powerful and strong Russian man said, "If I were left more years, St. Petersburg will become another Amsterdam." "Give me 20 years, and I'll give you back a

---

① 周安华、苗晋平,《公共关系:理论、实务与技巧(第4版)》。北京:中国人民大学出版社,2013年。

miraculous Russia." This is Putin's promise. In Moscow's Kremlin, Putin hangs a portrait of Peter the Great in his office. Many Russians even equate Putin with Peter the Great.

Putin, 60, is serving his third term since 2000. Since 1999, Putin took the highest authority of Russia for the first time. How to transform Putin's reserved, uncommunicative image to a charming international idol through a series of PR activities is urgent.

Due to the crisis in Ukraine, relation between Russia and the United States has fallen to the freezing point since the Cold War of the last century. Putin's PR team needs to tread a fine line to avoid making conflicts with the interests of US.

Objective

Shape Putin's image and promote his reputation and influence in world affairs, safeguard national interest of Russia through a series of arranged PR activities.

Practice

To attract public highlights, Putin has done a lot to shape an outdoor, sporty, tough guy public image, demonstrating his physical prowess and taking part in unusual or dangerous acts, such as extreme sports and interaction with wild animals. For example, in 2007, the tabloid *Komsomolskaya Pravda* published a huge photograph of a bare-chested Putin vacationing in the Siberian Mountain under the headline: "Be Like Putin."

Other notable examples of Putin's macho adventures include: flying military jets, demonstrating his martial art skills, riding horses, rafting, fishing and swimming in a cold Siberian river (doing all that mostly bare-chested), descending in a deepwater submersible, tranquilizing tigers with a tranquiliser gun, tranquilizing polar bears, riding a motorbike, co-piloting a firefighting plane to dump water on a raging fire, shooting darts at whales from a crossbow for eco-tracking, driving a race car, scuba diving at an archaeological site, attempting to lead endangered cranes in a motorized hang glider, and catching big fish.

On 11 December 2010, at a concert organized for a children's charity in Saint Petersburg, Putin sang "Blueberry Hill" with Maceo Parker's jazz band

and played a little piano of it and of the Russian patriotic song "С чего начинается Родина" from his favorite spy movie *The Shield and the Sword*. After that he took part in singing of a Russian song about cosmonauts, "Grass by the Home."

Putin's painting "*Узор на заиндевевшем окне*" (*A Pattern on a Hoarfrost-Encrusted Window*), which he had painted during the Christmas Fair on 26 December 2008, became the top lot at the charity auction in Saint Petersburg and sold for 37 million rubles. And there are a large number of songs about Putin.[①]

Besides, some services that Putin's PR team arranged were purely routines, such as doing journal investigation for Russian officials and contacting pro-Russian group in the documents submitted to the US Department of Justice. In addition, Putin and his team also called for the weakening of the US State Department's criticism on Russia's human rights record.

In April 2011, an American reporter asked Russian Prime Minister Vladimir Putin a very pleasing question: "Are you the coolest politician?" The following content was published in the website of *Outdoor Life* magazine. In fact, this is a deliberately arranged interview by Putin and his PR team.

Documents of the US Justice Department showed that since 2006, to raise Putin's reputation and tough man image, Putin's PR team including Russian government invest great efforts. For instance, from 2006 to 2012, Ketchum, the main PR Company that serves Putin and Russian government, received $ 23 million funds from Russia. In addition, Ketchum contributed a lot for brand promotion of Russian state-owned energy company Gazprom, getting $ 17 million reward.

The US NBC's business channel CNBC and the popular online newspaper site, *Huffington Post* published a series of columns for complementing Russia. The article praised the Russian government owning "modernization strategy ambition" and "law enforcement to reduce corruption and better protect business." There is an article concluded that "Russia may be the most vibrant continent."

---

① https://en.wikipedia.org/wiki/Vladimir_Putin#Public_image 2015年11月20日。

These articles were written by two businessmen, a lawyer and a scholar. All of them claimed that the article were purely on behalf of their own views. There is no remuneration received. However, media reports noted that, Putin's PR team approached these people, facilitating their column in the media.

In addition, Putin and his PR team work hard for promoting Sochi Winter Olympics in Russian city. They took the full charge of the operations of the website: *ThinkRussia*.com, "Twitter" and "YouTube" account.

Evaluation

A dramatic reversal of the image of Putin happened: transforming from the original reserved, uncommunicative person, to a man of muscle and strong will. Putin has already successfully made himself an international idol through a series of elaborately arranged PR plans, which helped Russia achieve a high degree of international exposure.

Putin was *Time* magazine's Person of the Year for 2007. In April 2008, he was put on the *Time* 100 most influential people in the world list. In 2013, 2014 and 2015, he was ranked as the world's most powerful person by Forbes.

According to public opinion surveys in June 2007, Putin's approval rating was 81%, the second highest of any leader in the world that year, following British Prime Minister Tony Blair, who received a 93% public approval rating in September 1997. In January 2013, Putin's approval rating fell to 62%, the lowest point since 2000 and a ten-point drop over two years. In May 2014 his approval rating rose to 85.9%, a six-year high. Observers see Putin's high approval ratings as a consequence of the significant improvements in living standards and Russia's reassertion of itself on the world scene during his presidency. One analysis attributed Putin's popularity, in part, to state-owned or state-controlled television. A 2005 survey showed that three times as many Russians felt the country was "more democratic" under Putin than it was during the Yeltsin or Gorbachev years, and the same proportion thought human rights were better under Putin than under Yeltsin.

As a result of a series of PR activities and promotion, the image of Putin is now becoming an uncontroversial tough man. It is not only good for his individual reputation, more importantly, very favorable for the Russian government to promote its international policies and actions.

公众人物国际公关 | International Public Relations of Public Figures

> **Case Study 案例分析**
>
> This is a successful pro-active case of public figure. According to the classification, Putin belongs to the group of political public, international public, voluntary public, complete public and accomplished public. In this case, Putin and the company that he hired are the PR subjects, through which we can see one of the biggest differences between public figures and common people is that public figures have abundant PR resources. Apart from Putin's personal efforts, his PR team takes a significant role. Governments and people from all over the world are the PR audiences.
>
> Maintaining Putin's hard-man image is not only important for him to win supports domestically, it also plays an important role for the Russian government in promoting its foreign policies. To shape an outdoor, sporty, tough guy public image, Putin has done a lot such as extreme sports and interaction with wild animals, moreover, Putin and his PR team have arranged many interviews with pleasing topic, for example, "Are you the coolest politician." Therefore, Putin's personal effort and his PR team made his "hard-man" image successfully shaped.

8.2.2 刘翔退赛危机公关

案例调研

刘翔退赛是北京奥运会上最大的冷门。2008年8月18日上午11点50分,当刘翔出现在鸟巢110米栏预赛跑道的时候,现场沸腾了。但当第一枪发令枪响,有对手抢跑后,刘翔在跑出5米远的时候收住步伐,并转身离开。那一刻,鸟巢里显得有些茫然。无数中国人的心里都留下一串串疑惑。

公关目标

"当危机爆发的那一瞬间,当公众的怒火一旦被点燃,就有迅速蔓延的可能性,控制形势的发展是当务之急,而最好的手段,就是道歉先行。"所以,打消公众的疑虑和误解成为首要公关目标。

公关实施

快速反应,真实披露信息

观众的这个疑惑也迅速地得到答案。在当天中午12点25分的新闻发布会上,中国田径队的总教练冯树勇和刘翔的教练孙海平道出了刘翔退赛是由于右脚的跟腱末梢炎症这一常年累积下来的老伤所致。冯树勇和孙海平还介绍刘翔在赛前训练的一些情况,使得退赛一事慢慢明朗起来。

道歉先行,赢取公众理解

公众很在意自己的感受。诚恳的道歉,向公众显示勇于承担和认真对待的负责态度,这样的举动一般能够起到减弱火势的作用。

8月18日晚间,刘翔退赛后接受央视采访。在短暂的采访中,刘翔真诚地向全国观众道歉,并且说明了退赛的历程以及受伤的情况。

权威支持,引导主流舆论

刘翔退赛后,医学专家或医生们纷纷从专业的角度向公众详细介绍刘翔的伤病。各大门户网站以及电视媒体分别用图解或者动画的形式来展示刘翔的伤病,这让公众能从最简易、最直观的方式了解到病情及它的危害。让医学专家从医学的角度来分析刘翔的"右肌腱末端病"更具说服力。而医学专家们基于刘翔的伤病做出"刘翔早就应该放弃"的判断,让公众对刘翔能够坚持要参加奥运会,出现在鸟巢,以及在比赛开始前大力踢墙以麻醉脚部神经的做法肃然起敬,深表感动。

全国主流媒体同样也对刘翔的退赛表示理解。在8月19日的《南方日报》上,题为《我们爱金牌,但我们更爱刘翔》的新闻引起读者的共鸣。在8月20日的《人民日报》海外版上,题为《刘翔养好伤从头再来》更是发出了媒体自己的声音。

代言企业力挺,消除刘翔后顾之忧

"金牌=广告",这是"奥运商战"中的潜规则。北京奥运会在家门口作战,广告商更希望自己的代言人刘翔能够一举夺冠,那么刘翔金牌带来的经济价值高达4.8亿元。但是,竞技体育的残酷让代言企业始料未及。飞人折翼退赛后,代言企业开跑危机公关110米栏。代言企业均快速反应,临时换新广告或者是继续采用刘翔的广告,力挺刘翔到底。耐克的动作最为迅速。在刘翔退赛的第二天,《南方都市报》封面有两张大图:一张是刘翔退赛后失落的背景;另一张是刘翔坚毅的正面特写,左侧是广告词:"爱比赛,爱拼上所有的尊严,爱把它再赢回来。爱付出一切,爱荣耀,爱挫折。爱运动,即使它伤了你的心。"耐克火速换上新广告并且在北京、上海、成都等地媒体显著位置上投放。其他企业也表态不会改变与刘翔的合作。中国平安发表声明称:"退出也是一种勇敢,我们不要舍命的一搏,平安就好。"

公众人物国际公关 | International Public Relations of Public Figures

公关评估

在刘翔及其公关团队采取一系列较为成功的公关措施以后,全国主流媒体同样也对刘翔的退赛表示理解。在8月19日的《南方日报》上,题为《我们爱金牌,但我们更爱刘翔》的新闻引起读者的共鸣。《刘翔养好伤从头再来》《理解刘翔退赛见证国民成熟心态》《刘翔因伤退赛依然是英雄》《有一枚最感人的金牌叫"宽容"》等媒体评论登上了新华网、《人民日报》等主流媒体的平台。医学专家们基于刘翔的伤病做出"刘翔早就应该放弃"的判断,让公众对刘翔能够坚持要参加奥运会,出现在鸟巢,以及在比赛开始前大力踢墙以麻醉脚部神经的做法肃然起敬,深表感动,彻底化解了危机。

> **Case Study 案例分析**
>
> 刘翔这个案例属于公众人物危机公关,根据其产生影响的不同阶段来分类,此案例属于既成公关,且是一个较为成功的主动型公关,其公关主体是以刘翔为中心的团队,目标公众包括粉丝、观众以及各大新闻媒体。
>
> 刘翔退赛成为2008年北京奥运会上最大的冷门,如何处理好这一事件既是对全国观众和媒体负责,更关乎刘翔本人今后的事业发展。在这个案例中,刘翔及其公关团队采取了一系列有效的措施保证刘翔的个人形象及商业前途受到最小的影响。包括快速反应,真实披露信息;道歉先行,赢取公众理解;找到权威支持,引导主流舆论等等实施公关策略都是刘翔及其公关团队的精彩应急之策。

刘翔的退役演讲稿[①]

作为一名运动员,我真的备感荣幸。上海是我的家,也是我的田径梦想开始的地方。今天很高兴在这里,有机会和大家说再见。

十几年来,跨栏成就了我的梦想,也给予了我无数的快乐和荣耀。我也努力把最好的自己表现给大家。人生总有高峰和低谷,在顺境中不失自我、不忘初心;在逆境时更能禁得起考验,勇于挑战梦想,敢于去做。虽然不是每次梦想都能成为现实,但孜孜追求的过程将成为我人生中一笔宝贵的精神财富。

跨栏是我所热爱的事业,陪伴我度过了最好的青春年华。每当我走上跑

[①] http://www.chinanews.com/ty/2015/05-17/7281715.shtml 2015年11月3日

道，我心中的热火仍在，不服输的斗志依然。但伤病困扰，让我感觉心有余而力不足，我只能坚强面对，选择离开自己心爱的田径赛场。

今天，我站在这里，心中有很多的不舍：不舍这条跑道、不舍那10个栏架，更不舍的是，支持我、陪伴我一路前行的朋友们。没有你们的支持和陪伴，我的人生不会如此精彩。你们的关心、理解和鼓励，让我感动、感激并感恩。今天，面对支持我的朋友们、面对跑道、面对栏架，我想告诉大家的是，在我个人职业运动生涯中，当我碰到过困难、挫折和对手时，我从来没有退缩过、逃避过、害怕过。我始终尽我所能，去努力、去挑战、去拼搏。在这里，真的有点激动。

感谢中国田径和上海市体育局，在我挫折和困难时，始终与我一起攻坚克难、不离不弃，没有你们的支持与培养，我也不会站在世界最高领奖台上。相信你们今后会培养出更多更优秀的世界田径健儿，在世界赛场为国争光。

最后，祝大家工作顺利、生活愉快。让我们一起祝愿，中国田径明天更美好。谢谢大家。

8.3 Further Reading 拓展阅读

8.3.1 Lewinsky Scandal PR

Research

After the 1998 elections, the House voted to impeach Clinton, based on alleged acts of perjury and obstruction of justice related to the Lewinsky scandal. This made Clinton the second US President to be impeached, after Andrew Johnson. Impeachment proceedings were based on allegations that Clinton had illegally lied about and covered up his relationship with 22-year-old White House intern Monica Lewinsky. After the Starr Report was submitted to the House providing what it termed as "substantial and credible information that President Clinton Committed Acts that May Constitute Grounds for an Impeachment," the House began impeachment hearings against Clinton before the mid-term elections. To hold impeachment proceedings, the Republican leadership called a lame-duck session in December 1998.

While the House Judiciary Committee hearings ended in a straight party-line vote, there was lively debate on the House floor. The two charges passed in the House (largely with Republican support, but with a handful of Democratic votes as well) were for perjury and obstruction of justice. The perjury charge arose from Clinton's testimony before a grand jury that had been convened to investigate perjury he may have committed in his sworn deposition during Paula Jones's sexual harassment lawsuit. The obstruction charge was based on his actions to conceal his relationship with Lewinsky before and after that deposition.

Objective

To decrease the negative effect on Bill Clinton, the public relations group must practice from both public and secret approaches.

Practice

News of the scandal first broke on January 17, 1998, on the Drudge Report, which reported that Newsweek editors were sitting on a story by investigative reporter Michael Isikoff exposing the affair. The story broke in the mainstream press on January 21 in *The Washington Post*. The story swirled for several days and, despite swift denials from Clinton, the clamor for answers from the White House grew louder. On January 26, President Clinton, standing with his wife, spoke at a White House press conference and issued a forceful denial in which he said:

> Now, I have to go back to work on my State of the Union speech. And I worked on it until pretty late last night. But I want to say one thing to the American people. I want you to listen to me. I'm going to say this again: I did not have sexual relations with that woman, Miss Lewinsky. I never told anybody to lie, not a single time; never. These allegations are false. And I need to go back to work for the American people. Thank you.

Pundits debated whether or not Clinton would address the allegations in his State of the Union Address. Ultimately, he chose not to mention them. Hillary Clinton stood by her husband throughout the scandal. On January 27, in an appearance on NBC's *Today* she said, "The great story here for anybody willing to find it and write about it and explain it is this vast right-wing conspiracy that has been conspiring against my husband since the day he announced for president."①

For the next several months and through the summer, the media debated whether or not an affair had occurred and whether or not Clinton had lied or obstructed justice, but nothing could be definitively established beyond the taped recordings because Lewinsky was unwilling to discuss the affair or testify about it. On July 28, 1998, a substantial delay after the public break of the scandal, Lewinsky received transactional immunity in exchange for grand jury testimony concerning her relationship with Clinton. She also turned over a semen-stained blue dress (that Linda Tripp had encouraged her to save without dry cleaning) to the Starr investigators, thereby providing unambiguous DNA evidence that could prove the relationship despite Clinton's official denials.

Clinton admitted in taped grand jury testimony on August 17, 1998, that he had had an "improper physical relationship" with Lewinsky. That evening he gave a nationally televised statement admitting his relationship with Lewinsky which was "not appropriate."

Evaluation

The scandal obviously affected the 2000 US presidential election. Democratic Party candidate and sitting vice president Al Gore said that Clinton's scandal had been "a drag" that deflated the enthusiasm of their party's base, and had the effect of reducing Democratic votes. Before and after the 2000 election, John Cochran of ABC News connected the Lewinsky scandal with a voter phenomenon he called "Clinton fatigue." Polling showed that the scandal continued to affect Clinton's low personal approval ratings through the election.

Bill Clinton's Speech to the American Public: Monica Lewinsky

Good evening,

This afternoon in this room, from this chair, I testified before the Office of Independent Counsel and the grand jury.

I answered their questions truthfully, including questions about my private life, questions no American citizen would ever want to answer.

Still, I must take complete responsibility for all my actions, both public and

---

① https://en.wikipedia.org/wiki/Monica_Lewinski_scandal 2014年9月13日

公众人物国际公关 | International Public Relations of Public Figures

private. And that is why I am speaking to you tonight.

As you know, in a deposition in January, I was asked questions about my relationship with Monica Lewinsky. While my answers were legally accurate, I did not volunteer information.

Indeed, I did have a relationship with Miss Lewinsky that was not appropriate. In fact, it was wrong. It constituted a critical lapse in judgment and a personal failure on my part for which I am solely and completely responsible.

But I told the grand jury today and I say to you now that at no time did I ask anyone to lie, to hide or destroy evidence or to take any other unlawful action.

I know that my public comments and my silence about this matter gave a false impression. I misled people, including even my wife. I deeply regret that.

I can only tell you I was motivated by many factors, first, by a desire to protect myself from the embarrassment of my own conduct.

I was also very concerned about protecting my family. The fact that these questions were being asked in a politically inspired lawsuit, which has since been dismissed, was a consideration, too.

In addition, I had real and serious concerns about an independent counsel investigation that began with private business dealings 20 years ago, dealings I might add about which an independent federal agency found no evidence of any wrongdoing by me or my wife over two years ago.

The independent counsel investigation moved on to my staff and friends, then into my private life. And now the investigation itself is under investigation.

This has gone on too long, cost too much and hurt too many innocent people.

Now, this matter is between me, the two people I love most—my wife and our daughter—and our God. I must put it right, and I am prepared to do whatever it takes to do so.

Nothing is more important to me personally. But it is private, and I intend to reclaim my family life for my family. It's nobody's business but ours.

Even presidents have private lives. It is time to stop the pursuit of personal destruction and the prying into private lives and get on with our national life.

Our country has been distracted by this matter for too long, and I take my responsibility for my part in all of this. That is all I can do.

Now it is time—in fact, it is past time to move on.

We have important work to do—real opportunities to seize, real problems to solve, real security matters to face.

And so tonight, I ask you to turn away from the spectacle of the past seven months, to repair the fabric of our national discourse, and to return our attention to all the challenges and all the promise of the next American century.

Thank you for watching. And good night!

Thinking:

1. Clinton addressed forceful denial in the beginning "I did not have sexual relations with that woman, Miss Lewinsky. I never told anybody to lie, not a single time; never." and the "speech to the American public: Monica Lewinsky," which speech do you prefer? Please explain it.
2. What's the attitude of the public towards Clinton's denial of Lewinsky Scandal in the beginning?
3. Please conclude some PR experiences on celebrity's crisis management.

8.3.2 陈光标慈善公关

案例调研

陈光标,1968年出生于江苏省泗洪县天岗湖乡,祖籍安徽省五河县,先后毕业于南京中医药大学、南京大学,中国企业家、慈善家,中国致公党党员,江苏黄埔再生资源利用有限公司董事长。

公关实施

2014年6月25日,陈光标在美国曼哈顿中央公园举行慈善午餐。陈光标为这顿宴请数百人的午餐亲自挑选菜品,包括芝麻金枪鱼、牛排、浆果等,他与三十多名身穿雷锋装的志愿者一起,举起"为人民服务"的标语,还与流浪汉们同唱英文歌"天下一家"。

宴会前,陈光标展示了装在篮子里的成捆美钞。宴会采用中式围桌的吃法,摆设圆桌、台布和瓷碗。

陈光标说,他想改变人们对中国有钱人只会花钱买奢侈品的印象。美联社说,他参加这次活动使用的名片上标注的英文头衔是"中国最有魅力的慈善家"。

公众人物国际公关 | International Public Relations of Public Figures

陈光标美国之旅发放的名片,上面印有"中国首善""中国最具影响力人物""中国精神领袖""中国最具号召力的慈善家""地震救援英雄""最著名最受爱戴的精神模范"等,陈光标英文名片上的一连串头衔令人震撼并引发争议。

陈光标表示,印刷在名片上的头衔都是有证书的,令网友误会,可能是因为将英文名片再度翻译成中文之后产生的误差。

陈光标结束纽约之行回国。7月1日上午,他出现在辽宁抚顺雷锋墓前,向雷锋墓献上了鲜花,同时还献上了《纽约时报》等外媒报纸,上面有关于他美国慈善之行的报道,并向"雷锋叔叔"汇报美国之行的成果。在雷锋墓前,他汇报多年来自己如何践行雷锋精神,以及这次去美国如何通过国际媒体,把雷锋精神传播到世界各地。陈光标认为首先是发自内心的,另外自己认为肯定能上头条,从没见过有人给雷锋墓磕头的,自己是第一个,又开创了历史。

此外,陈光标的出名事件还有很多。陈光标曾经携家人和公司员工,在贵州毕节举行了一场名为"一路慈善一路歌"的"个人演唱会"。在近两小时的演唱会中,民营企业家陈光标用他不太专业的嗓音,演唱了《好人一生平安》《爱的奉献》等共计9首歌曲。只要坚持听完全场的群众,就可以牵走一头猪或一只羊。

在演唱会前一周,陈光标还做了另外一件看上去很疯狂的事情:为了响应"9·22"中国城市无车日的活动,陈光标在他的公司内举办了一场活动,不仅亲手砸掉了他的一辆大排量奔驰车,而且还为集团的员工购买了200多辆自行车,提倡大家骑车上班。①

公关评估

陈光标的美国之行被美联社、法新社、路透社、新华网、人民网、凤凰网等多家媒体报道,登上了各大媒体的首页或APP客户端。新华社2013年4月22日发布了《"陈光标式慈善",你怎么看?》到22日17时,有4136名网友进行评论,8898名网友进行了转发,一些网友对高调慈善持保留态度,一些网友则力挺"标哥"。②虽然在美国的活动引起激烈讨论,但不少网友表示,应当在活动中寻找积极元素。一名叫科尔凯亚·艾卡的网友在CNN网站留言:"在这个充满私利和贪婪、逃税成风、种族隔阂的世界,这老兄至少想到了别

---

① http://www.doc88.com/p-8748593474886.html 2015年2月3日
② 《"陈光标式慈善",你怎么看?》http://news.xinhuanet.com/mrdx/2013-04/24/c_132333578.htm 2015年10月20日。

人。谁又会在乎他是不是个怪人呢？我希望更多的富人像他一样。"另一名网友留言："谁还记得特朗普上一次请流浪汉吃饭是什么时候？我想,当时特朗普被人赞扬无非是因为他是个白人。现在,一个中国有钱人请吃饭就得挨批？"[①]美国有线电视新闻网CNN援引陈光标的话报道："我不后悔,也不怕别人说什么,我会继续释放正能量。"

思考：

1. 按公关人物类型分类,陈光标属于什么类型的公众人物？试写陈光标慈善公关的案例分析。
2. 搜索一则陈光标的公关演讲讲稿和视频,结合公关演讲的理论分析陈光标公关演讲的特点和优缺点。
3. 比较普京的硬汉形象塑造和陈光标的慈善形象塑造,总结公众人物形象塑造的公关经验。

8.4 Simulation 情景模拟

8.4.1 Jolie's Breast Surgery PR

Angelina Jolie published a piece in the *New York Times* about her decision to undergo a preventive double mastectomy last month. As a carrier of a gene mutation called BRCA1, Jolie cut her chances of contracting breast cancer from 87 percent to fewer than 5 percent by undergoing the procedure. Her advocacy for all the women around the world to gain access to the too-expensive tests and procedures has empowered her to fight for her own life.

Jolie, for her part, addressed aesthetic concerns straightforwardly in her op-ed. (She also made a worrisome reference to "wonderful holistic doctors working on alternatives to surgery," which I can only hope won't steer readers away from the valid medical treatment they may need.) "There have been many advances in this procedure in the last few years, and the results can be beautiful," Jolie wrote. "On a personal note, I do not feel any less of a woman. I

[①] 陈光标纽约行善 有人叫好有人骂 http://news.xinhuanet.com/world/2014-06/27/c_126677140_2.htm 2015年10月21日

公众人物国际公关 | International Public Relations of Public Figures

feel empowered that I made a strong choice that in no way diminishes my femininity."

After hearing this breaking news, people held different attitudes toward it, though there're more understandings and approvals, some people still query about Julie's real intention. To respond that, Jolie's surgeon announced some details of the surgery。①

Simulation:

1. Simulate Angelina Jolie's PR team. Have a meeting to discuss what you will do before, during and after she published this news according to your research.
   Actors: Angelina Jolie, PR team, the fans and so on.
2. A newspaper which is going to interview Angelina Jolie. What questions are journalists going to rise? How will Julie answer?
   Actors: Angelina Jolie, journalists, audience, the fans and so on.
3. If you were a well-known breast doctor, how would you evaluate this news to make it more advantageous to your career?
   Actors: breast doctor, patients, the public and so on.

Angelina Jolie Tells Kids "Different Is Good" in a Passionate Speech

Angelina Jolie had a big night on 29 March 2015 at the Kids' Choice Awards, where she gave an inspiring acceptance speech after winning favorite movie villain for Maleficent. The actress started off by thanking all her fans, saying,

"When I was little, like Maleficent, I was told I was different and out of place ... never good at fitting in."

Angelina paused before adding,

"And then one day, I realized something, something I hope you all realize: different is good."

During the show, Angelina was seen smiling and laughing with her cute dates, daughters Zahara and Shiloh, and the two girls gave their mom a big hug

---

① http://vitals.nbcnews.com/_news/2013/05/16/18296909-doctors-detail-angelina-jolies-breast-surgery?lite. 2015年6月10日。

before she walked on stage to accept her award. The show marked her first public appearance since writing a powerful op-ed in *The New York Times* about her decision to remove her ovaries and fallopian tubes in order to prevent ovarian cancer.

8.4.2 名人吸毒危机公关

2014年8月,青年演员柯震东与房祖名在北京吸毒被抓。30日,柯震东在台湾二度举办道歉发布会,因为头一天北京的道歉发布会招来不少恶评,此次他不仅未声泪俱下,还拉近与媒体的距离,并正面回应尖锐问题,成功处理了公关危机。①

首先,及时调整姿态:缩减保安人数、近距离与媒体对话。

8月14日,柯震东在北京吸大麻被捕,遭行政拘留14天后,29日凌晨获释。29日下午,柯震东在经纪人柴智屏和父母的陪同下,在北京就吸毒一事举行道歉发布会。当天柯震东方面阵仗颇大,首先要求所有记者提前一天报名,需核对身份证件后才能领到入场帖,必须要贴在左臂并通过两道关卡方能入内,然后不准随意进出。

30日的台湾记者会,阵仗小了很多,除了父母未陪同外,保安也缩减为6人,同时柯震东也选择近距离与媒体对话。其经纪人柴智屏也就在北京要求媒体举右手保证维持秩序一事进行解释,称绝没有要在场媒体宣誓配合秩序,在北京也完全没有任何特权管道。

然后,否认表演痛哭,强调未提前准备声明稿。

北京道歉发布会上,柯震东发表了763个字的道歉声明,但因泣不成声,中途多次哽咽到无法说完整的一句话,足足说了十多分钟,被不少网友质疑"演戏"。

或许是吸取了教训,柯震东在台湾记者会上收起泪腺,神情镇定地道歉,再次强调自己犯了"非常严重的错误",做了"最不好和错误的示范","很抱歉在这时间让大家担心,我跟所有的人说对不起"。

同时,柯震东否认29日的痛哭流涕是"演戏",解释称因获释后情绪激动,难以控制,"没有办法想象到我所带来的错误有这么大影响,我很难过,我没必要去演这场戏,因为就是非常害怕"。

对于29日的演讲稿,柯震东坦言并非提前准备,"(内容)是这14天以来,

---

① http://ent.sina.com.cn/s/h/2014-08-31/00144201250.shtml 2015年1月29日

公众人物国际公关 | International Public Relations of Public Figures

我一直想要表达的,从一开始无助害怕不知所措,到后来沉思反省,心里想了很多事情,只是想把我认为的正确信息和错误示范让大家知道"。

再次,二度谈及房祖名,立场鲜明:不责怪,未来还是朋友。

在北京道歉会的采访环节中,柯震东否认被房祖名带坏,强调称:"是我自己做了不好的选择。"30日,他在台湾也独自扛起责任,谈到好友房祖名时表示,对方非常善良,"他一直以来很照顾我,给我很多正面能量,我们都犯错,但我相信他是个好人,也知道他是一个好人,他改错之后会是朋友"。

由于两人被捕后,又被曝出同场还有两位女星,柯震东承认认识其中的常一娇:"我们都犯错,这个时候就希望都一起改错。"

最后,复出态度谨慎,重回校园或服兵役。

提及何时能重返演艺圈,柯震东不予回应,他仅说,现在只能让自己更好,越来越好,"这种事情我会尽力去做,尽我可能去做,对粉丝,我非常抱歉,拜托他们不要模仿我,希望传递正面信息,对他们我非常抱歉。"

其经纪人柴智屏也回答了关于柯震东未来计划的问题,"公司跟他个人讨论后,有没有可能去当兵,或者继续完成学业,还都有待讨论"。

针对网友关注的《小时代4》,柴智屏表示,《小时代4》剧组已在第一时间跟柯震东方面沟通,她称:"因为该片是大家的同作品,不会因为震东个人的问题毁于一旦,电影应该可以上映,但震东会不会去做宣传,还需要讨论。"

虽然柯震东吸毒行为依旧饱受热议,但不少业内人士都称赞其团队专业,能第一时间提供消息,也积极配合媒体采访。

模拟:

角色分配:柯震东,其经纪公司团队,柯震东父母,柴智屏,娱乐八卦报记者数名,成龙。

场景设置:北京和台北两场新闻发布会,柯震东出狱回家路上。

剧情安排:演绎背景场景,并结合事件发展走向,设计模拟出该事件相关方从各个层面应对此事件时如何开展公关的。

要求:结合公关演讲技巧知识,先草拟出你认为可能的柯震东新闻发布会上的演讲稿,再通过对比分析柯震东的演讲稿。在依据事实的前提下可以适当增加戏剧性,充分展示此次公关的难点和可取之处。模拟后总结名人危机公关事件处理的过程、原则和方法。

Exercises
本章练习题

Gap Filling 填空题

Directions: Fill in the blanks with the correct form of the words and expressions provided.

impeach	commit	allegation	definitively
term	contract	breaking	advocacy
deputy	high-profile		

1. After the 1998 elections, the House voted to _____ Clinton, based on alleged acts of perjury and obstruction of justice related to the Lewinsky scandal.
2. The perjury charge arose from Clinton's testimony before a grand jury that had been convened to investigate perjury he may have _____ in his sworn deposition during Paula Jones's sexual harassment lawsuit.
3. Pundits debated whether or not Clinton would address the _____ in his State of the Union Address.
4. Nothing could be _____ established beyond the taped recordings because Lewinsky was unwilling to discuss the affair or testify about it.
5. Some services that Ketchum Company did for Russia were purely _____.
6. Putin, 60, is serving his third _____ since 2000.
7. In addition, Ketchum also called for the _____ of the US State Department's criticism on Russia's human rights record.
8. As a carrier of a gene mutation called BRCA1, Jolie cut her chances of _____ breast cancer from 87 percent to under 5 percent by undergoing the procedure.
9. After hearing this _____ news, people held different attitudes toward it.
10. Her _____ for all the women around the world to gain access to the too-expensive tests and procedures have empowered her to fight for her own life.

公众人物国际公关 | International Public Relations of Public Figures

Multiple Choice 选择题

Directions: In this part there are 5 sentences. For each sentence there are four choices marked A, B, C and D. Choose the ONE answer that best completes the sentence.

1. Which one can be described as the first reaction of Liu Xiang's public relations after his quit in Olympics?

   A. Dodged about and evaded the truth

   B. Inactive and Passive

   C. Quickly reacted to face the issue

   D. Showed no interest on the query and doubt from the outside

2. Which one played an irreplaceable role after Liu Xiang's doctor gave an authoritative explanation?

   A. The media

   B. His family

   C. The enterprises that he acted as the spokesman

   D. The officials of the National Sports Bureau

3. How did Clinton react after the scandal was exposed to the public?

   A. He made a presentation that ends with a short commentary on the Monica Lewinsky scandal, which admitted his affairs with Monica.

   B. He made a presentation that ends with a short commentary on the Monica Lewinsky scandal, and said that: "I did not have sexual relations with that woman, Miss Lewinsky."

   C. He never truly directly replied the scandal to any media.

   D. He used some channel to blockade the scandal to further spread out.

4. Which of the following media is relatively the most uncontrollable one in nowadays society?

   A. Newspaper   B. Television Station

   C. Radio Station   D. We-Media

5. From 2006 to 2012, ( ) the main PR Company that serves Putin and Russian government.

   A. Pravda   B. Vladimir

   C. Ketchum   D. Gazprom

Table Completion 表格题

请按照公共人物公关的不同类型填充下列表格。

分类标准	类型
	政治性公众人物 Political Public 社会性公众人物 Social Public
行为人主观意愿	
	完全的公众人物 Complete Public, 有限的公众人物 Limitative Public
产生影响的不同阶段	

Paraphrase 释义题

Directions: Explain the following sentences in your own words.

1. However, if celebrities carry out inappropriate public relations work, or take an inactive attitude towards public relations, there's a high chance that not only their situations be further deteriorated, but also produce a "chain reaction", resulting in image crisis the region, industry and even the nation to which they belong.

2. Due to the crisis in Ukraine, relation between Russia and the United States has fallen to the freezing point since the Cold War of the last century.

3. Every move of public figure may produces large responses from the society, and may has a direct influence on public affairs.

4. Because public figures have this extraordinary influence in society, we usually regard them as special social organizations.

5. Vice president Al Gore said that Clinton's scandal had been "a drag" that deflated the enthusiasm of their party's base, and had the effect of reducing Democratic votes.

公众人物国际公关 | International Public Relations of Public Figures

思考题：

1. 请结合本章理论，探究公众人物公关和普通人物公关在基础、实施和效果平息等不同方面的优劣势。
2. 通过对本章案例的详细分析以及情景模拟的具体实施，你能再搜索并分析几个典型的公众人物公关案例吗？

International Public Relations of Ordinary Figure
普通人物国际公关

Gist
内容概览

People reinvent themselves all the time to take on new challenges, shift into more-meaningful work, or rebut perceptions that have hindered their career progress. Taking control of your personal image may mean a rewarding career, different from an unfulfilling job. As Longfellow[①] noted, "We judge ourselves by what we feel we are capable of doing, while others judge us by what we have already done." Your path may make perfect sense to you, but how can you persuade others to embrace your new brand—and take you seriously?

This chapter will discuss the necessity and significance for an ordinary figure to manage public relations in the new media age and by explaining the principles of interpersonal communication, and giving examples of each, students may acquire the ability to effectively and skillfully implement public relations and build their image whether regionally or globally.

人们总是在迎接一个个新的挑战，转向更有意义的工作，或反驳阻碍了职业生涯进步的观念中重塑自我。掌握你的个人形象可能意味着区别没有成就感的工作和成功的事业。Longfellow指出，"我们是根据自己能做什么来定位自己，而别人是根据我们已经做的来评价我们。"你的道路可能完美，但你怎么能说服别人接受你的定位，并认真对待你呢？

随着网络时代的到来，信息传播速度以及覆盖面积正以惊人的速度疯狂蔓延，使得普通人物公关具有突发性、爆炸性、无国界性等特点。充分认识

---

① Henry Wadsworth Longfellow (February 27, 1807— March 24, 1882) was an American poet and educator whose works include "Paul Revere's Ride," The Song of Hiawatha, and Evangeline.

普通人物国际公关 | International Public Relations of Ordinary Figure

普通人物公共关系管理的重要性和必要性,进而把公共关系作为一种有效的管理思想和方法,已成为当前促进个人发展的一个重要方面。本章以普通人物为公关行为主体,介绍了普通人物国际公关的定义、属性、分类和技巧,选取了有代表性的普通人物公关双语案例,学生在学习完本章后,了解到普通人物公关的技巧与方法,更好地培养自己的形象意识、传播沟通意识和公众意识,强化技术技能、人际关系技能等。

9.1 Basic Knowledge
基础知识

9.1.1 Definition 定义

Public relations of ordinary figure, to some extent, is a kind of interpersonal communication and personal brand (image) building process. It is an exchange of information between different people through media, during which there is message sending and message receiving. This can be conducted using both direct and indirect methods. Successful PR of ordinary figure is when the message senders and the message receivers understand the message.

By comparison to the PR of public figures, the PR of ordinary figures is relatively more self-dependent and self-protection-oriented. The reasons can be traced back to their natures:

(1) Different in Resources

Ordinary people usually do not occupy so sufficient PR resources like a professional PR team which may consist of manage company or entrepreneurial organization, for organizing and implementing specific strategies and tactics to shape their image. Therefore, it happens more in passive situations.

(2) Different in Methods

As a result of limited resources, ordinary people usually choose economic methods to spread ideas or to improve reputation, especially we-media like blogs and other social media websites.

Essential to an understanding of PR activities are the following elements: source—receiver, encoding—decoding, messages (including meta-messages, feedback and feed-forward), channel, noise (physical, physiological, psychological, and semantic) and context (physical, social—psychological, temporal, and cultural).

Also, there are some points the players should notice: if a message can be understood in different ways, it will be understood in just that way which does the most harm.

There is always somebody who knows better than you what you meant by your message. The more communication there is, the more difficult it is for communication to succeed.

These tongue-in-cheek maxims are not real principles; they simply humorously remind us of the difficulty of accurate PR communication.[①]

公共关系活动的含义是指一个组织或个人为了塑造自身的良好形象,以传播沟通为手段,对公众采取的一种持久的策略行动。公共关系必须是塑造形象和面对公众两者的密切结合,缺一不可……只要是塑造形象和面对公众两者相结合,无论是组织或个人均可成为公共关系活动的主体[②]。因此,所谓"普通人物公关",是指作为个体的人为了更好地服务公众、实现自我价值而塑造自身的公众形象,为自己创造一个良好的人际环境的活动。

普通公众:具有普通公民身份的、不具有广泛社会影响力的公民。

国际性普通公众:属于普通公众,但由于其特殊的跨地域身份,可能形成跨国家影响力的公众。

普通公众群体:通常在某一事务中以群体身份被认知,其影响力和被影响力都与其整体形象有十分紧密的联系。

普通个人作为社会组织的重要组成部分,不能离开社会而独立存在,个人的管理——即公共关系塑造及维护是在同社会各方面的交往中进行的。随着网络时代的到来,信息传播速度以及覆盖面积正以惊人的速度疯狂蔓延,使得普通人物公关具有爆发性、无国界性等特点。

普通公众的公关与公众人物的公关既有相似之处,也有不同之处。相同点在于他们的目的可能都是为了传播某种思想、塑造某种个人或组织形象、改变或提升某种公众普遍认知等等,而不同点往往在于以下几点:

(1) 实施公关的资源不同

普通人物公关不像公众人物先天具有良好的公关资源,如经济支持、专

---

① Livingstone, Sonia, Wang, Yinhan, "Media Literacy and the Communications Act: What has been Achieved and What Should be Done?" London: Department of Media and Communications, 2013.

② 方宪玕,《公共关系学教程(第六版)》。杭州:浙江大学出版社,2004。

普通人物国际公关 | International Public Relations of Ordinary Figure

业团队、丰富经验等等,因此普通人物的公关往往是被动的,为了维护某种声誉或权利而不得已发起的公关。

(2)实施的方式不同

由于普通人物资源有限,他们往往选择经济便利的方式,尤其在网络和自媒体发展迅猛的今天,博客等社交网站等已成为普通人物公关的主要根据地。

虽然这两者之间有很大的差异,但普通人物若进行良好的公关策略实施,极有可能演变成为公众人物,所以这两者在前期有很大不同,但在后期又有很多相似之处。

9.1.2 Nature 属性

Public relations of ordinary figure, by its very nature, is still part of public relations.

Purposeful

(1) To learn. Interpersonal communication enables you to learn, to better understand the world of objects, events, and people—whether you do this face to face or online. In fact, your beliefs, attitudes, and values are probably influenced more by interpersonal encounters than by formal education.

(2) To relate. Interpersonal communication helps you relate to others and to form meaningful relationships whether it's face to face or online. Such relationships help to alleviate loneliness and depression, enable you to share and heighten your pleasures, and generally make you feel more positive about yourself.

(3) To influence. Very likely, you influence the attitudes and behaviors of others in your interpersonal encounters—to vote a particular way, to try a new diet, to see a movie, or to believe that something is true or false.

Power-involving

No public relationship exists without a power dimension. You cannot communicate without making some implicit comment on your power or lack of it. When in an interactional situation, therefore, recognize that on the basis of your verbal and nonverbal messages, people will assess your power and will interact accordingly.

(1) You hold legitimate power when others believe you have a right—by

virtue of your position—to influence or control their behaviors.

(2) You have referent power when others wish to be like you. Referent power holders are often attractive, have considerable prestige, and are well liked and well respected.

(3) You have reward power when you control the rewards that others want. Rewards may be material (money, promotion, jewelry) or social (love, friendship, respect).

(4) You have expert power when others see you as having expertise or knowledge. Your expert power increases when you're seen as unbiased with nothing personally to gain from exerting this power.

Ambiguous

Ambiguity is a condition in which a message can be interpreted as having more than one meaning. Sometimes ambiguity results when we use words that can be interpreted differently. Informal time terms offer good examples; different people may interpret terms such as soon, right away, in a minute, early, and late very differently. The terms themselves are ambiguous.

Punctuated

There's no clear-cut beginning or ending. As a participant in or an observer of the communication act, you engage in punctuation: you divide up this continuous, circular process into causes and effects, or stimuli and responses.

A Process of Adjustment

Content and relationship messages serve different communication functions. Being able to distinguish between them is prerequisite to using and responding to them effectively.

普通人物的公关仍然属于个人公关活动，从这个角度，它仍有个人公关的局限性、易操作性与易受影响性。

个人作为一个单薄的社会力量，在社会活动中要想成功地塑造、维持或扭转成为一个为人接受的状态，需要付出极大的努力。一方面是因为个人的力量微小，社会影响对其危害极有可能是其不易承受的；另一方面是因为社会对个人的关注度十分有限，若该个人不及时更正，则可能永远被保留该恶劣形象。

普通任务的公关又应当区别于公众人物的公关，因为他们不具备公众人物的影响力和公关经验，往往是处于被动的。

普通人物国际公关 | International Public Relations of Ordinary Figure

9.1.3 Classification 分类

Based on different criteria, the classification can be divided into various types. Generally speaking, there are positive and negative types:

（1）根据不同目的可分为

个人身份转变公关/主动型公关（Positive PR）：公关事件与活动中的普通个人由于主观想要被认知或需要维护其形象而进行的公关措施，体现为为了达到某种目的而通过各种手段提升自己的知名度，俗称炒作。

个人维权公关/被动型公关（Negative PR）：公关事件与活动中的普通个人由于客观被迫不得不被认知或需要维护其形象而进行的公关措施。在新媒体迅猛发展的今天，这种被曝光而进行的公关逐渐突显，体现为个人权益受到损害而发起的不得已的公关行为。

（2）根据不同态度可分为

回避型公关：在被迫需要进行公关活动以应对危机时，往往采取"挤牙膏"式的手段，不直接开展应对措施。

直面型公关：积极主动地面对事件，从各方面动用资源开展各类公关活动以扭转局面，改善其形象。

（3）根据不同方式可分为

传统公关：在开展公关的方式上，通常选择传统的宣传工具，如口口相传以及纸质媒体，或是利用实体活动，如新闻发布会等进行。

新媒体公关：在开展公关的方式上，通常选择新型电子领域的宣传工具，如微博等较为普及与活跃，影响力较大的互联网领域进行。

9.1.4 Evolution 演变

Phase One

In the early stage, there are few or no systematic public relations of ordinary figure. The general form of PR of ordinary figure is interpersonal communication, and there are four principles of it.

Inescapable

The very attempt not to communicate communicates something. Through not only words, but through tone of voice and through gesture, posture, facial expression, etc., we constantly communicate to those around us. Through these channels, we constantly receive communication from others. Even when you sleep, you communicate. Remember a basic principle of communication in general: people are not mind readers. Another way to put this is: people judge you by your behavior, not your intent.

Irreversible

You can't really take back something once it has been said. The effect must inevitably remain. Despite the instructions from a judge to a jury to "disregard that last statement the witness made," the lawyer knows that it can't help but make an impression on the jury. A Russian proverb says, "Once a word goes out of your mouth, you can never swallow it again."

Complicated

No form of communication is simple. Because of the number of variables involved, even simple requests are extremely complex. Theorists note that whenever we communicate there are really at least six "people" involved: 1) who you think you are; 2) who you think the other person is; 3) who you think the other person thinks you are; 4) who the other person thinks /she is; 5) who the other person thinks you are; and 6) who the other person thinks you think s/he is.

We don't actually swap ideas, we swap symbols that stand for ideas. This also complicates communication. Words (symbols) do not have inherent meaning; we simply use them in certain ways, and no two people use the same word exactly alike.

Contextual

In other words, communication does not happen in isolation. There is:

Psychological context, which is who you are and what you bring to the interaction. Your needs, desires, values, personality, etc., all form the psychological context. ("You" here refers to both participants in the interaction.)

Relational context, which concerns your reactions to the other person—the "mix."

Situational context deals with the psycho-social "where" you are communicating. An interaction that takes place in a classroom will be very different from one that takes place in a bar.

Environmental context deals with the physical "where" you are communicating. Furniture, location, noise level, temperature, season, time of day, all are

普通人物国际公关 | International Public Relations of Ordinary Figure

examples of factors in the environmental context.

Cultural context includes all the learned behaviors and rules that affect the interaction. If you come from a culture (foreign or within your own country) where it is considered rude to make long, direct eye contact, you will out of politeness avoid eye contact. If the other person comes from a culture where long, direct eye contact signals trustworthiness, then we have in the cultural context a basis for misunderstanding①.

Phase Two

In recent years, with the emerging and booming of social media, there are very few aspects of modern life and business that haven't been changed profoundly by the rise of social networks and other new forms of communication and connections.

In this period, three characteristics often considered together are PR of ordinary figure's inevitability, irreversibility and unrepeatability.

Inevitable: often it is intentional, purposeful, and consciously motivated. Sometimes, however, you are communicating even though you may not think you are or may not even want to.

Irreversible: in online communication, the PR activities are written and may be saved, stored, and printed. Both face-to-face and online messages may be kept confidential or revealed publicly. But computer messages can be made public more easily and spread more quickly than face-to-face messages, because

(1) E-messages are virtually impossible to destroy. Often e-messages that you think you deleted will remain on servers and workstations and may be retrieved by a clever hacker or simply copied and distributed.

(2) E-messages can easily be made public. Your words, photos, and videos on your blog or on a social networking site can be sent to anyone.

(3) E-messages are not privileged communication and can easily be accessed by others and be used against you. And you'll not be able to deny saying something;

---

① Four Principles of Interpersonal Communication http://www.pstcc.edu/facstaff/dking/interpr.htm 2015年12月23日

it will be there in black and white.

Unrepeatable: everyone and everything are constantly changing. As a result, we never can recapture the exact same situation, frame of mind, or relationship dynamics that defined a previous interpersonal act.[①]

虽然这普通人物公关和公众人物公关之间存在各种差异,但在良好周全的公关策略下,一旦提升了知名度,普通人物就会成为名人,其公关手段从而极有可能与一般公众人物重合,这就是普通人物公关的大体演变过程。这里我们主要介绍普通人物个人身份转变公关和维权公关两种。

(1) 个人身份转变公关的演变

在最初阶段,普通人物由于资源和条件限制,不具备实施大范围、大规模宣传和公关的可能性,因而会选择低成本、低消耗的媒介进行操作,如丰富的自媒体平台。而当其通过自身手段成功使名气得到提升时,相关利益方会为其提供更丰富可靠的支援,从而手段和目的也会随之发生改变。

(2) 维权公关的演变

由于本质上这属于被动型的公关,该普通人物的根本目的是维护其自身权益或声誉,因此总是会经历开始的威胁,然后才做出反应,接着调整策略的过程。其公关思想可能也会因此而经历从被动到主动的演变。

普通人在公关活动开展过程中,面临着新媒体网络时代电子领域影响日益加强的局面,新媒体的诞生和发展促使越来越多的普通人面临着公关的压力,因此,普通人的公关无论是主动型还是被动型,都在前期、中期与后期各个阶段对新媒体有日益加深的利用和依赖。

9.1.5 Process of Practice 实施过程

Step 1 The problem or the purpose. View a public relations interaction as a problem to be resolved, as a situation to be addressed or the attention you want to exert. Here you try to understand the nature of the PR situation, what elements are involved, and, in the words of one PR model, who did what to whom with what effect. Let's say that your "problem" is that you said something you shouldn't have and it's created a problem between you and your friend, family member or the public. You need to resolve this problem.

---

① Adapted and reorganized from *My Communication Lab*. http://www.pearsonmylabandmastering.com/northamerica/mycommunicationlab/ 2015年9月21日

普通人物国际公关 | International Public Relations of Ordinary Figure

Step 2 The criteria. Here you ask yourself what your specific public relations goal is. What do you want your message to accomplish? For example, you want to admit your mistake, apologize and be forgiven. Or you want to surprise or shock the audience and become an overnight success.

Step 3 The possible solutions. Here you ask yourself what some of your PR communication choices are. What are some of the messages you might deliver?

Step 4 The analysis. Here you identify the advantages and disadvantages of each public relations choice.

Step 5 The selection and execution. Here you communicate what you hope will resolve the problem and get you forgiveness or fulfill your goal of becoming famous.

普通人物公关不同于已具备良好条件的公众人物,其传播影响力有限的原因可能导致其公关效果缓慢或微不足道,当然这也正是它的优势所在:往往可以有充分的时间将公关策略考虑周全。通常,普通人物要做到化劣势为优势,要做到:

(1)研究环境变化,选择有利时机。普通人物建设公共关系,选择时机非常重要,选择好的时机可以让其搭上"顺风车",借局势和时机的优势为自己打造一个良好的"第一印象"。

(2)选择恰当方式。普通人物公关的方式有限,因此充分利用资源,合理规划操作方式显得尤为重要,比如纸质媒体和社交媒体面对的受众不同,通过恰当的方式选择来达到自己面向不同受众的不同目的本身就是一种公关策略。

(3)礼貌待人,注意礼节。

由于普通公众文化水平有限,公关经验不丰富,可能因为过于通俗的语言和强烈以个人为中心的心态导致与公关目的背道而驰的局面。因此,普通人物的公关一定要在措辞和形象上保持高度警惕。

另外,考虑到普通人影响力极小,且以被动型为主的客观特点,其公关活动在实施过程中的真实可信以及诚恳态度的地位就尤为重要。

普通人物国际公关所采取的基本手段是传播沟通,通过各种传播沟通手段使公众了解、理解、信任并支持自己,它往往遵循一种公事公办的原则。传播存在不同的方式,如人际传播(个人与个人之间的信息沟通与交往)、小范围传播(群体内的人际沟通活动)、公众传播(传播主体向相对集中的较大公众群体进行的传播)和大众传播(职业的传播者通过大众传播媒介而进行的传播)等。普通人物公关人际传播和小范围传播为主,大众传播和公众传播为辅。近年来,随着新媒体的发展,后者的运用更多,作用更明显。

9.1.6 Interpersonal Relationship 人际交往能力

普通人物公关过程中,如何与公众打交道,塑造良好的个人形象,树立良好的人际关系至关重要,本章专题将探讨普通人物公关技巧之提高人际交往能力。

(1) 什么是人际交往

社会学将人际关系定义为人们在生产或生活活动过程中所建立的一种社会关系。心理学将人际关系定义为人与人在交往中建立的直接的心理上的联系。人们常指人际交往是人与人交往关系的总称。人是社会动物,每个个体均有其独特之思想、背景、态度、个性、行为模式及价值观,然而人际关系对每个人的情绪、生活、工作有很大的影响,甚至对与公众沟通有极大的影响。

(2) 什么是人际交往能力

人际交往能力是指妥善处理组织内外关系的能力。包括与周围环境建立广泛联系和对外界信息的吸收、转化能力,以及正确处理上下左右关系的能力。

(3) 人际交往本质

人际交往也称做"人际传播",这是一种人类传播的特殊样式。其特殊性在于人际交流强调交流者的传播境遇与交流关系的独特性是把传播看做建构自我身份的一个过程,看做发生在具有不同个性特征,不同的社会与文化认同的人之间精神上的对话。

(4) 人际交往主要方式

现代人际交流有许多种形式,如会见、往来、倾谈、争论、讲演、会议、教学等,随着新媒体的发展,博客、微信公众号等成为人际交往的主要方式,成为普通人物进行公关最重要的手段之一。

(5) 互联网空间中的人际交往

网络空间的突显,创造了人际交往的新平台、新模式。网络世界展示的新生活质态,对传统的人际交往产生的实质影响,不仅体现在使人际交往成本减低,交往效率提高,联系速度加快,而且体现在创造了人际交往的全新空间,使人际交往从原来"点对点""点对面"的熟悉的强联系人群拓展到了

普通人物国际公关 | International Public Relations of Ordinary Figure

遥远、陌生的弱联系人群,呈现出"面对面"的人际交往所没有的新形态。这使得从前几乎不可能实现的普通人物公关萌芽、发展、兴起。其特点有以下几点。

① 不同于现实社会人际交往

现实社会的人际交往,可以不依赖媒介而面对面地展开,而网络人际沟通则完全依赖互联网这个媒介。网络空间的人际交往,是一种经由网络媒介的沟通(computer-mediated communication),互动双方并不像在现实社会中那样面对面地亲身参与沟通(in-person communication)。

② 更加自由

互联网的匿名性和开放性特征,使人们在网络空间的自我呈现比在真实世界更为自由。人们可以充分利用网络的匿名和连接功能,扩展自己的人际交往,充分地在陌生人面前展示自己。

③ 广阔无国界

一个完全开放的空间,其中存在着无数的不确定因素与无限的可能性,任何国家的人都可以在其中按照自己的意愿和喜好与别人交流和沟通,因此,网络空间亦提供了比以往任何交往方式都要广阔得多的对话界面,这为普通人物进行国际公关提供了可能。

(6) 提高人际交往能力的技巧

① 共享

共享突出体现在微博中。微博上绝大部分的发布,包括转发和评论,就是一种通常并不特定发生在两个对象之间的分享,往往同时向其他关注者和网友公开,它像是一个麦克风,一个用户发布信息的点对面的舞台式话语传播平台。普通人物通过共享,语言辐射面更广,人际交往更有效,公关效果更好。

② 理解

每个人都有个性、文化、社会这个传播共同体所赋予我们的特殊认同。我们在待人处世,表达自我与理解他人时,会有与众不同的特性,甚至会出现许多不和谐之音。理解对于良好人际交往至关重要。

③ 线上线下联动与整合的立体化塑造

仅仅依靠网络,人际交往与普通人公关的效果有限。因为,人们对于网络平台的信任度往往低于传统媒体,人们更习惯抱着围观心理和娱乐心态来看待发生在网络上的事情,半信半疑多于坚信不疑。如果能够很好地运用整合策略,用心地将线上发布和宣传与线下的实际行动,乃至与传统媒体的跟踪报道结合起来的话,往往会收到事半功倍的效果。

此外,普通人进行人际交往、国际公关时还应注重真诚原则、宽容原则、互利合作原则、平等原则、信用原则等技巧,树立可信良好的个人形象。①

9.2 Bilingual Case Studies
双语案例

9.2.1 David Chang: The Road to Fame

Research

David Chang is a Korean-American chef and entrepreneur. He is the founder of the Momofuku restaurant group, which includes Momofuku Noodle Bar, Momofuku Ssäm Bar, Má Pêche, Milk Bar and Momofuku Ko in New York City, Momofuku Seiōbo in Sydney, Australia and the Momofuku Toronto restaurants Momofuku Noodle Bar, Nikai, Daishō, Shōtō and Milk Bar.

The burly Mr. Chang, whose previous careers included junior golf champion (he burned out at 13) and entry-level Park Avenue financial functionary (he got drunk at the office Christmas party and burned his bridges) never plotted to become a celebrity chef. An ambassador of celestial ramen noodles and all things porcine at the place he calls his baby, Momofuku Noodle Bar, "Maybe."

How did Chang make his restaurants popular and himself a super chef? To a large extent, his success owes to the serial PR activities he generated.

Objective

The objective of David Chang's PR activities can be divided into three aspects. First, spreading his culinary philosophy; second, achieving his career pursuit; and third, publicizing his restaurants and gaining profits.

Practice

Cooking in His Way

Chang's website states momofuku means "lucky peach," but it is likely a reference to Momofuku Ando—the inventor of instant noodles. In August 2006, Chang's second restaurant, Momofuku Ssäm Bar, opened a few blocks away. In

---

① 王怡红,《关系传播理论的逻辑解释——兼论人际交流研究的主要对象问题》,《新闻与传播研究》,2006年第2期,第21-26页。

普通人物国际公关 | International Public Relations of Ordinary Figure

March 2008, Chang opened Momofuku Ko, a 12 seat restaurant that takes reservations ten days in advance, online only, on a first-come-first-served basis. The highly limited seating, along with Chang's popularity in New York, has caused a furor, generating frustration for both influential and ordinary people who have failed to secure a reservation.

Mr. Chang has not structured the new dinner menu to distinguish between appetizers and entrees, instead grouping his dishes. He has real imagination, coupling sea urchin roe with litchi-flavored tapioca pearls and a snowy cloud of whipped tofu on which bonito flakes, sesame seeds and bits of dried vegetables are sprinkled. He has standards: the grilled slices of pork sausage and hanger steak provided for different lettuce wraps were juicy and flavorful enough to be eaten on their own.

His advice to vegetarians and snooty diners is to go eat someplace else. Not here at the Ssam Bar (a Beard Foundation nominee for best new restaurant), nor at Ko (it means "child" in Japanese), which will open in Noodle Bar's spot when the mother ship moves to larger quarters at the end of the summer. Noted for his "bad-boy attitude (no reservations, no vegetarian options)," Chang created a controversy in 2009 by making dismissive remarks about California chefs, telling Anthony Bourdain: "They don't manipulate food, they just put figs on a plate." In the same year, it was reported that Momofuku Milk Bar's Crack Pie, Cereal Milk and Compost Cookies were in the process of being trademarked, which aroused heated discussion.

"We just want to make great food at an affordable price. And we don't copy. I've got the Emersonian take on that: Imitation is suicide."

Enter the Public Eyes Initiatively

Chang likes trying different things, which provides him with more opportunities to enter the public eye.

He participated in several episodes of the 2010 HBO television show Treme, together with other famous chefs. In September of 2013, David appeared on a skit on the Deltron 3030 album, Event 2. In the fall of 2012, David—along with executive producer Anthony Bourdain — launched a 16 episode series on PBS called The Mind of a Chef. In December 2013, during the third annual Mad Symposium, the acclaimed founder of the Momofuku restaurant empire talks candidly about having the courage to follow his own path and the theme of his speech was Guts.

Cooking Is a Kind of Culture

In October 2009, Chang and former *New York Times* writer Peter Meehan published *Momofuku*, a highly anticipated cookbook containing detailed recipes from Chang's restaurants.

In summer 2011, David Chang released the first issue of his Lucky Peach food journal, created with Peter Meehan and published by McSweeney's. The theme of Issue 1 was Ramen. The theme of Issue 2 was The Sweet Spot, and this issue became number 3 on *the New York Times* bestsellers list. Issue 3: Chefs and Cooks, was released on March 13th, 2012, and was also a *New York Times* Bestseller. The fourth issue was published on July 3 and was entitled the American Food issue. These printing greatly spread his cooking philosophy.

Free Recipes and Open Classes

In some popular or professional websites, such as *New York Times* and *Eater*, David Chang's recipes are offered free of charge to the public. In addition, he recorded an episode of the podcast Science and Cooking.

Evaluation

Reviews from *The New York Times* said that "David Chang is a terrific cook, a pork-loving, pickle-happy individualist whose integration of Asian flavors and his own unbound sense of what's delectable makes for some deliriously enjoyable meals. At Momofuku Noodle Bar, which he opened in 2004, and at Momofuku Ssam Bar, which came along in 2006, he has proven himself one of this city's brightest culinary talents."

PBS says that "Chef and restaurateur David Chang is enjoying an incredible run in the culinary world," and that, "Whether cooking in his kitchens in New York and Australia, or traveling for inspiration to Japan, Denmark, Spain or Montreal, David brings a voracious appetite for food knowledge and a youthful exuberance to cooking and travel."

David is the creative force behind New York City's wildly popular Momofuku restaurants. Along the way, he's racked up just about every major cooking award: In 2007, he was the recipient of that year's James Beard Foundation rising star award for best new chef; In 2009, one of his restaurant

普通人物国际公关 | International Public Relations of Ordinary Figure

was awarded 2 Michelin stars, which it has retained each year since; He was listed on the 2010 list of the *Time* 100 Most Influential People.

In addition, Chang has served as a guest judge on Top Chef: All Stars; In 2011, he was a guest judge on MasterChef Australia. And David Chang now has opened 16 restaurants in New York, Sydney and Toronto.

> **Case Study** 案例分析
>
> This is a proactive PR and a new media PR of an ordinary figure. The purpose or the objective of David Chang's PR activities is to attract public attention with his culinary philosophy and to make his restaurant popular.
>
> As an ordinary person with limited PR resources, David Chang chose economical methods to spread ideas and improve his reputation like we-media blogs and other social media websites. Through this, he is successful in thinking from the customers' point of view, and providing them with free online resources about how to cook. With the spread of information on Internet, he and his restaurants have subsequently become famous worldwide.
>
> The emergence of new social media has transformed traditional public relations and is providing the common people with countless new opportunities to attract the attention of public. Sharing food recipes and classes on Internet, David Chang attracted many fans and became an overnight success.
>
> In a word, David Chang's PR campaign is well-prepared successful PR.

9.2.2 "布鞋院士"李小文

案例调研

2014年4月18日,院士李小文在中国科学院大学做讲座时被拍的一张照片走红网络。照片里,蓄着胡须的李小文穿着黑色外套,没穿袜子的脚上蹬着一双布鞋,不经意地跷着二郎腿,低头念着发言稿。据了解,67岁的李小文专长于遥感基础理论研究,他曾创建Li-Strahler几何光学模型,成名作被列入国际光学工程协会"里程碑系列"。李小文传奇的经历一层层被剥开,网络上充满了排山倒海的惊叹之声。山村老人形象与院士身份形成的强烈反差,让网友惊叹,"一派仙风道骨,完全就是古龙笔下的侠士"。

自照片发布,"布鞋院士"已登上新浪微博热门话题榜首,讨论量达8万。"李小文"作为关键词,迅速排在了搜索引擎的第一位;他在科学网开设的博客,成了一周热门博客第一名,点击量迅速超过了400万次。

发表在《光明日报》2014年6月11日第9版上的一篇文章更是直指要踏踏实实向李小文学习。

众人多惊叹李教授学术造诣之高与衣着打扮之朴素形成强烈反差,不少人直白地表达敬佩之情,"这才是真正的学者"等夸赞的话语高频出现,有网友说,照片里的李小文像《天龙八部》里的扫地僧,低调、沉默,却有着惊人天分和盖世神功。

公关目标

作为国内遥感领域泰斗级专家,李小文在学术界早就是人尽皆知的"技术宅"和"优质叔"。然而对于普通大众来说,李小文是以"布鞋院士"加以那张广为流传的照片走红的。面对突如其来的"成名",李小文要做的似乎并不是趁热打铁,提升知名度。相反,潜心做学术、淡泊名利的他要做的是一场与媒体、大众周旋,逃离公众热捧的公关。

公关实施

接受采访:"冷一冷"

在科学网打去的电话里,李小文说:"冷一冷"。媒体和网友的持续关注成了他的负担。他希望用这种方式让舆论的山洪消退。李小文的声音低沉而果断,这种气场与照片里"看似做脱贫报告的老人"似乎格格不入,只有在提到网友对他的评价时,他才哈哈一笑:"谢谢网友们。"

走红照片与讲座:"没什么特别"

2014年4月18日的那场讲座在李小文看来,这只算一次与学生们的闲谈,没什么特别。如果不是因为那张照片,媒体蜂拥而至,他能平静地研究遥感领域"流形"与"分形"的区别,或者继续研究环保部和国土部发布的全国土壤污染状况调查公报。

对付新闻:有高招

67岁的老人有自己对付新闻的高招。有时,他会在电话里陪笑,"理解一下,理解一下";有时他会用商量的语气说,"再等等,等这波热点过去吧"。

李小文了解新闻的传播规律,希望赶紧出个新闻,为自己那张被热炒的

普通人物国际公关 | International Public Relations of Ordinary Figure

照片降降温,过了两天温度没降,他又略带委屈地向记者解释,"本以为这两天热度会过去的",然后在邮件里和记者商量,能不能以文会友。李小文说记者四处寻他让他很不好意思,自己文字不好,写文章有些词不达意,向记者请教文章该写成什么样子才算合格。其实李小文在谦虚,他用几句简单的古文,就可以解释复杂的遥感原理。

博客留言:视线转移

博客里,近百名网友给李小文留言,说他红了。李小文不做回应,只以"敬答好友"为题留下博文,里面只有一个链接,是河南贫困县舞阳县的贴吧。2014年4月初,舞阳县中小学数千名教师停课罢工,抗议政府克扣工资,一直没得到回应。有网友揣测李小文的本意,他不希望自己作为院士因为一张照片走红,而是希望更多的普通教师的合法权益,得到应有的关注。

公关评估

李小文院士淡泊名利、执着科研,为日趋浮躁的科研界重树了榜样和信心。面对突如其来的走红,他反其道行之,以一位学者的智慧巧妙地与媒体记者、公众、粉丝周旋,实施的是一场让人由衷钦佩的公关,事实业已证明,这是一场成功的公关。

李小文院士去世后,科学网建立专题专门悼念李小文,其科学网博客也将永久保留,网友的悼念文章笔者仅在目录部分就翻了十几页。国庆、中秋佳节时,众多网友也纷纷留言怀念、祝福老师。Boston University Earth & Environment机构也发表专题文章说道:"The 'Cloth Shoes' Academician, Li Xiaowen has passed away. From now on the 'Humble Sage' is no longer with us."

> **Case Study 案例分析**
>
> 这是普通人物回避型公关。新媒体时代的到来,使得普通人物公关具有爆发性、无国界性等特点。网络上随便的一句话、一张图片可以捧红一个路人,缔造一个又一个的社会公众人物。李小文院士就是其中之一。
>
> 回顾李小文院士与媒体、公众进行的公关活动,我们可以总结为以下两个特点:一、李小文院士所进行的公关活动是被动公关和回避型公关。面对突如其来的走红,他反其道而行之,公关目标是逃离媒体和公众的热捧,一心一意做学术。二、李小文院士的公关活动中有

着丰富的与学生的人际交往活动。在科学网博客上,李小文院士经常与网友亲切互动,为学生答疑解惑。纵观李小文院士个人公关活动的实施,他所展现的是朴素率真的性格,谦虚低调的品质。

9.3 Further Reading
拓展阅读

9.3.1 Luxor Temple Carving Issue PR

A Picture of Graffiti Uploaded to Weibo

On May 24, 2013, a Chinese traveler logged on to the social media site Weibo and posted a snapshot of a 3500-year-old Luxor Temple carving that had been scratched over with the phrase, "Xiao Ming (not his real name) was here" on the original Weibo post, the traveler also wrote, "The saddest moment in Egypt. I'm so embarrassed that I want to hide myself. I said to the Egyptian tour guide:'I'm really sorry,'" "We want to wipe off the marking with a towel. But we can't use water since it is a 3500 relic."

A Topic of Great Concern

The photo quickly went viral, prompting online outrage, and netizens reposted a picture of the scrawl alongside their outraged comments. "Reading this disastrous news this morning is heartbreaking. I despise this behavior, especially in Egypt—the place I love. Now, I just want to say 'Sorry' to Egypt," commented weibo user "Net bug jing jing." "It's a disgrace to our entire race!" said another angry micro-blogger.

The original Weibo post was re-posted almost 90000 times, received over 18000 comments and was widely distributed across international and local media.

The Vandal Was the Subject of a Cyber-Manhunt

On the evening of May 24, this issue was ranked first in the events hot search list of Sina micro blogging. On May 25, a Chinese netizen unearthed personal information pertaining to Xiao Ming, a 15-year-old middle school student from Nanjing, through the Human flesh search engine and posted it to

普通人物国际公关 | International Public Relations of Ordinary Figure

Weibo. Xiao Ming's behavior was slammed online and exposed further in the mainstream. The calls for Xiao Ming should apologize roared online.

On May 26, a website of Xiao Ming's elementary school was hacked by vigilante netizens and defaced with a pop-up window on the website mimicking Xiao Ming's vandalism. When opening the website, visitors saw "Xiao Ming was here" pop first, and only when clicking "yes" could the visitor continue browsing.

Objective

The objectives of Xiao Ming's PR activities can be divided into two aspects: first of all, save and rebuild the image of Xiao Ming by begging the public for their forgiveness; second, help Xiao Ming to restore his normal calm life, and avoid any further negative consequences of this action.

Considering the fact that Xiao Ming is still a minor, the PR measures mainly carried out by his parents.

Practice

Contact the Media and Issue a National Apology

Amid online declarations of national disgrace and social-media death threats, Xiao Ming's parents reacted quickly and then on May 25, 2013, they contacted the media outlets.

Xiao Ming's family came forward to express their regrets in the local newspaper *Modern Express*. They said that they shouldered the responsibility for what their son did, adding that Xiao Ming had learned his lesson. "We want to apologize to the Egyptian people and to people who have paid attention to this case across China," Xiao Ming's mother stated, adding that the boy had "cried all night" out of shame over the incident. "He has realized he made a mistake, and we beg your pardon; please give him a chance to correct his act."

Reporter reminded people that Xiao Ming's home was in an old district, and he and his parents were ordinary people. Within the over-one-hour interview, the mother was emotional and crying, "I feel that they are at a loss," the reporter added. At first, they wanted to contact the central media and openly publish a letter of apology in the newspaper. However, it was too late.

Xiao Ming's parents came forward and the apology was covered by the media at home and abroad.

Release a Letter of Apology in the Micro Blogging

At 22:00 on May 26, 2013, the Sina Weibo user "Xiao Ming 1999" released a letter of apology, and the letter led to heated discussions among users.

The Chinese Graffiti Has Been More or Less Removed

On May 27, Xinhua News Agency's official micro blogging "Xinhua Viewpoint" reported that local Egyptian staff had worked to try to clean the sculpture according to a photo taken by one of the agency's photo journalist. While there was some improvement, the graffiti could not be totally removed.

Evaluation

The Chinese people are very sensitive about their international reputation. That explains why a single act of tourist vandalism—committed by the Chinese citizen while overseas—has created social-media uproar in the country. Although the subsequent PR measures Xiao Ming's parents took were passive, their timely response and sincere apology stopped the further spread of the Luxor Temple carving issue, which turned out to be a relatively successful international PR effort of ordinary people.

To a large extent, such measures divert public attention from criticism of an individual to criticism of the improper supervision of the parents and the phenomenon of uncivilized tourist behavior which happens frequently in overseas travel. Thus some local and international media have covered the apology and some pointed that "A Chinese teenager defaced the Luxor Temple. That's bad, and scribbling is as old as tourism," illustrating the ubiquity of the vandalism.

Thinking:

1. In the case Luxor Temple Carving Issue, what did Xiao Ming's parents do? Did they realize the objective of PR?
2. Why did the "Cloth Shoes" Academician want to avoid media and public's attentions? What did he do to achieve his goal?
3. As reactive PR, what's the difference between the two cases Luxor Temple Carving Issue and "Cloth Shoes" Academician?
4. What characters of ordinary figure's IPR revealed in the two cases Luxor Temple Carving Issue and "Cloth Shoes" Academician?

普通人物国际公关 | International Public Relations of Ordinary Figure

9.3.2 斯诺登:"棱镜门"前后的系列公关

案例调研

2013年6月5日,英国《卫报》报道:美国国家安全局有一项代号为"棱镜"的秘密项目,要求电信巨头威瑞森公司必须每天上交数百万用户的通话记录。6月6日,美国《华盛顿邮报》披露,过去6年间,美国国家安全局和联邦调查局通过进入微软、谷歌、苹果、雅虎等九大网络巨头的服务器,监控美国公民的电子邮件、聊天记录、视频及照片等秘密资料。美国舆论随之哗然。随后,爆料又称,美国政府不仅对国内实行监控,其盟国及中国在内的其他国家都未能幸免。白宫政府陷入"棱镜门"监控丑闻。

这一事件的爆料人正是爱德华·斯诺登,只是美国中央情报局(CIA)前普通雇员的他迅速走进了全世界人民的视野,成为众多媒体竞相报道的对象。斯诺登随即遭美国政府通缉。

公关目标

斯诺登本人身份经历了巨大的转变,他从无人知道的普通人到一夜之间全球关注,他在爆料前后积极采取系列公关措施,主要目的分为:爆料前,1.引起世界舆论关注;2.获得媒体公众信任;爆料后,1.应对来自美国政府的压力;2.寻求政治庇护;3.获得美国民众支持;4.寻找世界舆论支持。

公关实施

主动公开身份

爆料后不久,英国《卫报》在他的授权下公布了一段事先录制好的视频专访。在视频里,斯诺登不仅公布了个人信息,还告诉全世界,"我为什么要这么做"。他说,过去四年,他一直为美国国家安全局的军事承包商工作,因此有机会接触到安全局的秘密项目。泄密者在秘密披露主动公布自己的身份,这需要勇气和谋略。

选择合适的记者与媒体

第一个被斯诺登找上门的,是美国纪录片女导演劳拉·波伊特拉斯。她的作品常以"美国政府侵犯人权"为主题,代表作《祖国、祖国》讲述美军占领下的伊拉克。近年来,劳拉也在着手调查美国政府是否广泛监视、监听。斯诺登还研究过劳拉的政治立场、社交圈子、行为特点等,最终抛出绣球——拍摄他泄密逃亡的整个过程。

第二个"被敲门"的是英国《卫报》专栏作家格伦·格林沃尔德。格林沃尔德专长民权自由、美国国土安全等领域,曾出书批评美国前总统布什滥用

"爱国者法案"。斯诺登向他转交了近2万份美国政府的秘密文件。除此之外,香港本地英文媒体《南华早报》的记者 Lana Lam 也是由斯诺登钦点的,她长期从事网络犯罪报道。

身为美国人,斯诺登为什么没有找上《纽约时报》?据悉,斯诺登记得2005年《纽约时报》压下记者揭露小布什政府未经授权监听的报道,次年才发,斯诺登以此为鉴,绕过《纽约时报》。

塑造爱国形象

斯诺登用一系列言语和细节为自己塑造爱国形象。对于被怀疑当了俄罗斯间谍,爱德华·斯诺登在莫斯科接受美国杂志《纽约客》的采访,坚决否认自己是俄罗斯间谍,并称这种猜测是荒唐而可笑的。2014年5月29日,斯诺登接受了美国全国广播公司(NBC)的独家采访。斯诺登就在俄罗斯申请政治避难给出回应,称自己并未受俄罗斯政府指使,并且在1年的避难期间没有向俄当局提供过任何情报信息,自己与俄罗斯政府毫无关系,俄罗斯没有在背后支持他,他没有受资助,也不是间谍。

2014年8月,美国《连线》杂志在最新一期封面刊登了斯诺登受访时拍摄的照片。照片中,斯诺登紧紧抱着美国国旗,两眼注重远方,表情严肃凝重,星条旗配上那若有所思的深邃眼神,真是十足的爱国范儿。照片一经发布,便引来外界普遍关注。《连线》杂志总编辑斯科特·达迪奇表示,斯诺登在整个拍摄过程中都很自然,本能地将美国国旗抱在怀中,并坚称自己是一名爱国者,强调其热爱美国。

与大众保持沟通

从2013年到2014年,斯诺登不时接受媒体访问,还以视频连线方式出现在世界各大活动中。2014年1月24日,爱德华·斯诺登举行网上直播答问会,就网友关心的监控相关问题回答了提问。他在回答中强调,自己"没有盗取过任何密码"。 2014年7月20日,斯诺登从莫斯科通过视频连线到纽约举办的黑客(HOPE)大会,呼吁与会黑客开发简单易用的反监控技术,在世界范围内消除监控行为,并表示他将把自己的多数时间用于推广此类技术,包括允许人们匿名通信和邮件加密的技术。斯诺登在隐匿自己行踪的同时积极保持着同大众的沟通。

声东击西

斯诺登离开香港前开始放风,说冰岛是他流亡的目的地。外界质疑香港飞冰岛途中需要转机第三国,很可能遭到扣押。最后斯诺登踏上俄航班机飞往莫斯科,到了俄罗斯,又说买了去古巴的机票,料到记者们一窝蜂飞去,

普通人物国际公关 | International Public Relations of Ordinary Figure

结果自己悠哉悠哉地逗留莫斯科中转站。斯诺登声东击西,巧妙地转移了媒体记者注意力,更好地隐藏自己行踪。

公关评估

尽管仍然饱受争议,但斯诺登所进行的系列公关措施成效依旧显著,为他赢得了众多美国民众及世界舆论的支持。

自2013年6月9日《卫报》抛出专访,至次日下午2时,白宫请愿网页上要求赦免斯诺登的条目已迅速搜集到两万个签名。2013年12月11日,美国《外交政策》杂志评选美国国安局承包商前雇员爱德华·斯诺登为2013年全球百名思想家榜首;2014年1月2日,《纽约时报》发表社论,认为爱德华·斯诺登扮演的是检举人角色,其揭发的信息具有重要价值,呼吁对他予以赦免或从宽处理。2014年1月29日,挪威前部长索赫捷尔推荐斯诺登为诺贝尔和平奖提名人。

思考题:

1. 请从公关主体、目的、具体措施、效果等方面对比David Chang与斯诺登所做公关的不同。
2. 斯诺登在公关实施方面有哪些成功技巧?
3. 一些普通人物为什么积极开展主动公关?有哪些开展主动公关的方法?

9.4 Simulation 情景模拟

9.4.1 Jiang's Kiss in the Airport

Jiang is from Jiangxi, China. He went to the United States to study in 2004. He is now a doctoral student of molecular biology at Rutgers University in New Jersey. His girlfriend lives in Los Angeles. She came to see Jiang one day. In January 3, 2010, Jiang went to the Newark airport to see his girlfriend off, which resulted in him trespassing in a safety zone, leading to the terminal being closed for 6 hours. Thousands of passengers were forced to delay their flights to submit to a security check. Therefore, the night of January 8, 2010, America law enforcement officers arrested Jiang at his home. This became an international news story.

Airport surveillance video displays that Jiang secretly crossed through the security isolation of a channel to kiss and rendezvous his girlfriend. Then they went hand in hand into the passenger security check area before entering the area. Twenty minutes later, he left. The night of January 8, he was detained at home, on charges of trespassing. Jiang was released at midnight on January 8 and was scheduled to appear in court the following week, facing up to 30 days in jail.

The latest video that American officials published on January 7, 2010 showed the cause of the closure of New Jersey, Newark International Airport terminal was a man sneaking into the alert zone and kissing good-bye to a female passenger. This led to the airport being closed for several hours. More than 100 flights could not take off, and thousands of passengers' trips were delayed. Based on reports from CCTV news, the kiss which paralyzed American airport passengers is not an American's, but instead an overseas student named Jiang.

Although from an emotional point of view, Newark Airport's way to deal with this issue was a little extreme, but taking into account that the USA had just experienced "Christmas Eve terrorist attacks," and in consideration of all of the passengers' safety, closing the terminal, and "stricting" to Jiang's behavior is the implementation of flight crisis early warning management. It was to reduce the probability of an air crash accident. At the same time, the airport should strengthen site management work during this period, and avoid having relevant personnel to leave their post.

Simulation:

1. Scene reconstruction: Imagine that you were Jiang and his girlfriend. Please take us back to the day when this thing happened and the process of how it moved forward. Your team will need at least three actors to play the role of Jiang, his girlfriend, and policeman who arrests Jiang.
   Actors: Jiang, his girlfriend, the policeman, etc.
2. An interview: After this news widely reported by the Chinese media, Jiang's life must have been intensively affected. Simulate a press conference held by Jiang. Jiang wants to reduce public anger and reshape his image. How would

普通人物国际公关 | International Public Relations of Ordinary Figure

Jiang answer questions asked by journalists at home and abroad?

Actors: Jiang, the journalists, etc.

3. Investigation: As Jiang's girlfriend and his other friends, if you were asked about your opinion on Jiang's actions, how would you respond?

Actors: Jiang's girlfriend, Jiang's friends and a journalist.

9.4.2 请吃切糕：大学生最可爱的危机公关

案例调研

湖南岳阳的"切糕事件"曾经一石激起千层浪，网友对"切糕党"冷嘲热讽，不少人现身说法，痛斥天价切糕的万恶。一块切糕上升到了"民族问题"，加上地域歧视、个人仇恨式的感情宣泄，整件事以"切糕党"形象跌至谷底而告终。

"切糕党"的买卖不好做了，"党外人士"自鸣得意，但"一竿子打翻一船人"误伤了多少诚实守法的新疆人？没有准确的数据，证明不了新疆人做买卖的手法均是"强买强卖"，把"卖切糕的"等同于"切糕党"的逻辑是粗暴的。因为一粒"老鼠屎"否定一个群体，弥合不了本来就已存在的心灵裂缝，更让两者之间的距离越发疏远，使仇恨的种子深埋彼此心底。

被妖魔化的"切糕党"成了过街老鼠，切糕虽然还在卖，但少有人问津，他们的买卖受到了严重的冲击。虽然有媒体用一贯善用的"煽情"文章为"切糕党"正名，但一家之言回天无术，并不能改变这个群体今时今日在中国的窘况。良心媒体开始拨乱反正，而善良的人选择用自己的一言一行，为少数民族挽回声誉。

公关目标

让"切糕事件"应该成为一个反思的起点，让"新疆大学生请吃切糕"也成为一个友好的新起点。

公关实施

吉林财经大学的一个学生团体"Enactus"想让同学们认识一个真实的切糕，于是找到新疆班的阿布，阿布出了700元钱，找同乡做了一个大切糕，让同学们免费品尝。"大家对切糕有误会，我就是想让大家了解切糕。"这一举动受到了同学们的欢迎，他们赞阿布是"糕富帅"，那堵"互相提防"的墙顷刻间土崩瓦解。

这可爱的危机公关在提醒公众：对抗的情绪，破坏掉了整个社会、族群之间信任的基石。"切糕党"如此，"大嘴巴"也如此，别再株连无辜的人了。

模拟:

背景:还原和模拟吉林财经大学的学生团体"Enactus"所进行的"为切糕正名"的活动。学校广播站记者采访和宣传"为切糕正名"的活动。

角色:阿布、"Enactus"社团几名同学、学校记者、学生、路人等。

策划:如果是你们学校的学生团体想要开展类似"为……正名"活动,你应当如何策划这场公关活动?

角色:社团成员、学生、记者、路人等。

Exercises
本章练习题

Gap Filling 填空题

Directions: Fill in the blanks with the correct form of the words and expressions provided.

| rack | slam | restore | exuberant | divert |
| plot | flavor | forefront | prompt | uproar |

1. The photo quickly went viral, _____ online outrage.
2. Xiao Ming's behavior was _____ online and exposed further in the mainstream.
3. Xiao Ming wants to _____ his normal calm life, and avoid the bad effects this issue may bring.
4. Chinese are very sensitive about its international reputation. That explains why a single act of tourist vandalism has created a social-media _____ in the country.
5. Such measures _____ public attention to the criticism of the improper supervision of the parents and the uncivilized phenomenon repeatedly showing up in overseas travel.
6. He never _____ to become a celebrity chef.
7. The grilled slices of pork sausage and hanger steak provided for different lettuce wraps were juicy and _____ enough to be eaten on their own.
8. David brings a voracious appetite for food knowledge and a youthful

普通人物国际公关 | International Public Relations of Ordinary Figure

_____ to cooking and travel.

9. Along the way, he's _____ up just about every major cooking award.

10. The screen is covered almost the person's face, and their name began to occupy the _____ of the major topics on the list.

Multiple Choices 选择题

Directions: In this part there are 5 sentences. For each sentence there are four choices marked A, B, C and D. Choose the answers that best complete the sentence.

1. Which of the following jobs has David Chang never done?
   A. Golfer　　　　B. Official　　　　C. Chef　　　D. Banker

2. The following are examples of David Chang's "bad-boy attitude." Which one is not correct?
   A. He advises vegetarians and snooty diners to go eat somewhere else.
   B. His dismissive remarks about California chefs, "They don't manipulate food, they just put figs on a plate."
   C. There are no reservations and no vegetarian options in his restaurants.
   D. Momofuku Milk Bar's Crack Pie, Cereal Milk, and Compost Cookies were in the process of being trademarked

3. By saying "Imitation is suicide," David Chang refers that_____.
   A. Imitation is the highest form of flattery.
   B. They sold fast food to the people in the neighborhood.
   C. The food in his restaurant is unique.
   D. Imitation will hinder the restaurant's development in the long run.

4. Which of the following is the correct order of the events that happened to Chang?
   ① He participated in the several episodes of the HBO television show Treme, along with many other famous chefs.
   ② He appeared in a skit on the Deltron 3030 album, Event 2.
   ③ He launched a 16 episode series on PBS called The Mind of a Chef.
   ④ He talked candidly about having the courage to follow his own path and the theme of his speech was "Guts."
   A. ①②③④　　　B. ②①④③　　　C. ④②③①　　　D. ①③④②

5. From the PBS reviews that "Chef and restaurateur David Chang is enjoying an incredible run in the culinary world," we cannot infer that David Chang _____.

A. Enjoys running in a virtual world. [This doesn't quite make sense].

B. Achieve a lot in cooking.

C. Is a prestigious restaurateur.

D. Plays an important role in the culinary world.

Paraphrase 释义题

Directions: Explain the following sentences in your own words.

1. These tongue-in-cheek maxims are not real principles; they simply humorously remind us of the difficulty of accurate PR communication.

2. You have referent power when others wish to be like you. Referent power holders are often attractive, have considerable prestige, and are well liked and well respected.

3. We don't actually swap ideas, we swap symbols that stand for ideas. This also complicates communication. Words (symbols) do not have inherent meaning; we simply use them in certain ways, and no two people use the same word exactly alike.

4. E-messages are not privileged communication and can easily be accessed by others and be used against you. And you'll not be able to deny saying something; it will be there in black and white.

5. David Chang is a terrific cook, a pork-loving, pickle-happy individualist whose integration of Asian flavors and his own unbound sense of what's delectable makes for some deliriously enjoyable meals.

Thinking 思考题

1. 结合前几章的学习，请总结出普通人物国际公关的主要步骤。

2. 对比公众人物国际公关，分析普通人物进行国际公关的劣势有哪些？怎样克服？

普通人物国际公关 | International Public Relations of Ordinary Figure

3. 你认为当普通公众被迫曝光后,应当如何处理其与媒体的关系?
4. 普通人公关往往面临着向公众认识转换角色的过程,你认为在这种转换期间应当注意哪些公关技巧呢?请结合情景模拟,分阶段进行回答。
5. 在新媒体时代,个人可以从哪些方面提高自己的人际交往能力,塑造良好的形象?

参考答案

第一章

Exercises 本章练习题

填空题

1. settlers
2. press agentry; publicity
3. strategic communication process
4. Practioner
5. press release

判断题

1. True 正确
2. True 正确
3. False 错误
4. True 正确
5. False 错误

表格题

阶段	实施内容
调研——Research	了解该国在国际公众心目中的形象地位,对开展公关活动的条件、困难、实现目标的可能性等情况进行了解,可以为决策提供科学依据。
目标——Objective	组织通过策划和实施公关传播活动所追求和渴望达到的一种状态或目的,是国际公关全部活动的核心和公关工作努力的方向。根据国际公关的主要工作内容,派生出国际公关的三大基本目标,即形象设计与塑造、关系协调、传播与沟通。
操作——Practice	国际公关主体为了实现既定的目标,充分依据和利用实施条件,对国际公关的创意策划进行实施策略、手段、方法设计并进行实际操作与管理的过程。
评估——Evaluation	主要是在活动末期从准备过程、实施过程、活动影响等方面开展工作。准备过程中,要考虑到背景资料、调查形式等因素;实施过程要考虑媒体参与数量、信息发送数量、影响公众数量,活动影响则要将最终结果纳入考虑范围内。

阅读理解

D A C A A

第二章

Exercises 本章练习题

填空题

forecast	tore	broached	evacuated
drastic	swept	get...across	instantaneously
cost-prohibitive	resume		

选择题

C B C D C

阅读理解 China National Publicity Film（Feature）

D C A B C

第三章

Exercises 本章练习题

填空题

1. maintaining, dissemination 2. hard-power 3. reduction
4. infancy 5. catastrophic 6. distribution
7. official 8. consecutive 9. Brazil Cost

判断题

1. True 正确 2. True 正确 3. False 错误 4. True 正确
5. False 错误 6. True 正确 7. False 错误 8. False 错误
9. False 错误 10. True 正确

简答题

1. 三个阶段；第一个阶段以亚历山大、汉密尔顿为首的争取宪法获得批准的运动被称为"有史以来最杰出的公共关系工作"；第二个阶段公共关系先驱爱德华·伯纳斯的《舆论的结晶》（Crystallizing Public Opinion）；李普曼的《舆论学》。第三阶段：斯科特·卡特里普和艾伦·森特出版的《有效公共关系》

2. "Tell you own tale"（以我为主提供情况）；"Tell it fast"（尽快提供情况）；"Tell all"（提供全部情况）

3. 维护政府和国家的良好形象；获得民众的支持与理解。

阅读理解

B A B A B

第四章

Exercises 本章练习题

选择题

C　　C　　B　　C　　D

填空题

1. 政府间国际组织　　2. 世界政府,常设机构
3. 国际公共物品　　4. 价值共识
5. 上善若水　　6. 新中装

表格题

1. 双边的或多边的会议
2. 按与会的代表性
3. 单一议题的和多种议题的会议
4. 最高级会议(即首脑会议)、部长级会议、大使级会议和专家会议

释义题

1. In a legal sense, what differs international organizations from simple coalitions of states is whether these associations have been found by a constituent document. For example, G8, a simple grouping of states without formal charters, is only regarded as a task group.

2. The expected effects of IGO public relations practitioners lie in enhancing the bottom line, bonding harmoniously member states with each other, and taking care of its internal interests while considering various needs of external interests, which become more complicated.

3. The social media will be used by WHO on World Healthy Day to get people involved and change people's old opinions on aging. WHO's social media will provide many positive images stories, and precious roles of senior citizens in current society.

第五章

Exercises 本章练习题

填空题

1. improves　　2. rely on　　3. roam　　4. dependent
5. diverse　　6. Empowering　　7. awareness　　8. emphasizes
9. sophisticated　　10. differ

选择题

| D | B | B | C | C | D |

连线题：

国际奥委会	IOC
世界气象组织	WMO
绿色和平组织	Greenpeace
国际特赦组织	AI
世界自然基金会	WWF
乐施会	OXFAM
福特基金会	The Ford Foundation
国际野生生物保护学会	WCS

表格题：

Charitable orientation	Ford lFoundation, The Clinton Foundation, Acumen Fund
Service orientation	International Committee of the Red Cross, OXFAM
Participatory orientation	WWF, IFAW, WMO
Empowering orientation	BRAC, Mercy Corps

释义题

1. Charitable orientation means those well-organized paternal organizations that only a few "beneficiaries" can take part in. NGOs who target to meet the needs of the poor also are included in this group.

2. The local brickies and consignees have benefited from Sanishop model because the Sanishop has trained them to develop entrepreneurial skills. Except for creating employment, trained brickies and consignees get trained to construct sustainable sanitation for their communities. The Community-Led Total Sanitation(CLTS) workshops also undertake the training work for the Sanishop consignees.

3. The logo of WWF manifests the importance of giant panda. The idea of WWF logo came from a giant panda named Chi-Chi that was living at the London Zoo in 1961 when WWF was created. WWF's founders are conscious of the significance of the symbol. Only a strong, recognizable symbol would overcome all languages obstacles. They all knew that with appealing, black-patched eyes, the big furry panda would be an optimal choice.

简答题

1. 见非政府组织的定义与分类

    乡村发展、扶贫、教育、卫生、儿童、环境保护、人道主义救济、难民安置、和平主义运动等

2. 略

3. 略

思考题 略

第六章

Exercises 本章练习题

填空题

1. retained	2. recruiting	3. convey	4. term	5. economically
6. triggered	7. evaded	8. consultation	9. disastrous	10. compelled

选择题

B C D A D

表格题 略

简答题 略

释义题

1. Generally speaking, foreign TNCs carry out PR activities just for handling crises, which are very reactive; they should take the initiative to conduct PR activities for forecasting and preventing crises, maintaining and building their images as well.

2. Aimed at expanding the market in the third world, Nestle boosted that breast-feeding was primitive and inconvenient and can reduce lactation, while bottle feeding baby was a better choice, which altered people's existing common sense.

3. With the boycott escalating, Nestle was unable to decide what to do because it was in a dilemma of whether to spend a lot in satisfying customer' demands or not, and it also worried the subsequent influence on its finance.

4. Shell's main scope of business consists of the exploration, production, refining and marketing of oil and gas products, while there also exist a chemicals business and independent division for developing renewable energy sources.

思考题 略

第七章

Exercises 本章练习题

填空题

1. infancy, exploration, development   2. seeking   3. maintain
4. embarked   5. spread   6. on behalf of

判断题

1. False 错误   2. True 正确   3. True 正确   4. True 正确   5. False 错误

连线题

释义题

1. The Internet giant Tencent has launched an application called Wechat which people can use their mobile phones to sent texts, photos, videos and voice messages. Plenty of people in China become the WeChat fans due to its convenience, and now WeChat has more than 600 million users since its first release in 2011.

2. With brand image at the core of its business identity and strategy, Haier was aware of the significance of brand which was its most precious resource, so Haier's goal was to build a strong, leading national brand name in the early days.

3. Sany Group emphasized that the company is determined to fight back US president Barack Obama through judiciary proceedings. Sany will stick it out and they may appeal to the circuit court or the supreme court of the United States if there is a need.

4. The corporation public relationship in China has gone through three stages: the initial period; formative period and the development period. China's Corporate Communications started later than Western countries, therefore we need to learn oversea experience and combine our actual situation, and thus we can solve all kinds of crisis and shape a full-responsible image.

思考题 略

第八章

Exercises 本章练习题

填空题

1. impeach
2. committed
3. allegations
4. definitely
5. deputy
6. term
7. high-profile
8. contracting
9. breaking
10. advocacy

选择题

C　　C　　B　　D　　C

表格题

分类标准	类型
公法的角度	政治性公众人物 Political Public 社会性公众人物 Social Public
行为人主观意愿	自愿性公众 Voluntary Public 非自愿性公众 Involuntary Public
时间属性	完全的公众人物 Complete Public 有限的公众人物 Limitative Public
产生影响的不同阶段	潜在公众人物 Potential Public 既成公众人物 Accomplished Public

释义题

1. Nevertheless, when people who share high reputation confront muffed PR tactics and action, there's a great possibility that they would be affected personally. At the same time, the organization, or even the whole industry they represent, will have to take the responsibility as well.

2. The crisis in Ukraine has resulted in bad influence on the relation between Russia and the United States since the Cold War of the last century.

3. Society may gives selectively large responses to public figures' various manners, which have direct effect on public affairs.

4. Public figures are usually sorted as special social organizations due to their considerable social influence.

5. Vice president Al Gore claimed that Clinton's scandal reduced the party's enthusiasm and Democratic votes.

思考题　略

第九章

Exercises 本章练习题

填空题

prompting	slammed	restore	uproar	divert
plotted	flavorful	exuberance	racked	forefront

选择题

D D D D C

释义题

1. These ironical or joking sayings are not true fundamentals actually, and they just tell us the difficulty of launching effective PR communication in a humorous way.

2. The moment others want to be like you, you obtain referent power. People with referent power are charming and authoritative, and also own a high level of admiration and respect from others.

3. We usually exchange symbols standing for ideas rather than ideas, which makes communication complex. There are no intrinsic meaning in the symbols like words, and we just use them in some aspects and different people express differently.

4. E-messages are not exclusive and can easily be stolen by others and used against you. You are forced to admit that you've said something because the fact will be presented for certain.

5. David Chang is a marvelous cook with particular love for pork and pickle, and his combination of the Asian flavors with his free sense of deliciousness provides the customers with desirable dishes.

思考题 略

英文参考文献

1. Alison Theaker. (2004). *The Public Relations Handbook.* Bodmin :Great Britain by MPG Books Ltd.
2. Cornelius B. Pratt and Akari Yanada. *Risk Communication and Japan's Fukushima Daiichi Nuclear Power Plant Meltdown: Ethical Implications for Government-Citizen Divides.* Temple University, Philadelphia, Pennsylvania, USA http://www.prsa.org/Intelligence/PRJournal/Documents/2014PrattYanada.pdf 2015-1-11
3. Danny Moss and Barbara DeSanto.(2010).*Public Relations Cases: International perspectives* (2 edition). London: Routledge.
4. Darrell Hayes and Jerry A. Hendrix. (2009).*Public Relations Cases.* Belmont: Wadsworth Publishing Co Inc.
5. Edward L. Bernays.(1961).*Crystallizing Public Opinion.*New York: Liveright.
6. Frederick Lipman and L. Keith Lipman. (2006).*Corporate Governance best practices: strategies for public, private and Not-for profit organizations.* New Jersey: Hoboken.
7. James. E. Grunig. David M. Dozier. (2002). *Excellent Public Relations and Effective Organizations: A Study of Communication Management in Three Countries.* New Jersey: Lawrence Erlbaum Associates Inc.
8. Jim Dunn.(1999).*Public Relations Techniques that Work.* London: Hawksmere.
9. John Doorley. Helio and Fred Garcia.(2007).*Reputation management the key to successful public relations and corporate communication.* New York :Routledge.
10. Krishnamurthy Sriramesh and Dejan Vercic. (2009).*The Global Public Relations Handbook, Revised and Expanded Edition: Theory, Research, and Practice.* London: Routledge.
11. Kieran Knights. (2001).*Strategic Planning of International Public Relations.* London: Thorogood Professional.
12. Livingstone, Sonia, Wang, Yinhan. (2013). *Media literacy and the Communications Act: what has been achieved and what should be done?*London: London School

of Economics and Political Science Department of Media and Communications. http://eprints.lse.ac.uk/38613/1/LSEMPPBrief2.pdf 2015-02-13

13. MathiasKoenig-Archibugi.(2004).*Transnational Corporations and Public Accountability.* New Jersey: Blackwell Publishing.

14. M. Salwen, d. Stacks (eds.). (1996).*An integrated approach to communication theory and research.* New Jersey: Lawrence Erlbaum Associates.

15. Michael G.Roskin, Robert L.Cord, James A.Medeiros and Walter S.Jones. (2012). *Political Science an introduction*(12th). London: Pearson Education.

16. Otto Lerbinger. (2008) *Corporate Public Affairs Interacting with Interest Groups, Media, and Government,* Taylor& Francis: Lawrence Erlbaum Associates.

17. Scott.M.Cultip, Allen.H.Center. (2005).*Effective Public Relations.* London: Pearson Education.

18. Sriramesh, Krishnamurthy and Verčič(eds.). (2003). *The Global Public Relations Handbook: Theory Research, and Practice,* New Jersey: Lawrence Erlbaum Associates.

19. Terence Timothy Flynn. (2004). *Organizational Crisis Relations Management in Canada and the United States: Construction A Predictive Model of Crisis Preparedness.* The Graduate School Syracuse University.

20. Andre Broome. (2010). The International Monetary Fund, crisis management, and thecredit crunch. In *Australian Journal of International Affairs* Vol. 64, No. 1.

21. Blair Bernstein. (2012). Crisis Management and Sports in the Age of Social Media: A Case Study Analysis of the Tiger Woods. In *Elon Journal of Undergraduate Research in Communication,*VOL. 3 NO. 2.

22. Bishop, R. L. (1998). What newspapers say about public relations. In *Public Relations Review.*

23. Daniela V. Dimitrova, Adam Shehata, Jesper Strömbäck, and Lars W. Nord. (2014). The Effects of Digital Mediaon Political Knowledge and Participation in Election Campaigns: Evidence From Panel Data. In *Communication Research.*New York.

24. Juan-Carlos Molleda. (2009). Global Public Relations. In *Institute for Public Relations.*

25. Mike Muller. (1974). A War on Want investigation into the promotion and sale of powdered baby milks in the Third World. In *War on Want.* London.

26. Youngmin Yoon, Heather Black. (2003).Learning about Public Relations from Television: How is the profession portrayed? In 커뮤니케이션 과학 28권 2호.
27. Andrew Gavin Marshall. (2010). 9/11 ANALYSIS: 9/11 and America's Secret Terror Campaign.*In Global Research.*
http://www.globalresearch.ca/
9-11-analysis-9-11-and-america-s-secret-terror-campaign/209752015-06-12
28. Heather Yaxley. (2015). An international view of crisis management of the Chile mine disaster. In *PRConversations.*
http://www.prconversations.com/author/heather-yaxley/. 2015-01-20
29. Lynn Lawry. (2009). Guide to Nongovernmental Organizations for the Military. In*Center for Disaster and Humanitarian Assistance Medicine.*US.
30.*Public Relations Society of America.*
https://www.prsa.org/. 2015-01-20
30. T*he International Public Relations Association.*
http://www.ipra.org/. 2015-01-26
31. *The institute for Public Relations.*http://www.instituteforpr.org/global-public-relations/. 2015-02-11
32. *Public Relations conversations.*http://www.prconversations.com/author/heather-yaxley/. 2015-02-16
33. Wikipedia,*thefreeencyclopedia.Intergovernmental Organization.*https://en.wikipedia.org/wiki/Intergovernmental_organization. 2015-02-19
34. *World Health Organization.*
http://www.who.int/en/. 2015-03-12
35. *The United Nations Oil-for-food Program.*
http://www.un.org/. 2015-03-20
http://fas.org/irp/doddir/dod/ngo-guide.pdf. 2015-09-12
36. *Paris Hostages Survived Hidden In Fridges And Beneath Sinks.*
http://www.businessinsider.com/
afp-paris-hostages-survived-hidden-in-fridges-and-beneath-sinks-2015-1#ixzz3QH7z7nDn. 2015-03-12
37. Wikipedia, *the free encyclopedia. Lewinsky_scandal.*
https://en.wikipedia.org/wiki/Lewinsky_scandal
38. *MARINA LIAO. Angelina Jolie Tells Kids "Different Is Good" in a Passionate Speech.*

http://www.popsugar.com/celebrity/Angelina-Jolie-Kids-Choice-Awards-Speech-37182800. 2015-03-28

39. *WWF.Giant Pandap.*

    http://www.worldwildlife.org/species/giant-panda. 2015-07-20.

40. *BBC News. Fifa corruption crisis: Key questions answered.* http://www.bbc.com/news/world-europe-32897066. 2015-12-06

41. *Sany Group. Corporate Overview.* http://www.sanygroup.com/group/en-us/about/group.htm. 2015-09-18.

42. *Alibaba. Alibaba Group.*

    http://www.alibabagroup.com/en/global/home. 2015-11-03

中文参考文献

1. 郭慧民主编:《当代国际关系教程》,上海:复旦大学出版社,1995。
2. 杰里·A.亨德里克斯编:《公共关系案例》,北京:机械工业出版社,2003。
3. 莱斯特·M.萨拉蒙等主编,贾西津、魏玉等译:《全球公民社会——非盈利部门视界》,北京:社会科学文献出版社,2002。
4. 李文斐、建军编著:《企业公关策划》,武汉:华中科技大学出版社,2011。
5. 罗子明、张慧子编著:《新媒体时代的危机公关:品牌风险管理及案例分析》,北京:北京清华大学出版社,2013。
6. 唐钧著:《政府公共关系》,北京:北京大学出版社,2009。
7. 汪锦军:《走向合作治理:政府与非营利组织合作的条件、模式和路径》,浙江:浙江大学出版社,2012。
8. 【美】沃尔特网·李普曼著:《舆论学》,北京:华夏出版社,1989。
9. 俞可平主编:《治理与善治》,北京:社会科学文献出版社,2000。
10. 赵麟斌:《公关理论与实务培训用书:国际公关》,北京:北京大学出版社,2013。
11. 钟宏武编著:《中国企业社会责任报告2014》,北京:经济管理出版社,2015。
12. 周安华、苗晋平:《公共关系:理论、实务与技巧(第4版)》,北京:中国人民大学出版社,2013。
13. 安世民:"政府公关的特征和实施条件",《甘肃理论月刊》1999(1),第44-46页。
14. 《公关世界》编辑部:"APEC峰会中的公关亮点",《公关世界》,2014。
15. 黄河:"跨国公司的公共外交决策",《公共外交季刊》,2011(2),第21—26页。
16. 何包钢:"跨国公司并购需要公共外交",《公共外交季刊》,2011(2),第33—39页。
17. 经营管理者编辑部,"H370失联危机公关重创马航",《经营管理者》,第5期。
18. 李永辉、周鑫宇:"企业公共外交:宏观战略与微观管理",《公共外交季刊》,2013(2),第14—18页。

19. 梁婷婷"分享：企业践行公共外交的基础"，《公共外交季刊》，2013(2)，第25—30页。
20. 刘新："公关危机管理中的非政府组织研究"，外交学院，2010。
21. 鲁巧玲："政府间国际组织发展演变规律初探"，青岛：青岛大学国际关系专业，2005。
22. 马宁三："全球性媒体如何在推动公共外交中发挥更大作用"，《公共外交季刊》，2014(1)，114—120页。
23. 毛红华，王瑞红："非政府组织资金来源的一个保障问题"，《西昌学院学报(社会科学版)》，2006(2)，第95—98页。
24. 莫盛凯："公共外交的跨国公司载体：热话题与冷思考"，《公共外交季刊》，2013(2)，第19—24页。
25. 齐小华，殷娟娟："政府公共关系案例精析"，北京：中国人事出版社，2012
26. 汤锋："全球背景下的政府公关与国家形象塑造"，2008，第1—54页。
27. 王林生："当代西方跨国公司理论的演变及其新动向"，《经济学动态》，1990(8)，第50—55页。
28. 王璐，孙学峰："从'走出去'到'融进去'——中石油开发建设融入苏丹的条件"，《世界经济与政治》，2013(3)，第99—114页。
29. 谢岷："跨国公司的发展及其基本概念：跨国公司经营与管理讲座第一讲"，《国际贸易》，1989(1)，第48—51页。
30. 谢婧："杭州城市品牌国际公关策略"，《公关世界》，2014(7)。
31. 许莎："名人危机公关策略技巧探析"，北京林业大学，2012，第11—13页。
32. 姚建明："构架企业公关信息系统的探讨与分析"，《管理科学》，2002(3)，第67—70页。
33. 于桂琴："中国企业跨国并购政治、法律风险分析与防范对策"，《企业发展论坛经济界》，2008(3)，第65—68页。
34. 余万里："跨国公司公共外交的三大功能"，《公共外交季刊》，2011(2)，第16—20页。
35. 袁王珏："全球化时代公共外交的国家领导人品牌构建研究"，上海外国语大学，2013，第8—13页。
36. 约翰·劳埃德，曹劼："社交媒体时代的新闻与公关"，《国际公关》，2015(3)，第20页。
37. 周弛："新新媒介环境下的名人网络危机传播：危机公关策略与效果研究"，上海交通大学，2013，第7—10页。
38. 周虎城："国际公关的五种媒体策略"，《公共外交季刊》，2010(1)。

39. 周批改,周亚平:"国外非营利组织的资金来源及启示国外非营利组织的资金来源及启示",《东南学术》,2004(1),第91—95页。
40. 周晓丽:"论政府公共关系与公共危机的治理",《理论月刊》2008(5),第97—101页。
41. 上海亚太经济合作组织(APEC)第九次领导人非正式会议. http://www.eventer.cn/. 2015-03-12
42. 新华网.
   http://www.xinhuanet.com/xhwenchuan/. 2015-01-12
43. *2011西安世界园艺博览会历程回顾展.*
   http://review.expo2011.cn/album_photos.aspx?album=14. 2015-03-20
   2015 Tempe Sister Cities Cowboy Christmas Party.
   http://www.tempesistercities.org/. 2015-03-20
44. 壳牌2013年可持续发展报告英文完整版(*Royal Dutch Shell plcSustainability Report 2013*)
   http://reports.shell.com/sustainability-report/2013/servicepages/welcome.html. 2015-02-19
45. *科学网博客*
   http://blog.sciencenet.cn/. 2015-02-21
46. 增祥国.体育明星代言当避免"刘翔现象".
   http://www.globrand.com/2008/84843.shtml. 2015-03-20
47. *Natalya Krainova. Putin's Latest PR Stunt Comes Under Fire.*
   http://www.themoscowtimes.com/news/article/putins-latest-pr-stunt-comes-under-fire/483739.html. 2015-03-16
48. *专题:罗永浩与西门子的微博之战.*
   http://www.domarketing.org/html/special/sp_lyh/. 2015-04-21
49. *陈坤呼吁理性看捐款:勿把爱心当比赛.*
   http://ent.sina.com.cn/s/m/w/2013-04-22/01293905093.shtml
50. *中国十大杰出慈善家陈光标主旨演讲——企业家如何履行社会责任.*
   http://news.cyol.com/content/2010-06/19/content_3285096.htm. 2015-04-12
51. 腾讯网.绿色和平拯救森林"筷行动我本是一棵绿树". http://news.qq.com/a/20101220/001696.htm. 2014-09-26.
52. 世界自然基金会.能见蔚蓝
   http://www.earthhour.org.cn/. 2015-06-11.
52. 新华网. 国际组织人才十大核心素养. http://news.xinhuanet.com/politics/

2015-01/29/c_127435546.htm.2015-10-12.
53. *阿里巴巴成功上市*.
http://news.163.com/14/0923/12/A6R0COO300014AED.html.2015-05-12.
54. *中国网.国际非政府组织：概念、分类与发展*[OL].
http://www.china.com.cn/node_7000058/2007-04/02/content_8047369.htm, 2015-12-06.